GROWING UP
PATTON

GROWING UP
PATTON

---- ★ ----

Reflections on Heroes,

History and Family Wisdom

---- ★ ----

BENJAMIN PATTON

with JENNIFER SCRUBY

BERKLEY CALIBER, NEW YORK

THE BERKLEY PUBLISHING GROUP
Published by the Penguin Group
Penguin Group (USA) Inc.
375 Hudson Street, New York, New York 10014, USA
Penguin Group (Canada), 90 Eglinton Avenue East, Suite 700, Toronto, Ontario M4P 2Y3, Canada
(a division of Pearson Penguin Canada Inc.) • Penguin Books Ltd., 80 Strand, London WC2R 0RL,
England • Penguin Group Ireland, 25 St. Stephen's Green, Dublin 2, Ireland (a division of Penguin
Books Ltd.) • Penguin Group (Australia), 250 Camberwell Road, Camberwell, Victoria 3124, Australia
(a division of Pearson Australia Group Pty. Ltd.) • Penguin Books India Pvt. Ltd., 11 Community
Centre, Panchsheel Park, New Delhi—110 017, India • Penguin Group (NZ), 67 Apollo Drive,
Rosedale, Auckland 0632, New Zealand (a division of Pearson New Zealand Ltd.) • Penguin Books
(South Africa) (Pty.) Ltd., 24 Sturdee Avenue, Rosebank, Johannesburg 2196, South Africa

Penguin Books Ltd., Registered Offices: 80 Strand, London WC2R 0RL, England

This book is an original publication of the Berkley Publishing Group.

The publisher does not have any control over and does not assume any responsibility for author or third-
party websites or their content.

Copyright © 2012 by Benjamin Patton
Book design by Tiffany Estreicher

FIRST EDITION: March 2012

Library of Congress Cataloging-in-Publication Data

Patton, Benjamin, 1965–
Growing up Patton / Benjamin Patton, with Jennifer Scruby.—1st ed.
p. cm.
Includes bibliographical references and index.
ISBN 978-0-425-24351-0 (alk. paper)
1. Patton family.   2. Patton, George S. (George Smith), 1885–1945—Family.   3. Patton, George S.
(George Smith), 1923—Family.   4. Generals—United States—Biography.   5. United States. Army—
Biography.   6. Fathers and sons—United States—Biography.   7. Patton, Benjamin, 1965—
Family.   I. Scruby, Jennifer.   II. Title.
CT274.P384P37 2012
355.0092'273—dc23
2011037637

PRINTED IN THE UNITED STATES OF AMERICA

10   9   8   7   6   5   4   3   2   1

Penguin is committed to publishing works of quality and integrity.
In that spirit, we are proud to offer this book to our readers;
however, the story, the experiences, and the words are the author's alone

ALWAYS LEARNING   PEARSON

For Tiger, Miranda, and Nicholas

CONTENTS

FOREWORD BY BOB WOODRUFF

WAR CHANGES PEOPLE. It defines them and sculpts their personalities and histories. Growing up in the family of a famous and
influential person can also have a profound impact. The combina-
tion of these two forces can shape a life in powerful ways.

The book *Growing Up Patton* offers us an insider's look at the
effects of war on a famous American military family, and how the
limelight and legacy of greatness influenced its members. It's a fascinating, panoramic view of three very different generations. All of
them struggle with war, and with the realities and burdens of living
with the expectations that come with bearing an iconic last name.

As a journalist, I have covered conflicts for well over a decade,
and have seen the fallout of war on families. In 2006, when I was
seriously injured by a roadside bomb in Iraq, it became personal. In
the subsequent months it took me to get back on my feet and then
ultimately return to the career I love, my family and I experienced
firsthand the devastation and legacy of war up close and at home.

Our own experiences dealing with the consequences of war have marked my children in ways that are perhaps still too unformed and unarticulated to discover. What they witnessed and felt and worried about in the aftermath of my injury will no doubt have a profound effect on how they move through the world and choose a place in it. These complex emotions are ones the Patton family knows all too well.

As Ben Patton relays, the "expectations for all the Patton children ran ridiculously high." And so it is from that iconic benchmark that the descendants of America's most famous military man had to set out and make their mark.

This book beautifully illustrates the arc of the journey as the children and grandchildren of General Patton feel compelled to make sense of their military legacy through the eras of the Korean and Vietnam wars, right up to the wars in Iraq and Afghanistan. In the end, however, the members of each generation of Pattons learn to define themselves in their own right. Part of this means tackling the questions about what it means to live in a family whose history is tied up in "war and killing."

In the process of learning about the Patton family, we also see the evolution of war in America, from the ticker-tape parades that welcomed home World War II's "Greatest Generation," to the Vietnam era of Ben's father, when returning soldiers were spat upon. And Ben—understanding that his legacy will not be one of war but of documenting history through the lens of filmmaking—brings us up to the present day. Through him, we see what's being done to treat a syndrome that his grandfather famously discredited, post-traumatic stress disorder.

The narrative also details the compelling journey of how Ben's grandfather and father, and ultimately, Ben himself, found their footholds and beachheads in life. Along the way, a fascinating cast of characters intersects with their lives, triggering a ripple effect of courage. The participants and the reader come to realize that there are many ways to leave a legacy, many ways to serve.

PART ONE

FATHER TO SON

*To Ben, This is a picture of a member of your
family uniting his vocation with his avocation.
What all of us should strive to do! —Dad*

I keep a framed copy of this 1969 image of Dad as CO of "Blackhorse," the 11th
Armored Cavalry Regiment in Vietnam, on my desk. It was his favorite photo
of himself and he used to refer to it as his "obit photo" (which it later became,
when he was buried in his fatigues). This note came taped to the back.

Introduction

WHEN MY FATHER was dying, he couldn't stop worrying about his soldiers. Dad, a retired major general who hadn't been near a war in over three decades, had no control of his thoughts at that point. As a side effect of Parkinson's, he suffered from Lewy body disease, a form of dementia that takes your mind back to different times and places. So, in spirit, he was often floating around somewhere else, usually with his men.

To put my father's mind at ease, my mother set up an "officer of the day" calling network. In the military, an officer of the day is someone who temporarily represents the commander of a unit. It's a post that rotates among commissioned officers. In our case, it rotated among our family members and my father's closest friends.

For example, when it was my turn, Mom would call me up wherever I was—by arrangement, so I was never caught off guard—and say, "This is Mrs. Patton, I'm calling for my husband, Major General George S. Patton. He would like to speak to the officer of the day."

George S. Patton Jr. and my dad, aboard *Arcturus,* circa 1937.

"What rank should I be today, Mom?"

A whisper: "Try lieutenant." Then she'd pass the phone to Dad.

"This is Lieutenant _____, the officer of the day," I'd say. "You're talking on an unsecure line. What can I help you with?" With effort, he would say something like, "I want to make sure all your men are okay. Have you got the right gear? Enough hot food?" Or: "There are some problems at the motor pool that need to be taken care of right away."

"Yes, sir," I'd reply. "We'll take care of that right away, sir."

"See that you do, soldier," my father would say. "Carry on." Then he could close his eyes and go back to sleep.

Occasionally, Dad's complaint would involve scheduling issues. "The staff car is late—I need to be at a conference in Stuttgart in an hour." At first, my brother and sisters and I made the mistake of replying, "Oh, yes, sir. We'll send the car right away." But then our father would wait anxiously for the car that never arrived, getting more agitated by the minute.

So we learned to say, "Sir, there has been a priority emergency that will prevent the cars from getting there today. So the conference has been rescheduled for tomorrow and your car will pick you up first thing in the morning." Of course, by the next day the scenario had changed and the car was forgotten, my father having moved on to a whole new issue or group of soldiers to worry about.

In a weird way, the calling circle comforted all of us. It spoke volumes about my parents' marriage—about my mother's love for him, in particular. But in another sense, it was also a measure of my father, the soldier.

In December 1987, I sat down and did the first of a series of interviews with my father. I was twenty-two; he was sixty-four.

He had recently lost all of his journals. A year earlier, our home had been severely damaged by a fire that started in Dad's basement office—the result of a smoldering cigar butt he'd tossed in the wastebasket on his way to dinner. Even after the flames were finally put out, the firemen had to cut two huge holes in the roof to release the smoke.

The biggest casualty of that night was my father's diaries— dozens of identical volumes bound in red canvas that dated back several decades. Like my grandfather George S. Patton Jr.,[*] he was an inveterate and meticulous journal keeper—a lover of all history, including his own. My father actually suffered second-degree burns trying to rescue the journals, as well as his scrapbooks filled with

---

[*] Although my grandfather was christened George S. Patton, Jr., he was actually the third George Smith Patton. Thus, my father was christened George Patton IV.

photos of his soldiers and comrades. Yet almost all of his papers were reduced to ash.

Everything we owned had to be removed or cleaned (or in some cases, removed *and* cleaned). The house, Green Meadows, part of an estate that my grandparents bought in 1928, was renovated and modernized. In the process, my parents cleared away a lot of the stuff that had made it feel like a museum. The giant painting of my grandfather, for instance, featured in the movie *Patton,* was shipped off to the National Portrait Gallery. Most of the war artifacts were donated to the Virginia Military Institute, West Point, or the Patton Museum at Fort Knox. As far as I was concerned, this was a good thing—it lifted the overwhelming shadow of my grandfather from the place. But I'd never seen my father more depressed.

He couldn't bring himself to try to re-create his diaries from the scraps the conservator had managed to salvage. I thought that if I could get his memories down on tape, it could serve as the basis for a new project—his autobiography. (He never wrote it, although our interviews were eventually used, along with extensive interviews conducted by his biographer, Brian M. Sobel, in *The Fighting Pattons*.)

I conducted the interviews with my father in our den—which we call the gun room. The ceiling beams are draped with weaponry: black-powder pistols, sabers, crossbows, helmets, even a rocket-propelled grenade launcher. For years, an assortment of World War II–era machine guns hung from either side of the fireplace—and most of them worked. (My mother was an Army brat, which is the only reason I can imagine that she would have gone along with this.)

Using a tiny microcassette recorder, we recaptured as many stories as we could. The interview sessions held a redemptive element for both of us: I was glad to help him; he was glad to see that I was interested and listening. I'd been too young to know him in his warrior days, and in any event, he was often away.

Also, up to then, I was too self-involved to truly appreciate what he'd done.

For as long as I can remember, I knew that my father labored under the weight of his name: If you're the son of a lionized yet controversial military hero *and* you choose to dive into his profession, what do you do next? The mountainous pressure was enough to drag anyone under: At my father's graduation from West Point, a guy famously walked up to him and said, "Well, George, you'll never be the man your father was, but congratulations."[1] Welcome to the world of George S. Patton IV. As his sister Ruth Ellen observed, "I always had the feeling he thought he let Daddy down by not becoming Jesus Christ II."[2]

Nonetheless, my father distinguished himself. Over the course of his career, he fought in two wars (including three tours in Vietnam), received two Distinguished Service Crosses (the second highest commendation for bravery in combat, after the Medal of Honor), two Silver Stars (the third highest), two Bronze Stars, and a Purple Heart. His framed commendations and medals still hang in the gun room at Green Meadows. And when I show people our house, I'm always quick to point out these dates: In one six-week period between August and September 1968, while head of a four-thousand-man regiment, my father received the two DSCs, a Silver Star and was wounded in combat—in three different engagements.

Dad led by example and led from the front, just like his father: During his major campaigns, my grandfather could often be seen in his command car driving toward the action, passing his troops and saluting and cheering them on as he went. Later, at the end of the day, he would take a small plane back to headquarters. My dad often used the term *visible personality* to describe this leadership technique.

Case in point: General Julius Becton, the subject of a chapter in this book, told me that when my father was the deputy corps commander of VII Corps, he always visited his units in an open jeep— even in the dead of winter. On closer inspection one frigid day, Becton noticed that my dad had cranked up the heat so that it was blasting hot air into the front seats. "I always felt bad for the aide riding in the back freezing his ass off," said Becton. But the men on the ground saw their leader, and it made a difference.

WHILE RECORDING MY father's memories, I didn't look into them too deeply. I was certainly conscious of the fact that I had disappointed him (and for a while myself) by not going into the military. Since I was the youngest son, one could say I was Dad's last hope. I'd only decided at the last minute not to attend the Naval Academy Prep School, dismissing the pros-and-cons chart my dad and I had compiled in which the pros of the military life had won out by a serious margin. My father worried—with reason—that I had not found a clear path or passion to follow, that I wasn't an expert at anything, that I had demonstrated no powers of concentration, and that my horizons looked decidedly murky.

Ironically, it was through the interviews that I stumbled onto my career as a documentary filmmaker.

By the time my father was fading, in 2004, I was in my thirties and had lived long enough to appreciate the richness and depth of his experiences. I'd also discovered a few things through my work: First, that your parents' memories provide a vital part of your own life story. Second, if you want to get a clearer view of someone, there's nothing like looking outside the family and gathering stories from the people they admired and drew into their circle of friends. Third, the negative lessons from the past are just as valuable as the positive ones.

When I started working on this book, it was with these facts in mind. I wanted to commemorate my father. I wanted a concrete way to deal with my loss. And I wanted to compile all of my father's life lessons, and the wisdom of his own beloved father and friends, for the sake of my own son.

Accordingly, the book is split into three sections. The first starts with a look at the relationship between my father and grandfather and finishes with excerpts from their lengthy correspondence between 1939 and 1945. If you've ever doubted what a kick-ass warrior my grandfather was, take a look—his advice to my father was as manly and witty and loving as it comes. As it turns out, he dispensed much of it while he and the Third Army were charging across Europe. It reveals a lot about my grandfather as a general, a parent, a raconteur, and possibly an insomniac: How he found the time to write all of this correspondence, plus the hundreds of letters and journal entries crammed in *The Patton Papers,* is beyond me.

The second section features profiles of twelve remarkable people who were closely connected with my father—and who, by extension, loom large in my own pantheon of personal heroes. The fact that I've included my mother, Joanne Holbrook Patton, may sound biased and sentimental, but just check out the countless hours of audio correspondence that my parents sent back and forth between Washington, D.C., and Vietnam during my father's last tour of duty in the late 1960s. To me, they offer more drama, romance, and honor than anything else in the book.

The third section focuses on Charley Watkins, my father's

beloved helicopter pilot, and my brother, the latest George S. Patton Jr.[3] Their story is a sort of summing-up for me: what a family's cultural legacy is, and what it means—deep down—to be a hero, whether you grab headlines or not.

Of course, we are just one instance of a family. My experience is that we all share the impulse to look into the past and find connections. Making sense of your lineage is one way of trying to understand yourself better—truly, an exercise anyone might benefit from.

Which brings me to one of my father's favorite quotations, which kind of strikes at the theme of this entire book: One of my father's favorite sayings came from the Book of Ecclesiastes in the Bible. He often included it in his speeches and offered it to me as a key to life: "Whatsoever your hand findeth itself to do, do it with thy might."

Dad, I'm trying.

ONE

Family History

IT'S INTERESTING WHAT the mind holds on to. During one of our last visits before he died, I read my father one of his favorite poems about the service, Rudyard Kipling's "Gentlemen-rankers." My mother sat next to his wheelchair in our dining room, holding his hand. Dad was only semiconscious at that point and hadn't spoken much in days, but as I reached the third stanza, he suddenly chimed in, startling me so much that I almost dropped my book:

> *Oh, it's sweet to sweat through stables, sweet to empty kitchen slops,*
> *And it's sweet to hear the tales the troopers tell . . .*[1]

My father—the namesake and only son of World War II general George S. Patton Jr. and a decorated general and famously tough warrior in his own right—felt born to the military the same way his father had felt destined for combat, as he wrote his future father-in-law, textile magnate Frederick Ayer, in 1909: "It is hard to answer intelligibly the question of 'Why I want to be a soldier.' For my own satisfaction I have tried to give myself reasons but have never found any logical ones. I only feel it inside. It is as natural for me to be a soldier as it is to breathe and would be as hard to give up all thought of it as it would be to stop breathing."[2]

My late aunt Ruth Ellen Patton Totten had a similar take on Dad: "I remember a little boy with a paper hat on marching around," she said. "A soldier was all he ever wanted to be. I don't think he could have done anything else."[3]

Surprisingly, my grandfather didn't encourage my father to enter the military, at least at first. He wanted to make sure that he'd given his son every opportunity to choose a different path. Still, he was thrilled when Dad—under his own teenage steam—decided to enter West Point in 1942. As a child, he'd been formed and fed by war stories and his father's own sixth sense of the battlefield. (Dad said that breakfast with his father consisted of cornflakes and military history.) My grandfather told him about *his* grandfather, Colonel George Smith Patton, a Confederate regimental commander who died—gloriously, of course—from wounds sustained during what is commonly known as the Third Battle of Winchester in September of 1864.[4] He gave my father books to read on everyone from Napoleon to Stonewall Jackson. He once pulled him out of school to hear a speech by T. E. Lawrence, the legendary Lawrence of Arabia. He frequently invited General John J. Pershing over to hang out with the family. ("What a marvelous-looking man," my father said later. "Straight as a damned string and with a little bristly mustache.")[5] My grandfather also taught Dad how to fish, ride, sail, and shoot, even climb volcanoes.

That close relationship lasted until 1937, when, at age thirteen, my father left Massachusetts for boarding school, as young men of means often did in those days. (My grandmother Beatrice Ayer Patton had inherited the vast wealth of her father, a self-made coal and textile tycoon who lived in Boston.) My grandfather, meanwhile, was rotating through a series of posts and ramping up for war. In fact, from the time Dad entered West Point until my grandfather died after a car accident in Germany in December 1945, they saw each other only twice.

The first time was in the fall of 1942, when my grandfather came to visit Dad during his plebe year at West Point. George Senior was about to leave on a troop-filled ship across the Atlantic, en route to the then top-secret Operation Torch—the Allied invasion of North Africa.

The late lieutenant general Dave Ott, a fellow cadet who was to become my father's commander at VII Corps, remembers my nineteen-year-old dad bringing his father to see his room in the barracks. In that era, plebes couldn't walk diagonally between the buildings. They had to walk in squares, along the seams of the large, gray granite pavers. "George was walking alongside [his dad], but always doing little rights and lefts," Ott said. "And that wasn't required—when you were with somebody you could cut across. But he was in a stiff military brace and trying to show his father 'I'm 100 percent plebe!'"

After commanding corps and armies in North Africa, Sicily, and the European theater of operations, my grandfather returned to the United States for a bond tour in early June 1945, on the heels of Germany's surrender. Even then, the amount of quality time my father had with him was minimal. By now, everyone wanted a piece of Patton.

In anticipation of his father's arrival, Dad headed home to the family farm, Green Meadows, in Hamilton, Massachusetts. "A couple of days later we all went up to Boston and the aircraft landed," he said later. "I'll never forget it. My dad got out of the aircraft and he really looked super; he was fifty-nine years old at the time. With him were a couple of division commanders . . . followed by eight or nine noncoms, not one of whom was wearing less than a Silver Star. All of this was followed by a ticker-tape parade through Boston. That evening my father spoke at the Shell on the Esplanade in Boston. We came home that night quite late and the next morning he came upstairs and woke me up and said we were going for breakfast. I ate breakfast with him and then I got on a train and went back to West Point. It was the last time I ever saw him."[6]

Newsreel footage from around that time shows my grandfather standing in a convertible staff car as it rolled through Los Angeles on a sunny summer day, with confetti filling the air and nearly two million men, women, and children waving American flags and cheering. Smartly dressed in his dress uniform with riding jodhpurs and gleaming steel helmet, he smiled, saluted with his riding crop, and blew kisses to the ladies along the route.

My grandfather's fatal accident occurred back in Germany, six months later. On December 9, 1945—the day before he was scheduled to fly back home to the States for Christmas, and for good—his Cadillac sedan was struck by an Army supply truck just east of Mannheim.

My father, then twenty-two, was in the middle of West Point finals when he was called to the tactical department office. "Colonel Russell 'Red' Reeder told me what had occurred," he said. "He went on to explain that my father had suffered a broken neck and was paralyzed. He also said they were in communication and would keep me informed. I went back to my room and wrote a cable, which I sent on December 10, 1945. It said: *"All of us here are praying*

General Patton in Los Angeles, June 1945.   PHOTO COURTESY OF GETTY IMAGES

for your speedy recovery and return home. I know you can do it. Your affectionate son, George."[7]

The trip to Germany was an arduous one at the time. Rather than have my father interrupt his studies with a long journey, my grandmother refused to let him come to the hospital in Heidelberg. Nor, thanks to a decision by the Department of the Army, was he allowed to attend my grandfather's Christmas Eve funeral service or his interment in the American Military Cemetery in Luxembourg. A few months later, however, he and my grandmother traveled to Normandy and retraced the Third Army's campaign across

Europe. And then it was back to the Army, where he had to figure out how to follow in my grandfather's footsteps.

IN 2001, I had the opportunity to meet Martin Blumenson, my grandfather's official biographer and the editor of *The Patton Papers,* two brick-thick books based on my grandfather's extensive diaries and letters. At the time I was researching the connections between our family and the family of Erwin Rommel, the famous German field marshal of World War II (which is discussed later in this book). I called Blumenson and we set up an interview at his small apartment in Washington, D.C.

A Harvard-educated historian who had served on the Third Army staff under my grandfather and later commanded a unit in Korea, Blumenson was then in his early eighties—a short, squat, balding man with a gift for spinning one story into the next. He sat in a swivel desk chair. We talked all afternoon about why he thought my grandfather was one of the greatest military geniuses of all time, and why Blumenson felt he'd been cast aside after World War II. We also talked about how my father had carved out his own place in history.

Blumenson obviously adored my grandfather and was quick to remind me of all the names Patton had for his superiors during the war—amounting to a kind of code in his letters home so that the censors wouldn't know whom he was talking about. Omar Bradley was the "tentmaker" because my grandfather felt he never moved his troops quickly enough. "D.D."—Eisenhower's first and middle initials—in Patton's parlance stood for "Divine Destiny": He'd intuited, justifiably, that Eisenhower had his eye on a political future.

"It sounds cold to say this," Blumenson told me, "but General

Patton really died at the right time. [His] death was essential for transfiguring him from an earthly figure of importance to a legend. It made a hero out of Patton in a way that a normal death wouldn't have done."

Blumenson marveled at the fact that despite the ticker-tape parades and the immense popularity of my grandfather at home and abroad, he was sidelined at the end of the war. No reassignment to the Pacific. (Two prima donnas in one theater were probably one too many for MacArthur.) No transfer to the War College or another major position stateside. But from the moment my grandfather was injured in the car accident, his name dominated the headlines until he died twelve days later. And amazingly, in many ways, his status in the public consciousness has continued to grow.

Of course, having war and command taken away from him would probably have killed my grandfather in a different way. At the very least, it would have crushed his spirit.

Yet he'd sealed his fate in the fall of 1945 when, as head of the Third Army and military governor of Bavaria, Patton insisted on allowing many of the local officials—several of whom had been members of the Nazi Party—to retain their positions. General Eisenhower promptly fired him, despite Patton's insistence that, Nazis or not, no one else knew how to run things.

Seven years later, when my aunt Beatrice—"Little Bee"—died of a sudden heart attack at age forty-one, Mamie Eisenhower called my grandmother to offer her condolences. It so happened that my mother, who was then recently married to my father, answered the phone. "Mrs. Eisenhower was calling from the presidential campaign train and couldn't have been more gracious," my mother remembers. "But Mrs. Patton was so mad at General Eisenhower that she refused to take the call." My grandmother was still bitter about what she perceived as Ike's disloyalty to her husband, his old friend, and the pain it had caused.

True to his roots, my father, who served in the Korean and Vietnam wars and returned home to become a farmer in New England, had a hard time adjusting to life outside the military. "Peacetime can kill you," he told me on occasion. He worried that being in the army had made him unfit for anything else.

THE PARALLELS BETWEEN my father and grandfather practically jump out at you. They looked alike and shared the same colorful vocabulary. They were both students of military history who felt confident in their tactical abilities, relied on bravado, and took risks that irritated their superiors. Both dressed well and took pains to look the pillar of leadership. (In the age before permanent press, my grandfather ironed his clothes practically every night at West Point, and actually had one uniform that he never sat down in.)[8]

The list goes on: They shared a love of poetry and the Bible and a belief in reincarnation. Both were held back a year at West Point for flunking math. Both spoke French and had an old-school sense of chivalry. Both had high expectations for themselves and set high standards. Both worried that they weren't good enough, that they hadn't measured up. And, ironically, both saw their careers cut short because of their outspokenness. (The military is so political that it's almost impossible for someone with opinions to get along for years in a system like that and not have a conflict. It shouldn't necessarily be held against my father. But it's something he regretted.)

One habit my father shared with my grandfather was respecting great soldiers—even if they happened to be the enemy. My father once advanced on an enemy position, wounded a Viet Cong soldier, and then pulled him out of a hole. As the man lay on a stretcher awaiting evacuation, Dad saluted him and said, in French, "You put up a hell of a fight."[9] (The soldier returned the salute.) In the same way, my grandfather respected Rommel and regretted the fact that they never faced off on the battlefield.[10]

Blumenson told me about one World War II correspondent who proposed, only half in jest, that my grandfather and Rommel climb into two tanks and duke it out to determine the outcome of the war. Some people even thought that Patton suggested the slugfest. "I don't think he did," said Blumenson. "But he liked it and he talked about it as though he were almost ready to go do this battle with Rommel.

"Patton had really a medieval view of military people," Blumenson added. "They were one big brotherhood. They went to war and they fought each other and they killed each other. But after the war was over, that was one big fraternity and they all drank together and joked together and sang together."[11]

A MAJOR OVERLAP that emerges is the way my father and grandfather stayed in the field with their men: "Not only must a leader be seen, but it's of vast importance that he be seen moving in harm's way," my father insisted.[12] Then there's the way they took care of their troops and looked out for their welfare. We saw that in my dad after he died, when hundreds of letters poured in from men who had served under him. On his first day in command of A Company, 140th Tank Battalion, in Korea, for example, he discovered that morale in the unit had plummeted, and that many of the men hadn't eaten a hot meal in weeks. As Dad said later, "I went back to my mess sergeant and said, 'We're gonna serve a hot meal . . . and we're gonna start on the right flank and end on the left flank of our position, and we're gonna carry that food in a trailer and it's gonna be piping hot. And you and I are gonna serve it.'"[13] He had five platoons at the time, set about a hundred yards apart. They started serving lunch at about eight o'clock in the morning and finished around nine hours later. By then, my father had won the soldiers' trust and respect, although that wasn't his original intention. "I did [it] because it was the right thing to do," he said.[14]

My grandfather's troops were devoted to him for similar reasons. Blumenson briefly served in the headquarters of Third Army before moving on to the Seventh Army for the last month of World War II: "There is a difference between the way I was treated in one Army and the way I was treated in another . . . I just wanted to go back to the Third Army all the time. There's a story of a division that came over and fought in Europe. They were assigned to Patton's Third Army and then the boundaries changed, and so they were placed under somebody else's Army. And they felt dejected because they thought they weren't good enough to be in Patton's Army. And I think that's how we all felt. We were all better than anybody else. We got treated better. The food was better. The lodgings were better. Everything. Everybody was looking out for you and . . . it was just a great place to be. Wonderful."

Once he became a commander, my father unspooled all the lessons he had learned from his father and his other great mentors. Andy O'Meara, who was the regimental intelligence officer when my father took the reins of the Blackhorse Regiment, remembers Dad's first day on the job: "After arriving and speaking with the troops, he called a staff meeting, and when we got through briefing Patton he pulled out a notebook and shared with us his style of operation. It quickly became clear to me that he had been preparing those notes his entire career. I found that to be a beautiful insight and testimonial of professional competence. He wasn't there to punch his ticket. He was there because he was a professional soldier and a leader who had prepared himself his whole life for that day."[15]

My father bore a recognizable link to my grandfather in his single-minded devotion to war and duty, too. "We gotta think about fighting, we gotta think about attacking, we gotta think about pursuing and exploiting, we gotta think about it all the time, whatever we do, wherever we go and whoever in the hell we talk to," he said in his final State of the Division speech to the officers and soldiers of the 2nd Armored Division in 1977. "Frankly I think about little else. I cannot drive by a piece of ground—even when I'm on leave or pass or taking my wife to the movies—without thinking how I would attack it."[16]

Finally, they both had an aversion to cowardice and battle fatigue that hit them at a visceral level and unleashed their volatile side. In my grandfather's case, this brought about the notorious slapping of two shell-shocked soldiers in field hospitals in Sicily.[17] Less well known, but certainly never covered up in our family, was an incident involving my father that took place in the Korean War in 1953.

My father had gone up to the 2nd Platoon of A Company, 140th Tank Battalion, on a routine check, only to find that the lieutenant in charge had deserted.

"He said he'd had enough of the shelling and he went back to his hooch," the platoon sergeant told him. My father charged down the hill in his jeep and, as he remembered it, found the missing lieutenant sitting on his cot smoking a cigarette.

"I've had enough of it," he said. "I left. I ran off."

"So I went over there and took my steel helmet off and beat the hell out of him," my father said. "I thought I'd broken his jaw. And I said, 'You get your ass back to that platoon or I'm going to try you for misbehavior before the enemy, and the penalty for misbehavior before the enemy is death.[18] Now git.'

". . . I whistled up a jeep for him and carried him back to his platoon . . . I think he did a satisfactory job from that time on until he left . . . Being the yellow bastard that he was, I could have sent him up to battalion or division or something, to work on the staff, but I wouldn't do that. I mean, why reward a guy with a station further from the front when other guys were up there [getting] seriously wounded?"[19]

Battle fatigue was little understood at the time, and my father described the scene for me without remorse: He insisted that rolling a fearful soldier back into action was the only way to restore his self-esteem, and only fair to the men who were out there putting their lives on the line.

The men he admired most were the ones who stood up for duty and honor even when their legs gave out. Around that same period in Korea, my father walked up to the same platoon to see how things were going. "It was cold and wet and awful and there was a lot of freezing rain," he said later, looking back. "We got an order down from division that we would have a foot inspection every night and to see to it [that] there were dry socks for everyone [and] Mickey Mouse boots. We were to take special precautions on trench foot and that type of thing that comes with standing in cold water for a long time."

When my father reached the command post, its leader, Sergeant Harold Potter, was out. "His driver was there manning the radio and I said, 'Where's Potter?' And he said, 'Sir, he's out inspecting the troops' feet.' I said, 'Well, I'm gonna find him,' and there was Potter on his hands and knees crawling along the trench line. I said, 'Why are you on your hands and knees?' He said, 'Sir, I've got amoebic dysentery so bad I can't stand up.' I said, 'Well, let me finish the inspection with these men and I'll send you down in my jeep to the medics.' And he said, 'No, sir, this is my job. I inspect the feet in this platoon, and when I finish my inspection, I'll be happy to ride down the hill with you.' He didn't have the strength to walk down the trench line. Now, I call that a sense of duty."[20]

ALL OF THIS is not to imply that my father was a clone. For example, I never knew my grandfather, but from the family anecdotes I've heard, I think I got a better deal in a parent. My father and his two sisters, Ruth Ellen and Bea, certainly loved and admired my grandfather, whom the older members of the family called Georgie. But he could be a complete jerk.

Per my aunt, Ruth Ellen Patton Totten, from her memoir, *The Button Box:*

> *[Georgie] bought us each a racquet and a can of six balls and he took us out to the practice court, which was up in the 19th Infantry area and near where he exercised his polo ponies. There was a backboard on that court ... Georgie told us to get in there and practice hitting the balls ... He took us there during the lunch hour, as he didn't want us to interfere with any real players. So, Bee and I, in the boiling sun, hit ball after ball at the backboard. Georgie would usually be riding nearby, circling and practicing polo shots, and if we stopped even for a minute, he would gallop up and yell at us to keep going. After a few weeks of this, my sister Bee and I wrote a paper which vowed that we would never*

play tennis as long as we lived, and we pricked our fingers and signed it in our own blood.[21]

Per Blumenson, writing in *The Patton Papers:*

Once when he was rehearsing his young daughter for a horse show, he berated her constantly, criticizing and cussing her, finding everything wrong, her posture, the way she handled her horse, her method of taking the jumps. He finally shouted in anger, "Get off that goddamn horse and let me show you how to do it." Meekly she climbed down, a chubby twelve-year-old, and he took her place. Resplendent and supremely self-confident in his horsemanship, he prepared to jump. As he spurred toward the obstacle, she was heard to say, "Dear God, please let that son of a bitch break his neck."[22]

To be fair, my grandfather had competed in the modern pentathlon in the 1912 Olympics—no wonder he could be an obsessive sports parent. My father, while a product of that upbringing, considered himself more of an enthusiast than an authority on anything beyond soldiering. Although he could be tough and opinionated and always expected us to do our best, I had the feeling that he didn't want us to feel the kind of pressure he'd grown up with: He made things fun. And, despite his devotion to his work, he made an effort to be present for his children in a way that his own father could not.

I was still a baby when my father left for his last tour of Vietnam. My first memory of him is when we flew to Hawaii on R&R to meet him when I was three. My mother recalls me tugging on her dress at the airport and asking, "What did you say his name was? Daddy?"

And yet, once my father came home, he made the most of his time with us. He took us camping and fishing. He taught us to build race cars and rockets for our Boy Scout derbies and make duck decoys that bore some resemblance to the picture on the box. He frequently attended my football games and tennis matches in high school. He and my mother flew to London to see my sister Helen play Regan in a production of *King Lear* at the Royal Academy of Dramatic Art. Though he was quick to comment on what he liked or didn't like—"Why the hell is Lear nude in Scene IV?"—time after time, he was there. Wherever he went, he brought the same bluster, audacity, bravado, and romantic streak. And for each of us, he carried forward his father's love of sailing, hunting, poetry, and, yes, history.

My grandfather and father's shared sense of history—and the importance of recording it—may have been genetic. It would be too easy to conclude that my grandfather kept his wonderfully detailed diaries, as well as copies of the countless letters he wrote from the front, simply to preserve his own legacy. As Ralph Waldo Emerson noted, all history is biography. But I think my grandfather felt that he was living through a momentous time and recognized the importance of recording everything that happened.

Both he and my father took extensive photographs and movies of important events in their lives. I recall the endless hours we spent splicing together Super-8 films of our family visits to Stephen Foster's home, or the O.K. Corral, or the presumed site of the Battle of Zama between Rome's General Scipio Africanus and Carthage's Hannibal the Great. As we stood in a huge valley bordered by a mountain range in Tunisia, Dad took us through each stage of the battle, then pointed to a gap in the mountains and reminded us that "dozens of battle elephants came through that pass." He made the scene come alive for us; back at school, plowing through our history textbooks, we felt like we were missing out.

HERE'S DAD'S RESPONSE to an article in *People* magazine entitled "George Patton, Chip off the Famous Block":

I am not a chip off the block and regardless of random comments concerning my upbringing and character, I went out of my way to be myself always and every time. Certain characteristics that did pertain to my father were simply not my cup of tea, and I went out of my way to discount them.[23]

In reality, my father couldn't have remade himself in his father's image even if he wanted to: They were both classic warriors but fought in very different types of wars. My grandfather intersected with history at precisely the right moment to make a name for himself. With its clear delineation between good and evil, World War II lent itself to mythmaking. In the Vietnam and Korean wars, in which my father fought, things got a lot messier. The Vietnam war, in particular, lacked public support, clear objectives, and an exit strategy; no one even knew exactly what success there would look like. Back at home, people weren't idolizing military leaders anymore. If anything, it was just the opposite.

Consider the contrast between my grandfather's triumphant victory parades and a lap my father and some of his soldiers—Vietnam veterans from the 10th Special Forces Group—took in Cambridge, Massachusetts, in the spring of 1975. The city's mayor had requested some troops for a bicentennial reenactment of

George Washington's commissioning ceremony as commander in chief of the Continental Army:

So I got these guys lined up and I mean they looked like a million bucks [my father told me later]. They were wearing camouflage fatigues with pistols and a couple of them had machetes and we came down there and it was really a super ceremony. The Philadelphia cavalry group . . . all dressed up in the Continental uniform . . . and they had a guy dressed as Washington—he looked more like Washington than Washington. He had a white wig on and buff and blue Continental uniform and a three-cornered hat.

[As the Washington impersonator came forward to accept his commission] a hippie broke loose from the crowd and . . . walked up in front of Command Sergeant Major Johnson . . . He had a flower and he stuck it under Johnson's nose. "Baby killer, nasty man," you know, that kind of talk.

Under his breath, Johnson said, "General Patton, what do I do now?" This little fart was under Johnson's nose with a flower—with a beard, you know, and peace symbols hanging off of him and all.

"Sergeant Major," I said, "you just use your best judgment."

He said, "Yessir," and hollered out, "Get lost, motherfucker! Before I waste your motherfucking ass!"

And Mayor Sullivan turned to me and he said, "My goodness, it sounds like he means business." "I guess he does," I said.

The problem was, it got on the PA system: The microphone was very close to Sergeant Major Johnson . . . and his voice blasted out over the entire group, which may have been four or five thousand [people]— here in the actual spot where Washington was commissioned, you know, by legend anyway. Well, it didn't even get in the paper . . . but, Jesus, that was quite a thing.[24]

On top of antimilitary sentiment, my father had to wrestle with guerrilla warfare, which blew open a whole new set of complications. Most of the military history he and my grandfather had absorbed had focused on classic formations and organized battles in which two armies clashed and you could identify your enemy on sight. Not anymore.

Another key difference: The way some of the soldiers who served under my grandfather have described it to me, they almost revered him like a god. Conversely—and perhaps because he fought in unpopular, intractable wars—my father didn't boast about his achievements, nor did he want to be seen as iconic. I think it's interesting that he never worked in my grandfather's custom-designed home office, with its voluminous library and perfect replica of Napoleon's desk. "Too much damn traffic," Dad would say, a sentiment that might be voiced by any father of five. Then he'd head off to his plywood-walled office in the basement, every surface a collage of photos of fellow soldiers and family.

I got the impression that my father was wary of fame in general. He and my grandmother didn't want the movie *Patton* to be made, for instance, feeling skeptical that Hollywood could capture the nuances of my grandfather's complex personality. Not that that discouraged Hollywood. After my grandmother's burial in 1953, under her favorite tree at Green Meadows, my mother was the first one to come inside and hear the phone ring. "The person on the other end was a Hollywood producer," she remembers. "He said, 'Well, now that the old lady is out of the way, let's talk about a movie!'"

Eventually, of course, the film was made. The family stayed out of it, but once *Patton* was released, everyone was dying to see the result. My father ended up taking my mother and my brother

The Patton family at their Fort Knox quarters in 1971, a year after the feature film *Patton* was released.   COURTESY OF THE PATTON FAMILY

Robert to watch it at a movie theater in Times Square where they could go incognito. His one complaint: The star of the film, George C. Scott, sounded nothing like the real General Patton, who had a high-pitched voice. As it happened, with his gruff, gravelly delivery, Scott sounded a lot like my father.

On a side note: The star of *Patton,* George C. Scott, came to dinner at my parents' house in Fort Knox a few years later, bringing along a print of the movie as a gift. (The film canisters were so heavy that when he handed them to my mother, she almost fell down.) As she remembers it, Scott asked for a Bloody Mary. "So my husband went out and fixed him one, and after a few minutes he asked, 'Is that Bloody Mary all right?'

"'Well, General, you wanna know the truth?' said Scott. 'Let me show you my way.' So the two of them went back over to the bar in our living room, and Scott picked up a tall highball glass. 'You got a quarter?' he asked my husband.

"'Sure,' George said. Scott dropped the coin in the glass, drizzled in just enough tomato juice to cover it, and then filled the rest of the glass with ice and vodka. It looked like pink lemonade. 'Now that,' he said, 'is a Bloody Mary.'"

TWO

Wartime Correspondence Between George S. Patton Jr. and George S. Patton IV

THE RELATIONSHIP BETWEEN my father and grandfather is notable not only for the amount of time they spent apart but for how many letters they wrote—about three in each direction a month throughout World War II—and how close they grew through that correspondence. Many of the letters were written while my father was a struggling cadet at West Point (like his father, he had troubles in math) and while my grandfather was marching across France on his way to Berlin. During this period, as commander of the Third Army, my grandfather earned his reputation as the Allied general the Nazis feared most: He and his troops liberated tens of thousands of square miles of territory and advanced farther in less time than any other Army in history.

Many of these father-and-son letters have never been published. Together, they make up all that remains of the relationship between

The Patton family, June 7, 1945. PHOTO COURTESY OF THE PATTON FAMILY

my grandfather and his grown son—except, of course, for what lives on in their children and grandchildren. As with all the excerpted correspondence and interviews in this book, I've omitted some passages and corrected spelling and punctuation in others. An ellipsis indicates where I've skipped a few words to be more concise.

My grandfather dictated his letters or composed them on his portable typewriter. My father's are written in small, decisive longhand. While there are some asides from the battlefield, I've chosen to focus on the heart of the material, which is the advice—on leadership, friendship, and life in general—that my grandfather, a wonderful character and hero, handed down to my father, another wonderful character and *my* hero.

For me, these letters sum up their relationship better than anything else.

Letter, GSP Jr. to his son George IV (at the Hill School, Pottstown, Pennsylvania) from Fort Myer, Virginia:

MAY 19, 1939

Dear George:

Your frank and manly letter was very pleasing to me, and I was glad to get it. If you can't like the Smith boy, leave him alone, because no matter how good a fighter he is, the people at the school consider him an underdog. It never pays to fight an underdog. You can fight for them, but never against them.

It is very foolish, but quite understandable, that one should run around raising h—l, but it gets one nowhere and betrays a lack of self-confidence. A man who is self-confident does not run around with a gang. It is much better to be a lone wolf than a coyote. Thanks for the money you sent me. I have already spent it. Hoping that you will not get into any more trouble.

I am, very affectionately,

Letter, GSP Jr. to his son George IV (at West Point). At this point GSP Jr. was at the headquarters of I Corps in Indio, California. Two days before this was written, Patton had learned that the War Department might move him and the armored corps overseas in the fall:[1]

JULY 13, 1942

Dear George:

Your mother and I are very proud of you because you have at last demonstrated [yourself] to be a money rider—to come across in a pinch. But you must realize how very close run the thing was as Lord Wellington said of Waterloo. God and Luck were on your side. Both are useful but remember the Virginia adage "That the best trainer is Old Doctor Work."

As to your conduct as a <u>CADET!!!</u> You do all the getting along. Don't talk or look smug as if it was an old story to you. Do your damndest in an ostentatious manner all the time. Make it a point to always be the best turned out plebe at any formation. Brass polished, trousers pressed, everything smart. Weapons spotless and get there on time—NOT JUST ON time but WELL AHEAD OF TIME. Never make excuses whether or not it is your fault.

If you want to be a high-ranking make you must start the first day. You must <u>NEVER KNOWINGLY</u> infringe any regulation. You will get skinned but they will be accidents[;] no man ever walks the area for an accident. He walks the area for a premeditated crime.[2]

If you truly want to be a make you must dispense with friends or "Buddies"[;] be friendly but let the other man make the advances. Your own classmates—the worthless ones will tease you about boning make—admit it.

I repeat to be a make you must be a man not a boy and you must never let up working. You must not be a good fellow or join in "HARMLESS LARKS"[;] they are the result of an unstable mind.

You will probably have no choice in initial roommates or tent mates. But keep looking for a quiet studious boy or boys for roommates for the winter. The older the men you can pick the better as roommates. It is usually best not to live with your friends—that makes you lose them. Remember you are a lone wolf.

If some little fart hazes you don't get mad do what he says and take it out on someone else next year. AGAIN, NEVER BE LATE, ALWAYS BE WELL DRESSED, DON'T BREAK THE REGULATIONS AND DON'T BE CARE-LESS ABOUT ROOM POLICE.

Well we are really proud of you for the first time in your life, see to it that we stay that way.

Affect,

Letter, GSP Jr. to his son George IV, from the headquarters of the Western Task Force in Morocco:

DECEMBER 22, 1942

My dear George:

I would not be too worried about missing the war for as far as I can see, it looks like a long job. At the present time I am in command of a Corps with considerable added equipment.

I wrote your Mother all about my various expeditions, in one of which some of our Allies fired 18 rounds of high explosives at my plane, mistaking me for an Italian. One of these came near enough to make a hole in the wing. It was certainly very unpleasant while it lasted.

Another time, I was caught in a storm and circled over the airport for an hour and a half before I was able to get in. For a time it looked as if we would all have to jump, which would be very unpleasant in this country as there are many rocks.

. . . If I am as famous as you seem to think, I really believe it is quite unfortunate. In a horse race you never want to make your race on the first turn. It is better to put on the speed in the stretch—and the stretch is some years from now.

[He had decorated two privates with military honors earlier in the day.]

Two of these privates were really very heroic men. In the storming of a fort they climbed up the wall and sat straddling on it under an intense fire at a few yards, and worked their light machine guns so effectively that the other soldiers were able to force the breach. It must have been a regular "Beau Geste" battle. Some day I will get some pictures and send them to you.

Some weeks ago I went boar hunting and succeeded in killing two boars and a jackal with a solid slug out of a shotgun. I had the most infernal luck as I hit all three running with one shot each, and got two through the heart, and one through the head at ranges of from fifty to ninety yards. Of course the French, not being good shots, thought that I aimed at the places I hit. Actually you know that in shooting running game you shoot at the whole hog, but the effect was very useful.

With best wishes for a Merry Christmas and a Happy New Year, and a successful life as a Cadet.

Very affectionately,

Letter, GSP Jr. to his son George IV. The younger George had just been "found deficient in mathematics" and would have to retake the exam before returning to West Point in the fall. Meanwhile, the Allied invasion of Sicily was just a few weeks away:

JUNE 20, 1943

My dear George:

General Eisenhower was good enough to send a telegram to find out the status of yourself, Gay, Keyes and Truscott. So far as we can note from the answer, you have been apparently turned back, but since everyone at West Point says that you did your best and since you also very loyally followed my example, not only in getting turned back but in getting turned back in the same subject, I cannot criticize you because no man can do more than his best, and it is highly probable that in your case, as in mine, the fact that you were turned back will militate to your advantage in giving you a broader outlook on life and in hardening your soul.

Everyone has to conduct himself according to his own understanding and in consonance with the usage of the Corps at the time. In my day the turnbacks had to room with the new Plebes, and I believe that this is for the best.

If I were you I would simply consider myself a member of the new class and without cutting myself off from my former friends would attempt to make friends in the class of which you are a member. If you do this, you will have the respect of both classes, whereas if you follow the example of certain men of my time and associate only with your former class, you will be looked down on by them and by your new class.

It is also very important not to become a young Solomon and spend all your time telling the new Plebes just what is going to happen. It is best to let them find out for themselves. In other words, keep your mouth more religiously shut than you did the first year . . . Above all you must not make excuses for being turned back any more than you make excuses for failing in a horseshow. It is a fact and must be accepted as one. On the other hand, do not make fun of yourself for being a turnback.

So far as your future in the army is concerned, it makes no difference because I am sure that you will still have a chance to get in this war upon graduation, and you will be very much better fitted for the military profession, which during your lifetime will be the leading profession of our time, than had you come in through an officers' training camp.

... Yesterday, Bradley, Gaffey, myself, and Jenson, posthumously, were made honorary members of the 2nd Regiment de Marche de Tirailleurs Algériens, together with the Regiment's Fourragère of the Legion of Honor, so that we now wear a red Fourragère around our left shoulder on dress occasions.

Letter, GSP Jr. to his son George IV:

JUNE 28, 1943

My dear George:

I have already written you a letter as to your conduct in the ensuing year, but I hear so many fine things about your actions that I want to again congratulate you.

As you surmise, I realize better than anyone the acute pain which you are enduring, but I also realize that probably in your case, as it was in mine, it will be all the better in the long run. It is really very amusing that both of us failed in the same subject, and I certainly hope that while you are at Silverman's [an academic tutor] you can get such a mastery of mathematics as to be able to see them, rather than to memorize them.

Your devoted father,

[UNDATED]

Advise your mother to send your father to Trenton, the home for the insane, with a spike floor, many iron bars to kick until he cools off! He should be shot!! Only Hell is too good for him! Any Beast like your____father that would go to a U.S.A. army hospital[,] grab a sick dying U.S.A. soldier by the neck, throw him out of bed, and when he is "Down" kick him in the pants and say men like you should be shot! Is a crazy beast! Keep this card for a souvenir. It will remind you of what kind of conceited father you have. Men like him should be placed in a den of Lions. Thousands of boys have been tortured by your father's damn conceit! showing his authority! I hope someone pops him in the pants with a shotgun. The boys' friend.

[*Handwritten by GSP on the back:* This is a crank note I got and if you'll pardon me it's an S.O.B. Save it please]

Letter, GSP Jr. to his son George IV from Palermo:

OCTOBER 6, 1943

Dear George:

Self-confidence is the surest way of obtaining what you want. If you know in your own heart you are going to be something, you will be it. Now there is no reason on earth why you will not be a high-ranking Make so do not permit your mind to think otherwise. It is fatal.

So far as I am concerned, I do not know what is going to happen, but I am sure, with the same self-confidence which I am preaching to you, that something will happen, and that when it does I will make a success of it. With very affectionate regards, Your devoted Father,

---

Letter, GSP Jr. to his son George IV from Palermo. GSP Jr. had just turned fifty-eight:

NOVEMBER 14, 1943

Dear George:

It is getting pretty cold here and we have no fires in the palace, so we dress and undress fast. I wish I could find out what I am going to do and when, but so far none of us know a damned thing.

... If they have cadet Rifle teams—voluntary—turn out, or if you like the pistol better, go in for that ... Do they still have riding and polo? I hope so. Had I had a Division of American Cavalry in Tunisia and Sicily not a damned Hun would have escaped and that is no dream. As it was we had to improvise Cavalry on mules and donkeys and bulls etc. They looked like hell but did good work. With best wishes for a Merry Christmas and Happy New Year, Affect.

Letter, GSP Jr. to his son George IV from Palermo. GSP Jr. was still in limbo. His prolonged stay in Sicily made the Germans think that the Allies would soon invade southern France; they presumed that Patton would lead the assault:

JANUARY 14, 1944

Dear George:

Geoff and I almost got hit[;] we were in an O.P. [observation post] in the town shown in the picture and he said well I guess we have seen all there is to see, we stared down and one of our batteries fired just below us so I stopped to take a picture and then went on when a volley of four German shells, fairly big ones, hit all round us[;] we never heard a thing till they exploded and threw rocks and dirt on us. Col. Codman got hit on the helmet with a small fragment which did no harm[;] the nose of one bounced off something and lit within three inches of my [boot] but the funniest thing was when a fragment lit off some ammunition and hay piled in a cave[;] there were several soldiers in it too and you never saw men move so fast. One turned two somersaults in the air and lit running and he was doing a hundred in 8 flat as he passed me, being a general I had to walk[;] what we were really worried about was the W.P. [white phosphorus] in the cave which would have burned us but it did not catch. Not a man was hurt yet according to the rules of artillery we are dead as no shell hit further than thirty feet from us. Patton's luck still holds.

Well thus far I don't know where I am going to fight but hope it will be soon and seriously I have a lot of swell new ideas to kill Huns with.

In order to keep in shape I have become a hell of a mountain climber[;] there is an old Roman trail that goes up 900 feet in less than two miles and I can make it in 24 minutes and sweat like hell.

Tomorrow Hap Gay and I are going up to the middle of the Island to look at the battlefield of Troina where we had a big show. It was also the site of a very famous cast of Roger I, conqueror of Sicily in 1068 A.D.

Congratulations on being a make during Xmas[;] it is an especial honor since usually they are against Turnbacks so you must be doing a good job. Be so SPOONY that you not only get by but attract attention. Why do you think I pay so much attention to being well dressed. You must be different from the crowd but different in an efficient way, not in a sloppy way. You will find cadets who bone being blasé, too, but shun them. Never economize on your clothes or on having them pressed. When I was boning make I always had one uniform that I never sat down in.

I have had a couple of hundred letters on the D.P. case [the slapping incidents of August 3 and 10, 1943, first reported by newspaper columnist Drew Pearson on his radio show] and all but eleven were very much for me, I am not dead yet.

Letter, GSP IV to his father, who had just been moved into the European theater, but was still without a major command:

FEBRUARY 14, 1944

Dear Pop,

I got your letter the other day and heard about your new A. P. O. [Army Post Office address]. Well, I gather that you're probably glad about it all. Every one of your friends around here says they're glad about something but they either can't say or don't know what it is. Saw a picture of Ike today in the newsreel and he was looking pretty chipper with more decorations than a Xmas tree.

I guess I'm losing interest in most everything around here but graduating and getting out into life and getting a lick at those Japanese bastards. If I thought it would get me on the line any sooner, why I'd even take the Air Corps. It's the funniest feeling . . . to see my own ex-classmates about to become firsties, etc., but when I really get down to contemplation of the subject, I realize that I wouldn't have been a bit satisfied with myself as a West Pointer and a graduate next June. This is a long bitter way to come through and you know that. I have been told that I am 22nd ranking man in my class of 1001 or something like that. And brother I really worked for it. Now the idea is to hold it or try to gain more.

Letter, GSP Jr. to his son George IV (at West Point) from England. GSP Jr. was now commanding the fictional First U.S. Army Group—part of a plot to persuade the Germans that the Allies would invade France by way of Calais:

APRIL 19, 1944

Dear George:

. . . I appreciate your wishing that I would be Superintendent of the Military Academy, but after the war I am going to be through and spend my time sailing.

I am glad that you have taken up squash. Remember that the whole art in squash is to keep looking at the ball all the time. Keep your eye on it until the racket actually hits it. Also in nearside, that is backhand shots, do not change your racket as in tennis, but hit backwards the same as the forehand drive and face the wall.

I am sorry that 415 boys are going to the aviation school, but there is certainly quite a lot of glamour to it and very good promotion, although I still believe the ground people will win the next war.

I do not believe that you should go into the paratroops or airborne infantry because, while there is a great deal of glamour attached to them, they have as yet to prove themselves worth anything except a pain in the neck to the people who have to use them. They are very gallant and all that, but they do not have the equipment to fight after they land. However, keep these remarks to yourself.

Letter, George S. Patton IV to his father, GSP Jr.:

MAY 9, 1944

Dear Pop,

During furlough, instead of going home I'm going back to the Doc and let him poop me up on as much calculus as he can over a two-week period. I think it's a fairly good idea, as I don't want to have a "repeat performance" of last June. What do you think? Well I don't know myself although I'm just hoping that I might learn something. I hope you aren't suggesting that I should bone "air corps." Are you? I'll admit that they have been doing some red-hot work but I still don't think we can bomb Germany out of the war . . .

Drilled my first plebe squad the other day and did a pretty good job of it if I say so myself. Have more "balls" than I thought I would have—Thanks! At least that's something I inherited . . . Well, drop me a line if you have a chance. Always look forward very much to hearing from you.

Your devoted son,

Letter, GSP Jr. to his son George IV:

MAY 19, 1944

Dear George:

I think your going to the Doc instead of furlough is swell and whether you learn much or not the fact that you gave up that much for your ambition speaks very well for your future. If you go after what you want with all you have got you will always get it.

Remember that General Pershing told me once that SELF CONFIDENCE is the greatest thing a man can have. Joe Louis is not a great boxer but he thinks he is a great fighter so he is. Men are never beaten by anything but their own souls when the latter curl up.

As you say the Air is doing a lot but Germany is still there and so is her air force but we will kill them off[;] wait and see.

Before I went to Sicily I marked on my map the places I thought I would have battles and I was 100% right—I just got through marking a map of Europe today[.] I hope I come out as well both in winning and picking—I am sure I will . . . I am very proud of you,

Affect,

Letter, GSP Jr. to his son George IV on D-Day, the start of the Normandy invasions. The Allied ruse to make the Germans think that Patton would invade at Calais had worked; the Nazis were slow to respond to the Normandy attacks, allowing the Allied forces to form a firm beachhead:

JUNE 6, 1944

Dear George:

At 0700 this morning the BBC announced that the German Radio had just come out with an announcement of the landing of Allied Paratroops and of large numbers of assault craft near shore. So that is that.

This group of unconquerable heroes whom I command are not in yet but we will be soon—I wish I was there now as it is a lovely sunny day for a battle and I am fed up with just sitting.

I have no immediate idea of being killed but one can never tell and none of us can live forever, so if I should go don't worry but set yourself to do better than I have.

All men are timid on entering any fight whether it is the first fight or the last fight. All of us are timid. Cowards are those who let their timidity get the better of their manhood. You will never do that because of your bloodlines on both sides. I think I have told you the story of Marshall Touraine who fought under Louis XIV. On the morning of one of his last battles—he had been fighting for forty years—he was mounting his horse when a young ADC [aide-de-camp] who had just come from the court and had never missed a meal or heard a hostile shot said: "M. de Touraine, it amazes me that a man of your supposed courage should permit his knees to tremble as he walks out to mount." Touraine replied, "My lord duke, I admit that my knees do tremble but should they know where I shall this day take them they would shake even more." That is it. Your knees may shake but they will always take you towards the enemy. Well, so much for that.

There are apparently two types of successful soldiers: those who get on by being unobtrusive and those who get on by being obtrusive. I am of the latter type and seem to be rare and unpopular; but it is my method. One has to choose a system and stick to it. People who are not themselves are nobody.

To be a successful soldier you must know history. Read it objectively—dates and even the minute details of tactics are useless. What you must know is how man reacts. Weapons change but [the] man who uses them changes not at all. To win battles you do not beat weapons—you beat the soul of man, of the enemy man. To do that you have to destroy his weapons, but that is only incidental. You must read biography and especially autobiography. If you will do it you will find that war is simple. Decide what will hurt the enemy most within the limits of your capabilities to harm him and then do it. TAKE CALCULATED RISKS. That is quite different from being rash. My personal belief is that if you have a 50% chance, take it because the superior fighting qualities of American soldiers led by me will surely give you the extra 1% necessary.

In Sicily I decided as a result of my information, observations and a sixth sense that I have that the enemy did not have another large-scale attack in his system. I bet my shirt on that and I was right. You cannot make war safely, but no dead general has ever been criticized, so you have that way out always.

I am sure that if every leader who goes into battle will promise himself that he will come out either a conqueror or a corpse, he is sure to win. There is no doubt of that. Defeat is not due to losses but to the destruction of the soul of the leaders. The "Live to fight another day" doctrine.

The most vital quality a soldier can possess is SELF-CONFIDENCE, utter, complete and bumptious. You can have doubts about your good looks, about your intelligence, about your self-control; but to win in war you must have NO doubts about your ability as a soldier.

What success I have had results from the fact that I have always been certain that my military reactions were correct. Many people do not agree with me; they are wrong. The unerring jury of history written long after both of us are dead will prove me correct.

Not that I speak of "military reactions." No one is born with them any more than anyone is born with muscles. You can be born with the soul capable of correct military reactions or the body capable of having big muscles, but both qualities must be developed by hard work.

The intensity of your desire to acquire any special ability depends on character, or ambition. I think that your decision to study this summer instead of enjoying yourself shows that you have character and ambition—they are wonderful possessions.

Soldiers, all men in fact, are natural hero-worshippers. Officers with a flair for command realize this and emphasize . . . in their conduct, dress and deportment the qualities they seek to produce in their men. When I was a second lieutenant I had a captain who was very sloppy and usually late, yet he got after the men for just those faults; he was a failure.

The troops I have commanded have always been well dressed, been smart saluters, been prompt and bold in action because I have personally set the example in these qualities. The influence one man can have on thousands is a never-ending source of wonder to me. You are always on parade. Officers who through laziness or a foolish desire to be popular fail to enforce discipline and the proper wearing of uniforms and equipment not in the presence of the enemy will also fail in battle and if they fail in battle they are potential murderers. There is no such thing as "A good field soldier." You are either a good soldier or a bad soldier.

Well, this has been quite a sermon, but don't get the idea that it is my swan song because it is not. I have not finished my job yet.

Your affectionate father,

Letter, GSP Jr. to his son George IV:

JUNE 17, 1944

Dear George:

Your letter of June 4th reached me yesterday and found me reading about the Philippine war of 1899–1903 instead of fighting in this one. I feel like a slacker but it is all according to plan so I have to possess my soul in patience. However, I worry all the time for fear that it will be over before I get in, though I know damned well that it won't.

. . . It is hard to advise a man on what branch to take. You have to follow your own convictions. All I can say is that the Artillery live the longest but get the least glory and promotion. The Armored Force is fairly healthy but it is hard to get above a Major General (don't laugh[;] you will beat that grade). [In fact, George IV did not.] The Paratroops are used only on targets of opportunity and while they get a lot of honor they don't stay on a job long enough to get real promotion. The Air Force gets lots of excitement and promotion but I doubt if a C in C [commander in chief] ever will come from the air. I may be wrong in this but I can't see it. The bombing is not as effective as lots of people think and there is little chance for great leadership. As soon as you get rank you have to stop flying. Besides, there will be a lot of aviators with combat experience and only a few years older than you at the beginning of the next war. That would seem to leave only the infantry, as I fear that the cavalry is extinct—more is the pity. Also since the infantry always has and probably always will be the largest branch they naturally have a big say in selecting future commanders. But it is your life, not mine, and make your own choice. Whatever arm you take you must feel that it is the best.

A lot of us think that men should not choose arms but simply be commissioned in the U.S. Army and then spend a year or so in several branches before they are allowed to specialize. Such a course would make a much more homogenous army.

Letter, George S. Patton IV to his father:

JULY 23, 1944

Dear Pop,

I suppose that by the time you receive this letter, you will have gone into action somewhere in France. Well, they tell us here that fire and movement will win any war. And I guess it will. We have been having quite an extensive course this summer. We will have fired all basic weapons in the end.

Also the 42[,] which is quite an instrument[.] I have finished one week of battle practice on the inoculation to combat under live fire. Quite a skill.

But for all this—academics are foremost in my mind and I mean it. I have just got to get through and graduate. I have one more reason for doing this than I did in the past 2 years. I never thought it would happen but a certain member of the fairer sex has me in her grasp. Damn all women!

They tell you these creatures take the mind off the math but so far as I can see it makes for more studying.

. . . We are taking a course now that is right square out of this world. It is called Mechanics and has to deal with forces acting on a body. I can't see how it's going to help me to get my platoon out of Burma if I ever get there. Well, I see by today's paper that you have taken Trier and are pushing ahead. I guess the going is a little easier than before, eh?

. . . I'd appreciate it if you could send me a few of your out-of-date training memorandums for me to use with the yearlings and plebes this summer, for squads, mainly, and platoons. I would really love to have them and I think I could actually do something with them.

. . . We are also taking a very useless course on political science. Well, they were going round the class asking people the opinion of the President the other day. I told them that (when they came to me) I didn't care to voice my opinion, that it was none of my business, that so far as I was concerned, leave the army to the army and the politics to the people . . . I think the "p" [professor] got bitter but no matter—that was my idea and I don't worry what he thinks.

Letter, GSP Jr. to his son George IV:

Dear George:

As I write, several hundred bombers are going over to blast the Hun. We are moving up to a heavily mined area, so I hope that Willie [Patton's famous bull terrier] will not try and retrieve one of the new Mustard Pot mines, about as big as a pint jar. It would be most embarrassing to me and to him if he chewed the detonator.

Paddy Flint was killed four hundred yards ahead of his men in a lone hand fight in which he was using two carbines and an M1 at a range of twenty yards. He got it in the head right through the helmet and did not suffer at all. I sent your mother an account of the affair which you should read as he was one <u>HELL OF A MAN</u>. I think it is a Medal of Honor— I hope so.

I saw the deadest German yet the other day. He was shiny black because he had just been found. I should hate to have to bury him but he will be properly planted as we always do it for them and they for us.

Letter, George S. Patton IV to his father:

AUGUST 1944

I certainly enjoyed your D-day letter. It was really swell. I've read it and reread it and I get more out of it each time . . . I'm just counting the days . . . hoping against a failing hope that I'm going to get in this war. I'm really sweating it out and I don't mean maybe.

Letter, GSP Jr. to his son George IV from France, where he was leading the Third Army:

AUGUST 21, 1944

My dear George:

Your letter of August 8, duly dated, just reached me. I believe that by now you know where I am, but if you know what I am doing you are smarter than the Germans. We have been having a swell time and I trust that good fortune continues to attend our efforts.

I have used one principle in these operations which has been remarkably successful, and that is to—

"Fill the unforgiving minute
With sixty seconds' worth of distance run."

That is the whole art of war, and when you get to be a general, remember it!

I have never given a damn what the enemy was going to do or where he was. What I have known is what I have intended to do and then have done it. By acting in this manner I have always gotten to the place he expected me to come about three days before he got there.

We are having another try this morning, which is the most audacious we have yet attempted, but I am quite sure it will work.*

The great difficulty we have experienced here is that we have moved so fast and so far that we are nearly always out of communication. However, Colonel Muller and the Quartermaster and the Ordnance people have done a job which will be studied for years in supplying this Army . . .

With wishes for all success, I am, Devotedly yours,

 * [*Letter typewritten. Added in GSP Jr.'s handwriting:* It worked! We got the bridge at Sens before he knew it. That is worth a week.]

Letter, GSP Jr. to his son George IV:

AUGUST 28, 1944

Your letter of July 23 has just reached me. We are really having a swell time and have just captured CHATEAU THIERRY, which, while it was fought before you were born, you probably know about. We will be further along before dark.

At the present time, my chief difficulty is not the Germans but gasoline. If they would give me enough gas, I could go anywhere I want.

I am sorry that you have to damn all women, but if the woman you are damning is the one I think she is, then she is a very charming person, or at least she appears so in her pictures.

. . . I am sure that you are doing a fine job at West Point, and now that you have an incentive in the "damn women" to study, I think you will probably come out at the top of your class.

With affectionate regards, I am as ever,
devotedly yours,

Letter, GSP Jr. to his son George IV:

SEPTEMBER 17, 1944

Dear George:

Your mother writes me that you came out one (ONE) in the infantry assault course. Fine work.

We had to halt for a couple of days for certain reasons and as a result the Bosch built up west of the Moselle and we have had a time kicking them out. We got Nancy yesterday but Metz[,] which is one of the best-fortified cities in the world[,] is still holding out.

. . . I personally saw a nice tank fight the other day from a plum orchard where I was eating. There were two German tanks in the foreground burning brightly and beyond them were four of our tanks shooting into a woods. The Bosch were shooting back and it was all very merry.

These damned paratroops are more trouble than they are worth. They are great personal fighters but have no staying power or means of supply. I wish they would turn them all into Infantry and equip them in the normal way. In this campaign, which is in its 103rd day, they have been in combat seven days.

I have been going to the front so much and kicking so much about delay that I have the generals jittery so I am spending a Sunday in the truck with Willie. He sends his best. Well[,] good luck;

Affect.

> [*Letter typewritten. Added in GSP Jr. handwriting:*
> Box score to date for 3d Army:
>
> | | | | |
> |---|---|---|---|
> | PW [prisoners of war] | 87000 | Tanks out 850 | |
> | K [killed] | 20000 | Guns out 1600 | |
> | W [wounded] | 73000 | Vehicles 4200 | |
>
> Planes shot down by our AA 234 sure & 106 probable
> Of course we have paid too but only at less than one to five.]

Letter, GSP Jr. to his son George IV:

OCTOBER 4, 1944

My dear George:

Your letter of August 31 just reached me. With regards to the shoulder padding, you will notice every garment you own has padding in the shoulders. They are padded no more in my clothes than in yours. The reference to the padding was a nasty crack on the part of *Time* or *Life,* whichever one used it. You cannot make clothes fit without it.

Up until yesterday, we had very severe fighting on the front of this Army, but now we seem to have persuaded the Germans to quit and they are apparently wholly defensive.

Today, we are assaulting one of the old forts around Metz and have got two platoons of tanks inside the fort. However, this is not all you have to do because most of the defenders are under about 15 yards of concrete and the question of getting them out is difficult. I am trying an experiment of pouring gasoline down the ventilator pipes and then lighting them. I think this should at least keep the Germans from getting cold feet.

The fighting is at very close range, the tanks getting to within 50 yards of the pillboxes. We have lost some tanks but not many. In the last two weeks we have destroyed between 150–200 German tanks and killed a very large number of Germans.

The 6th Armored the other day in a counter-attack counted 700 dead as the result of 2 hours fighting. Seven hundred dead means 2800 wounded, very few of whom we captured. In fact, it was a very bloody fight and we only took 57 prisoners in the whole show.

I am glad that you are Second Corporal of your Company but wish you were First Corporal. Remember that there are two more makes before June, at least there were in my day. By the time you get this, you will have some news on how you are doing in the academic department. I trust that it will be satisfactory, and in fact, I am confident that it will be.

Your affectionate father,

This letter and the one that follows—written on the same day from Europe—record a pivotal point in George IV's life.

Letter, Major General Hobart R. "Hap" Gay to George IV:[3]

OCTOBER 25, 1944

Dear George:

It is a peculiar thing, when one really considers it, that most advice costs nothing and is worth exactly that much. I am afraid that the advice which I am going to give you falls in the same category. However, since talking with your Father on the subject, and also remembering that I too have an Honorable Son in the Military Academy, I am taking the privilege of writing you this short note.

Boys of your age (pardon me, I should have said, "men of your youthful years") take life, very fortunately, more seriously than do those of us who have seen perhaps more than our allotted number of summers. During that stage when one takes life so seriously, we are perhaps prone to give undue weight and consideration to certain subjects and problems, which are prevalent for the time being. Frankly, as I look back over my years before and after coming into the Army, I am sure that on many occasions I was entirely too serious, thus my judgment became slightly warped and I would have been much better off, if in the language of slang, I had "lit a Murad" and been slightly more nonchalant.

Now as to why this build-up paragraph, which you have just been forced to read. I think in the years to come you will find that you made a very serious error if you decided to leave the Academy at this time. I know that you feel that every young man in America today is not doing his duty unless he is in the Army, and perhaps in the language of the newspaper people and of the pseudo-historians, "baring your chest to the effects of the bullets and shell fragments of the enemy." This, I assure you, is not true—particularly the latter. There is no assurance whatsoever that if you left the Academy and enlisted in the Army that you would be given a chance to bare your bosom to the effects of the enemy bullets. I am not certain of the percentage, but I am convinced that not more than one young man out of four hundred in the Army gets that chance. The surprising thing about war to me after having seen it incessantly now for two years—which is about as long as any other officer in the American Army has seen it during this struggle—is how little fighting actually goes on and how few people actually become engaged in the struggle directly with the enemy.

This war will probably continue for some time after your graduation from the Academy. Unfortunate as this may be, I am afraid it is quite factual. Within a short time you will have completed two and one-half years at the Military Academy. During this time the Government has afforded you many opportunities, for which it rightfully should expect a commensurate return. This is an obligation on your part, and I feel that unless you do your best to complete your course and come into the Army as a Second lieutenant, you have not fulfilled your part of the contract. The Government could have gotten, and did get many thousands of young men to go directly into the Army. This they did without first giving them the instruction afforded by the facilities of the Military Academy for two years or more, as it has done for you.

In life most people find that a broken contract leaves forever in their mouth a bad taste, and once a contract is broken, it is practically impossible to fully repair it. My advice, which as mentioned before costs nothing and is probably worth that, is that you make a serious mistake if you let your conscience lead you into that false conception of duty which will culminate in your leaving the Military Academy before you complete your course. In doing so, you would breach a contract with the Government. No Army man wishes to do that.

Sincerely yours,

Letter, GSP Jr. to his son George IV:

OCTOBER 25, 1944

My dear George:

I have heard from your mother, and also from others, that you are feeling very miserable about not being in the army as an enlisted man. I can perfectly understand your feelings, and at your age I would have had a strong inclination to resign or get "found." However, at my present age, and with my present experience, there are certain points which I should like you to consider and then decide because you will be twenty-one next birthday.

In the first place, you are not playing fair with the Government by deliberately getting "found" or resigning. The

Government has spent a lot of money training you to be one of its future leaders. I know that few people have any feeling of responsibility for the Government, but I have, and my success has been largely due to the fact that I have had such feelings.

Next, there are a great many high-ranking generals, of whom I can name General Marshall, Hodges, Truscott, Eddy, and so on who are non-graduates, but—and here is the point—they are all college graduates and therefore had the background of knowledge and education necessary to carry on as a commissioned officer. You are not a college graduate and will not be until you have graduated from the Military Academy; therefore, you will always be deficient in education and always will be handicapped by this deficiency.

There is another thing: As far as I understand, there are not more Officer Candidate Schools, either in the Ground Forces or in the Air Forces[,] so that all men come in as enlisted men, and the only way for them to get commissions is to win a battlefield promotion. I do not doubt but with sufficient experience you would win a battlefield promotion. Of course, you could not win it in my Army, but I am sure you could demonstrate your ability in some other Army.

However, a battlefield promotion is temporary. At the end of this war there will be thousands of men, many of them college graduates, who have held temporary commissions, either through Officer Training Camps or through battlefield promotions. In order to get in the Regular Army, a series of examinations will be held and those who pass will be commissioned according to their seniority in the army. At least that is the way it was after the last war.

For example, a hundred of you got battlefield promotions on the same day. You all took the examination and passed, which, with your present deficient education would not be a certainty. Among these men you would find some with two or three years' service. You would certainly find that practically all of them had more service than you. Now, there will not be an unlimited number of vacancies for officers, so it may well be that at first people will be screened by making the examinations very severe, and second, the seniority in service will be such that men with only a short term of enlistment will be eliminated.

You should think of these things very seriously. One of the best officers I know, and also one of the greatest athletes, is Major Pfann, who is Secretary of the General Staff in this Army. He was All-American half-back (amateur) and also All-American (professional). He is a Rhodes Scholar, a Phi Beta Kappa, and a Ph.D. He was exactly your age at the beginning of the last war and had the same urge that you have to enlist. However, he didn't do so because he felt that he lacked the fundamental education. He told me only today that he never regretted it.

I am simply bringing these points to your attention because, as I said before, you are free, white, and twenty-one, and can make your own decision.

However, before making it, think of what I have written and also remember that even if you miss this war due to remaining at the Military Academy, which in the opinion of all of us is highly doubtful—that is, we think it will last longer than that—you will still have plenty of more wars and they will, I think, come much sooner than most of the people at home believe.

I trust that this is not too preaching an article, but it is my best-considered thought on the matter . . .

The other night the Bosch put three 11-inch shells around our house, none of them missing it by more than 25 yards and breaking all the glass in the windows. Since then we have discovered a very nice German bomb-proof shelter under the house which we intend to inhabit when they start shelling again, so unless they get us on the first round we ought to be alright.

The house right across the street was hit and one of the MP's told me that there were some people stuck in it, so he and I went over to pull them out. There was also one Frenchman there who had a man by the foot and was pulling on it, so I joined in and we pulled, but the man's cries became more and more feeble, so we decided to take a look and found he was caught by the neck and we were choking him to death.

After we got him out, an old lady, also buried, began to scream and said that her little grandchild was buried in the ruins. The Frenchman helping me was very polite and said, "I beg of you, Madame, do not derange yourself, do you realize that the famous General Patton is helping me to remove you from the ruins and that this famous General has also sent for a doctor and an ambulance"—and so on for the ten minutes it required for us to get her out, by which time a small boy came around from the back of the house, holding the baby, which had not even waked up.

With lots of love,
Your affectionate Father,

Letter, George S. Patton IV to his father:

{NOVEMBER} 1944

Dear Pop,

Thanks for the sympathy. I'm surprised that a man busy as you must be at this moment had time to sympathize with my obviously stupid meditations on this college. I'm sorry I caused you the concern I did and will not let it happen again.

It is no damn use in worrying and I'm here for 562 more days so that's that. I will not be found. Either intentionally or unintentionally I will not get found. I'm getting more hivey every minute and I think I'll pull through fairly well. Of course I won't have the stars but I will have a commission and that's what counts!

The reason I <u>was</u> deficient in History <u>was</u> that it came on the same day as Physics, which is my hardest subject. They'd ask us these damn fool questions on government and treaties and on absolutely none of the real history, which I learned to love from yourself. For example, they completely skipped over Wallenstein, Gustavus Adolphus, Tilly [sic] and many others. But the worst faux pas was the complete omission of the Peninsular War of Napoleon. Well, I got so peed off that I told my "pe" [professor] about it and we went round and round. He finally let me give a 20-minute speech on this campaign and I maxed it—It put me pro in History which was one of the reasons I asked him. How all these other jerks around here like this stuff. They don't care about Napoleon. All they care about is his governmental policies of liberty and fraternity etc. etc. We spent 10 minutes in a not too hot discussion of Russian campaign of 1814. That also made me mad.

... Thanks again for the advice—<u>it shall be done</u>

—Your devoted son,

Letter, GSP Jr. to his son George IV:

NOVEMBER 8, 1944

Dear George:

The statement that Dinah Shore got my pistol is an unmitigated lie. The only time I saw the girl was when I sat opposite her at a lunch in the Officers Mess. She probably did not make the statement either, but it was simply a publicity stunt by some of her hired assistants.

When you write, even to me, about a General Officer, you should not say, "Devine," but say, "General Devine." It is very cheap to speak of your seniors in the military profession behind their backs in a manner different from what you would speak to their faces. It was very nice of him to look you up, and I am certainly glad that you enjoyed hearing him talk.

... In one of the magazines—I think it was *Time*—I was attacked for attempting to accomplish the impossible. This was a very stupid attack because success is only achieved by accomplishing the impossible. However, it may interest you to know that I did it again last night when the Battle of Nancy—about which you will probably have read by the time you get this—started.

It was raining to beat hell, and had been for a week. All the rivers were flooded and the ground seemed impossible to move on. However, I figured the enemy would think exactly that, so we attacked, and although it is still early to say we have won a battle, we have taken every objective set for the first day ahead of time.

It was really quite a show. We jumped off at 6:00 this morning, with three divisions, backed up by over 400 guns. The firing could be seen from my room, and it looked just like heat lightning. The rumble of the guns is something which can only be appreciated after it is heard. It does not sound like artillery. It sounds like a continual slamming of a large number of doors in an empty house and makes the house shake in the same way.

I have been clear down to the front this morning, but nothing exciting happened as our artillery preparation, which lasted forty-five minutes, had apparently put the Germans into a complete tailspin.

... With affectionate regards,
Your devoted Father,

Letter, GSP Jr. to his son George IV:

JANUARY 16, 1945

Dear George:

I was glad to hear from a letter from your mother what a nice Xmas you had and I was also delighted to hear that you were rated so high in leadership. It is the thing that wins battles. I have it—but I'll be damned if I can define it: Possibly it consists in knowing what you want to do and then doing it and getting mad if any one steps in the way. Self confidence and leadership are twin brothers.

The Bastogne Operation which we terminated today by taking Huffalies is probably the most important one I have done. It certainly stopped the German breakthrough when all the defensive in the world would have had no effect and I think we accounted for some 80,000 Germans. The woods are full of corpses and it is going to stink some in the spring.

I am starting a new attack in a few days[;] it should have been launched sooner but I did not have the men. Even though I had seventeen divs that is the most I have ever used. In the battle of France I had 14 at the highest. It is just as easy to command 20 as it is one perhaps.

. . . One of these damned Jet Planes that goes 470 miles an hour just dropped a bomb. It shook this house—which is normally an old woman's home—and scared Willie. They also shoot rockets at us but one gets used to such things: It is like a thunder storm[;] you are not apt to be in the way and if you are[,] What the Hell—no more buttoning and unbuttoning. Hope your watch keeps running.

Your affect Father.

Letter, GSP Jr. to his son George IV:

MARCH 6, 1945

Dear George:

Who ever called you a draft dodger for coming back to WP to graduate was a fool and you need not worry about him. The added effort you have made to graduate will do you good all the rest of your life. Of course it will be hard to see your old class go, but in a few years you won't be able to remember to which class they belonged . . .

Affect.

Letter, George IV to his father:

MARCH 9, 1945

Dear Pop,

Well[,] I had to write you on account of the fact that you have <u>god damn</u> done it again. Excuse my emotional outburst but I couldn't help it. Now of all the things I've read about you that was the damnedest of all. That's what the leadership of an Army or higher echelon commander is. You define it about once a week in the papers and probably many times a day that doesn't get printed. It's got a lot to do with guts— just plain guts. I'm wondering how the hell I'm ever going to make out in this profession. About the only thing left for me is to charge out and nail a Medal of Honor somewhere in

Burma about two years from now. Leave that one open anyway.

... God knows I'll do anything because I feel so guilty about not being with my friends in the 2nd Armd.

... I hope you get along OK in Germany and will be home by Xmas—as I usually say when I'm excited, That'll be the god damn day—

Your devoted son,

Letter, GSP Jr. to his son George IV. This was written immediately after Patton's ill-advised attempt to liberate a prisoner-of-war camp near Hammelburg, Germany. His son-in-law, Lieutenant Colonel John K. Waters, was being held captive at the camp, which probably influenced Patton's decision to wage the attack. An ambush of the undersized task force followed; about three hundred soldiers died or were injured or taken prisoner in the attempt.[4] Waters himself was badly wounded and recaptured. The event stands out as perhaps Patton's only tactical military error in the war:

MARCH 30, 1945

Dear George:

Our mechanized cavalry regiments, as I wrote you before, have been doing a wonderful job, and I believe that for steady fighting without the certainty of immediate death, they are the best show going. The trouble with the paratroops is that they fight very little and then nearly always on the defensive, waiting for someone to extricate them. While this is very gallant, it does not promote rapid promotion, except to the grave.

. . . As you will see from the modest words of the enclosed General Order, we have won the greatest battle in the history of the 3rd Army, and I personally believe in the history of the world, as I know of no case where such a complete destruction of the enemy has been wrought in such a short time.

. . . I think it is a mistake to fight your subjects, which you seem to be doing. As you know, I did not like any of them and did not do very well in any of them, but it is a foolish thing to fight a problem. It puts you in the wrong frame of mind . . . You have repeatedly demonstrated that when it came to a pinch, you could succeed. Now you must remember that you have done this and keep on succeeding.

Affectionately,

Letter, GSP Jr. to his son George IV. This one captures Patton's belief in reincarnation—which was shared by his son:

MAY 21, 1945

Dear George:

Your V-Day letter just arrived. I am shocked at the number of cadets you say do not intend to go into the Army, but I think that most of them are talking through their hats.

What do you mean by the expression that you came pretty near knocking yourself out? Was that from over-study or an abortive attempt at suicide? I abhor suicide as it saves the Japanese a chance of shooting at you. I feel quite sure that you will get a chance to fight the Japanese.

It is my present opinion that the Third Army will not go over there for several months, perhaps six months if at all, although I doubt if they can keep me from going unless the Japs quit.

There is no use feeling sorry for the people who get killed. It is probably the greatest end they can have, and there is very little pain to it. It was tragic for the United States that Darby got killed, as he was a splendid soldier. The rest are probably looking down from heaven and making plans to get reborn so they can fight in another war.

This thing of having no war to fight is something of a let down, although for the moment, Marshal Tito is making faces at the Third Army, and the 3rd Cavalry has gone down to straighten him out . . . Your devoted father,

---

Letter, GSP Jr. to his son George IV:

AUGUST 12, 1945

My dear George:

What is your correct address now, if any? I presume if you are a Battalion Adjutant, the battalion should be named, or should I still make it to F Company?

I know that you will be very disappointed at not getting into the war. I am equally distressed that I did not have a chance at killing Japs, but it is one of those things that you can't help. Your education and heredity will certainly make you a very valuable officer in the next war, and there will certainly be another war in spite of what a lot of fool people say to the contrary.

The thing to do is to keep your mind open, find out what happened in this war, and think what may happen in the next war. Someone once said of the Regular Army officers that they knew everything about the last war and nothing of the present one. In the case of certain officers this is true. For instance, the thing to think about now is the effect that the atomic bomb and the rocket-type gun will have, but remember that no matter what weapons you fight with, men use them, and the art of war is the art of commanding men and knowing how they will react.

I am sending you the first chapter of my personal account of the war in France. This must not be left around or shown indiscriminately to your friends. There are many people who would give thousands of dollars to have that paper to publish. If published in the form in which you get it, it would simply make many people unhappy to no purpose.

I have thought of a fine trip for you and your mother when you graduate. If I am still here, which I probably will be, I will arrange for you two to come over, and we will take a car and start at Cherbourg and come over the entire route of the Third Army. I should think that in two weeks we could cover it very well, and you could learn a great deal about it. With affectionate regards, Your devoted father,

Letter, GSP Jr. to his son George IV. The senior Patton's show-down with Eisenhower was looming:

SEPTEMBER 3, 1945

Dear George:

Your opinion about the capacity of the atomic bomb is unduly large. In the first place, the Japanese had made peace overtures through the Russians at least a week before the first atomic bomb fell. The Japanese were not so much beaten as they were disillusioned. As you know, most Japanese are extremely local, even more so than the inhabitants of Myopia. When, around 1930, a good many of our college students signed pledges that they would not fight for the country under any circumstances the Japs believed it. They also believed a great many other things equally foolish, and based their attack on us upon such beliefs. Presently, they found out they were wrong. We used to read with great interest the reports from the Japanese Ambassador to Berlin, warning his people that the Americans were extremely dangerous and that they had better look out for them. The Japanese, therefore, surrendered not because they were beaten, but because they realized that they were unready to win.

So far as the atomic bomb is concerned, while it is a scientific invention of the first [order], it is not as earthshaking as you might think. When man first began fighting man, he unquestionably used his teeth, toenails and fingernails. Then someday a very terrified or else very inventive genius picked up a rock and bashed a man in the head while the latter was gnawing at his vitals. The news of this unheard-of weapon unquestionably shocked Neolithic society, but they became accustomed to it. Thousands of years later, another genius picked up the splintered rib of a mastodon and using it as a dagger stuck the gentleman . . . Again, pre-historic society was shocked and said, "There can be no more wars. Did you hear about the mastodon bone?" When the shield, sling shot, throwing stick, and the sword and armor were successively invented, each in its turn was heralded by the proponents as a means of destroying the world or of stopping war. Certainly the advent of the atomic bomb was not half as startling as the initial invention of gunpowder. In my lifetime, I remember two inventions, or possibly three, which were to stop war; namely, the dynamite cruiser Vesuvius, the submarine, and the tank. Yet wars go blithely on and will when your great-grandchildren are very old men.

I am glad that you had such a good time at Pine Camp and am sorry that your voice was not at its best, but I believe that you will get a good make and I am sure you will hold it when you do.

I am planning, if possible, to get you and your mother over here on your graduation leave so that we can take a car and drive over the route of the Third Army. I do not see any chance of any women getting over prior to the next spring. The situation as to food and accommodations here is too critical, but I think that possibly we could work it for a short time in the spring.

. . . Finally, my conclusion is that the Army is just as important as it ever was, and that people with imagination are needed . . .

Your affectionate father,

Letter, GSP Jr. to his son George IV:

OCTOBER 22, 1945

My dear George:

I am glad you are living up to the best traditions of the family in Military History. I stood 1 in it. Don't let Economics get you down because on your maternal grandfather's side you should be good at it.

. . . I did not know until you told me that Napoleon crossed near Oppenheim. I had picked this when I was still in England as the place to cross the Rhine because the terrain on my side dominated that on the other side as the former was far enough away from the Frankfurt hills to prevent direct fire on the bridges and because, above everything else, there was a barge harbor there from which we could launch the boats unseen . . . Your affectionate father,

Letter, GSP Jr. to his son George IV:

NOVEMBER 3, 1945

My dear George:

It is quite natural that my speeches should sound like Napoleon's because, as you know, I have studied him all my life. You are wrong in saying he found a different type of war—he and I fought the same way but my means of progress were better than his.

Letter, GSP Jr. to his son George IV:

NOVEMBER 10, 1945

... Napoleon, I think, started making mistakes in 1805 ... about that time he lost his old soldiers and his old officers and had to resort to heavy formations to make up for lack of discipline and leadership.

... I doubt very much if I get home for Christmas but hope to get home permanently shortly after that.

Affectionately,

George Patton Jr. died on December 21, 1945. The following letters to George IV arrived the following year:

MULHOLLAND FARM

HOLLYWOOD 46.

Dear Mr. Patton,

Many thanks for your letter, and particularly the obviously real sentiments which inspired it. If, as your name would seem to imply, you're some connection of the General, I don't imagine you'll find it very hard to find within yourself those qualities you rightly or wrongly ascribe to me—personally I feel like an imposter.

I never answer letters as a firm rule, and in fact avoid reading them as far as possible, but I am doing so now out of a sense of sympathy—because I know that to one in your chosen profession you must have the hell griped out of you every day to know that the big show's going on and you're not in it. I got left out too and it hasn't stopped griping me. I can only say I hope you have better luck and I'm sure you will.

Thanks again,
Errol Flynn

Oh yes—I'm glad you deliberately distinguished the complimentary things from my acting ability—if you hadn't I'd have known you were talking through your helmet.

Letter, William Hobson, Brigadier General, U.S. Army, to George S. Patton IV:

MAY 31, 1946

Dear George:

I have just been reminded by the Army-Navy Register of 25 May 1946 that you will be graduating in a few days. I wish very much that I were going to be present at the graduating exercises so that I might have the honor and pleasure of congratulating you and your Mother as you pass such an important milestone in your military career. How we all will continue to bemoan the untimely passing of your distinguished Father whose graduation I witnessed thirty-seven years ago and who, if he were living, would no doubt be prouder of having you graduate from his Alma Mater, West Point, than of any of the many great honors that came into his illustrious life.

Of course you too are fully aware of the fact that you have ahead of you the challenging experience of living up to the lofty standards that are associated in military talk, in and out of our Army, with the famous name you bear. And, from what I can learn about you, we who have had the privilege of enjoying the friendship of your Father and Mother over the years have every right to anticipate that in due time you too will measure up fully to the great name of Patton and the high expectations of our beloved Alma Mater, West Point, whose motto, "Duty, Honor, Country," has borne the test of time as an ever-present inspiration to her sons . . .

Faithfully yours,

Letter, from a Sergeant Newman to George S. Patton IV:

JUNE 4, 1946

Dear George:

I guess this is a big day for you as the time grows short for the Graduation Exercises tonight. I know you are glad that the time has finally got here after working so hard trying to complete your studies for the past few years. I bet that your mother and sister are proud to know that after tonight you can take up where your father left off. For my opinion and many others, we think your father was the greatest man who ever lived and, son, take the advice from me, work hard and be a straight shooter and you can be the man that your father was.

Letter, William Hobson, Brigadier General (ret.), to George S. Patton IV. George was now at the Infantry School at Fort Benning, Georgia:

SEPTEMBER 1, 1946

Dear George:

Words fail me in my attempt to express to you . . . my deep sense of appreciation for the honor and privilege which you accorded me by leaving with me your collection of original letters which your Father wrote to you in 1944 and 1945 while you were a Cadet at West Point during your Second and First Class years.

After carefully reading all of these letters, I am left with the impression that they reveal in themselves a truly unique and beautiful relationship between a father and his son, such as I have never read before. And, in this relationship, one perceives a nobility of soul upon the part of your Father of which, it seems to me, an expectant and admiring world ought to know more. For, while of course much is already known of Patton, the great military world hero and leader, only a comparatively small number of close friends of your family are familiar with the equally admirable role he played as a model Father and tried and true friend of his only son at a critical time in both of their lives.

At your request, or rather with your consent, I have had the originals of the letters photostated, so that perhaps personal copies of the collection might thus be made available to your Mother and two sisters and a few close relatives or friends. May I suggest therefore that both the originals and the copies be carefully guarded until perhaps the fitting time when, in your opinion, they might well be published in some form for either private or public distribution?

... The content of the letters is also quite obviously of great historical value, for they reveal a military leader while in the heat of battle, leading his famous Third Army through brilliant victories; and yet he had the inclination and found the time and opportunity to write such fine letters to his Cadet son at his own Alma Mater, West Point, picturing the Father's leadership experiences in the war, and at the same time passing on to his beloved son some of the soundest and most helpful advice that a son ever received, and especially during a period when that son obviously needed the guiding hand of a wise and devoted Father.

I have found great personal pleasure in compiling the attached loose-leaf booklet of photostatic copies of the letters ... May I suggest that you keep it close by always and read and reread it in the days ahead of you as an officer of our great United States Army, for the wisdom therein will surely inspire you to attain your noble ambition to prove yourself to be a worthy son of one of the worthiest Fathers of recorded history.

... Faithfully your friend and your
Father's and Mother's friend,

From the diary of George S. Patton IV on December 21, 1950, the fifth anniversary of his father's death. COURTESY OF THE PATTON FAMILY

PART TWO

STUDENTS, DOERS, TEACHERS

There are three phases of life: the Learner,
the Doer, and the Teacher.

—MY FATHER, GEORGE S. PATTON IV

If we take the generally accepted definition of bravery as a
quality which knows not fear, I have never seen a brave man. All
men are frightened. The courageous man is the man who forces
himself, in spite of his fear, to carry on.

—MY PATERNAL GRANDFATHER, GEORGE S. PATTON JR.

ONE WAS A World War II hero and my father's beloved mentor. One was a Korean orphan. One was the son of my grandfather's greatest military adversary. One was my father's professional rival. One was a nun. Together, all of these uncommonly courageous people knew my father from the start of his career to the end of his life. And they're as different and unique as the ways in which their lives intersected with his.

THREE

Creighton Abrams

*If Abrams gave me a mission with the chance of staying alive at
1 in 10, I'd ask, "When are we moving out?" I never felt that
way about an officer before or since, and I worked for some good
ones . . . He was the best soldier I have ever known, including
all the members of my family.*

—MY FATHER, GEORGE S. PATTON IV[1]

*The relief of Bastogne is the most brilliant operation we have thus
far performed and is in my opinion the outstanding achievement of
this war. Now the enemy must dance to our tune, not we to his.*

—LETTER, GSP JR. TO HIS WIFE, BEATRICE,
DECEMBER 29, 1944[2]

THE SUBLIME MOMENT of my grandfather's career came just before
Christmas 1944. Only a few days earlier, Patton's Third Army had
been racing east toward Germany. The Germans, meanwhile, were
throwing everything they had into a do-or-die thrust into Allied
lines across Belgium, Luxembourg, and northeast France—a struggle
that came to be known as the Battle of the Bulge. As part of their
offensive, German Wehrmacht troops had surrounded the Belgian
town of Bastogne, trapping the 101st Airborne Division and elements of other U.S. units inside.

Lieutenant Colonel Creighton Abrams (at left) just before the Bastogne offensive, December 1944.   PHOTO BY ROBERT CAPA, COURTESY OF MAGNUM PHOTOS

In a meeting with Eisenhower and his senior commanders on December 19, my grandfather mapped out a rescue plan. He would wheel three of his divisions—around forty-five thousand men—ninety degrees to the north, and march them over a hundred freezing, snowy miles to Bastogne . . . in just three days. He'd already put the preparations in place; acting on them would simply involve a phone call and a code word. As my grandfather's biographer, Martin Blumenson, put it, "Patton's proposal was astonishing, technically difficult and daring . . . Altogether, it was an operation that only a master could think of executing."

Eisenhower agreed. And my grandfather, luckily, had thirty-year-old Lieutenant Colonel Creighton W. Abrams Jr.—known as Abe—to help lead the assault. Dynamic and aggressive, Abrams had distinguished himself as a tanker, relying on speed and meticulously maintained vehicles to outmaneuver the often better-equipped German forces. (Abrams famously dubbed his own tank *Thunderbolt*.) Earlier that year, my grandfather had told reporters at Third Army headquarters about Abrams: "There's a great young officer in the 4th," he said. "But if you're going to write about him, you better do it right away. He's so good, he isn't going to live long."[3]

By the time the 4th Armored's task force (composed of Abrams's 37th Tank Battalion and the 53rd Armored Infantry Battalion, supported by the 94th Armored Field Artillery Battalion) approached Bastogne on December 26, it was nearly dark. Their orders were to cut through the nearby town of Sibret, capturing it on the way. But Sibret was well guarded, and after days of fighting, Abrams's ammunition was nearly spent. And on top of that, he was running short of both men and tanks. His battle map showed a secondary road to Bastogne that led through Assenois—a possible chance for a surprise attack. On the other hand, it could mean walking into an ambush. The path ran through enemy territory. There was no time for reconnaissance.

Abrams and "Jigger" Jacques, commander of the 53rd, paused on the roadside to weigh their options. Beyond them, they could see Allied cargo planes struggling, amid a barrage of ground fire, to drop supplies into the Bastogne garrison. (Inside, many members of the 101st Airborne, having assessed the bleak situation, had already said their good-byes to one another.)

Liaison Officer William A. Dwight later described the scene to Lewis Sorley, author of the terrific book *Thunderbolt: General Creighton Abrams and the Army of His Times*: "I saw these damn

C-47's coming in to drop their colored parachutes for the 101st. They . . . were taking one hell of a beating. We trembled standing there . . . After Abe watched that, he said, 'Well, if those fellows can take that, we're going in right now.' And that was it."[4]

When they reached Assenois, the fighting turned so intense that Abrams had to leave the infantry behind. But the gamble paid off. As he rolled up to Bastogne with just five tanks intact, the German soldiers were caught completely off guard. Some were just lining up for dinner. "They fell like dominoes," said Charles Boggess, who was in the first tank.

As Sorley reports, "Then Boggess spotted some foxholes with what looked like men in American uniforms. He called out to them. 'Come on out, this is the 4th Armored,' but nobody moved. 'I called again and again,' said Boggess, 'and finally an officer emerged from the nearest foxhole and approached the tank. He reached up a hand, and with a smile said, 'I'm Lieutenant Webster of the 326th Engineers, 101st Airborne Division. Glad to see you.'"[5]

Of course, if taking the route through Assenois had turned out to be the wrong call, Abrams would have been court-martialed for disobeying orders. Instead, he managed to punch through the German defenses and bring about what was hailed as the turning point in the Battle of the Bulge.

He was honored with his second Distinguished Service Cross in four months for his efforts—just one of his many achievements. Even my famously egocentric grandfather is reported to have said, "I'm supposed to be the best tank commander in the Army, but I have one peer—Abe Abrams. He's the world's champion."[6]

For my family, Abrams is no average military hero. He's the bridge between my father and grandfather. Not long after the senior Patton's death in 1945, Abrams became my father's commander, mentor, and de facto big brother. As compensatory moves go, it was entirely lucky. Abrams may have equaled my grandfather in leadership and tactical skills, but their styles were completely different, and my father benefited hugely from the difference.

A master of self-promotion, my grandfather filled dozens of journals, saved copies of all his letters, kept a wartime memoir (later published as *War As I Knew It*), dressed to impress (complete with jodhpurs and ivory-handled revolvers), and loved nothing more than an entourage. He brought courage, flamboyance, and eccentricity into an explosive balancing act. Consider the contrast: When, after a meteoric rise through the ranks, the perpetually rumpled Abrams eventually became the chief of staff of the Army—the highest military position in that branch of the military, a position that put him in charge of nearly a million Army personnel[7]—he spurned his predecessor's Cadillac limousine and instead chose an old blue Chevelle from the motor pool.[8] Even as a four-star general, he often walked the halls of the Pentagon alone. When it was suggested that he write his autobiography, he recoiled in horror. "Never!" he said. "Memoirs become larded with the vertical pronoun."[9]

My father often said that Abrams was the best man he ever knew, and wasn't alone in his bias. People who worked with Abrams still love to share stories about his integrity, compassion, and the fearless example he set. Once, in World War II, he was standing by the side of the road when enemy fire came roaring in. Two nearby soldiers leaped into the ditch. "Abrams looked down at them," writes Sorley, "and then, in his kindest and most solicitous voice, cautioned them: 'Please be careful. You guys might catch cold down there.'"[10]

In the end, my father claimed to have borrowed more of his

leadership techniques from Abrams than from his own father. And Abrams, who died of lung cancer at age sixty in 1974, said that he borrowed from everyone he ever worked with.

Abrams grew up in Springfield, Massachusetts. His father was a railroad worker. Creighton (a Celtic name meaning "creekside farm") and his younger sisters walked a mile each way to school. He turned fifteen in 1929, the year the Great Depression hit. But his intelligence, drive, and ability to rally the support of others were already emerging. By his senior year of high school, the stocky, five-foot-nine teenager was class president, editor of the school paper, and captain of the football team. He scheduled football practices and games around his farm chores. After their final, undefeated season, the team got permission to buy one letter sweater—that's all the school could afford. There was no argument over who would receive it. Abrams said it was only later, after he'd left home, that it occurred to him that he was poor.[11]

He had to turn down a full scholarship to Brown University because his parents couldn't afford to pay for books and extras. After he was accepted to West Point, he reluctantly borrowed three hundred dollars from an heiress in Springfield to cover his uniforms and initial expenses. Abrams paid it back upon his graduation.[12]

One of Abrams's first lessons out of West Point was a negative one. In 1938, as a first lieutenant, he was put in command of a cavalry troop in Fort Bliss, Texas. Soon after, the division went on its annual maneuver. This took place in a remote desert more than two hundred miles away: The troops had to drag all their supplies with them on horseback. Nonetheless, the division commander, Brigadier General Kenyon A. Joyce, insisted on having his own private mess tent in the field, with a canvas floor, proper dining table and chairs, china, and silver serving dishes—and for breakfast, fresh squeezed orange juice, whipped cream, and Canadian bacon. To secure the general's morning paper (yet another demand on the list), Abrams had to send out soldiers on motorcycles at 2 a.m.[13]

Abrams never got over it. Five years later, when he was made commander of the 37th Tank Battalion, 4th Armored Division, he did just the opposite. He had his men eat first, ushering them ahead of him in the chow line. When they entered the war in France, Abrams rode with his troops into battle rather than stay back at a secure command post. He also pulled three tanks and their crews from his tank companies and turned them into mobile offices for his intelligence, operations, and liaison officers. It was the only way they could keep up.

"Abrams believed that a commander could not do his job unless he could see what was going on, and that to see he had to be up and looking out of the turret," writes Sorley. "In the 37th Tank the hatches 'rusted open,' they said proudly."[14] This approach, along with Abrams's open concern for the soldiers' welfare, made his men fanatically loyal to him. As one of his tank drivers put it, "It made us feel more like fighting harder when you could see a great man like Abe right alongside of you."[15]

It was meaningful work done at a grueling pitch. In the fall of 1944, not long before Abrams's triumph at Bastogne, he confessed as much in a letter to his wife, Julie:

Things have been most pressing, the pace has been furious, the attack is ferocious, this over a period of weeks is fatiguing. I haven't had my clothes off, I haven't been dry, I haven't been warm, except for quick naps I haven't slept for two weeks. There's no time to eat right, there's no time to think—it's attack, attack, attack. That's why I don't write more—that's why there's no rest, and that's why you get so tired and weary that you almost don't care any more. When things are that way the men, God bless them, have got to be led—someone has got to be cheerful, confident and intelligent—someone has got to be first.

He wrote a follow-up note two days later:

Yesterday or day before I wrote you a letter and I guess it was a pretty sad one. I was quite tired and upset and [had] a cold and I guess it all contributed to a bad letter. I hasten now after a refreshing sleep and a bit of sunshine to let you know that I am in good health, good spirits and just getting along fine.

Back at headquarters, Abrams's superiors didn't perceive that he'd ever wavered. With his men, too, he exuded confidence. Many officers began their day by tuning in to Abrams's command frequency, just to hear him inspire and motivate the troops.

ABRAMS FIRST APPEARED in my father's life in 1949 in occupied Europe. My father, then twenty-five, had been assigned to the 63rd Heavy Tank Battalion in Mannheim, Germany. Soon afterward, Abrams, just nine years his elder, was put in command of the unit.

Forget the glorious battalion Abrams had commanded in World War II. The 63rd made *Animal House* look tame. "It had kind of a seedy reputation," admits Abrams's son John, a retired four-star general and former head of the Army's Training and Doctrine Command. "It had probably the highest VD rate in the command, the largest recurring scandal in black marketing. It had the most undisciplined activities of soldiers being AWOL—missing formations and training and the like—and the few tanks they had in the battalion weren't running, hadn't been running for some time."

Less than thrilled with his assignment, Abrams arrived with a swagger stick, the kind of short riding crop that had been one of my grandfather's favorite props. At that point, my father began a study of him. "In those first weeks after Abrams took command he did nothing but observe," my father remembered. "Then one morning he called a meeting of the company commanders and his battalion staff. When we assembled, Abe announced we would take a short walk. We started in the headquarters motor park and terminated in the C Company motor park. I'll never forget it. He had fifty or so officers on the tour and he said, 'Each time I raise my stick the problem I point to will be corrected in twenty-four hours . . . If you need more time to fix the situation, call [the executive officer] and give us a precise time when it will be corrected. But be damn sure you're right on that, because if you're not I'm going to fire you.' So we walked and observed tools rusting in the sun, spare tires and pieces of machinery, dirty glasses and dishes and broken furniture . . ."[16]

"Three days later [Abrams] retraced his steps," noted Sorley. "The one thing he found uncorrected was [a] jeep trailer with a flat tire. He relieved the company commander on the spot."[17]

The shock waves resounded throughout the unit. "Within about three to six months that was the best battalion in Europe," my father told me. "The best unit I've ever been in." From then on, in each of his assignments, he took the same approach.

At the time, of course, Abrams was whipping my father into shape, too. Abrams had a reasonable obsession with momentum; he'd seen firsthand how decisively German Panzer divisions shot along, and the edge it gave them. For the tankers of the 63rd, this meant near-constant speed drills. During one early maneuver, a simulated firefight near a German village, the umpires asked my father to herd his tanks off the road so they could evaluate the action. At the same time he received a call from Abrams. "Get 'em right off the road," Abrams said. "I'm going to pass through you [with B Company] to continue the attack."

"There was a hell of a lot of crops on the right side of the road," my father remembers. "I was a little slow. I was worried about maneuver damage, you know, running over the produce. And around the corner comes a jeep with Abrams in it. They were really moving, practically on two wheels. He got out and walked up to me and said, 'Goddamn you. You get these goddamn tanks off the goddamn road—you're moving too slow to suit me.' And he hauled back his fist and slugged me right in the face.

"I went down in the mud. Abrams turned around and walked back to his jeep and took off. Luckily, the only people who saw us were Abe's driver and my driver, a guy named Albert Cash. He came over and picked me up off the ground. 'Captain Patton,' he said, 'I know enough about the Army that that shouldn't have been done.'

"'Forget it,' I said. 'Don't say anything to anybody.'"

My father fully expected to be relieved of his command. And that night, right on time, Colonel Abrams summoned him to his office. "I'll never forget it," my father said. "He had a little tent pitched with a cot and a folding camp table, with one candle burning. When I walked in he was sitting at the desk, kind of glowering at me, and I said, 'Captain Patton reporting to the battalion commander as ordered.'

"'With regard to today, the incident over in that village,' Abrams said, 'I've written this up.' He handed me a set of court-martial charges, accusing Abrams of conduct unbecoming an officer. 'Sign it.'

"I picked it up, read it, and tore it up and threw it in the wastebasket," my father said. "I was the source of the problem," he told Abrams. For him, there'd been nothing personal about the attack that day. If anything, Dad respected Abrams's focus and intensity. "'I thought that's what you'd do,'" my father remembered Abrams saying. "'I want you to know that I was wrong in what I did today.'"

And, pulling out a bottle of bourbon: "Let's have a drink."

"Both of them were mortified by the experience," says John Abrams. "By this time they'd developed a relationship. There was no issue of credibility about young George Patton [or] about the battalion command. There was a real fondness."

From my father's diary, 1949:

Abrams is quite a guy, he can be described in one sentence: He means business. He is very forceful, rough, kind, generous, understanding, thinks of his men, has great personal attraction and the ability to inspire. I am possessed of the feeling that he wants men around him who respect him, but are not afraid of him in the end.[18]

GRADUALLY, AFTER TAKING on division command, Abrams reinvented training for the whole army in Europe: Instead of the structured exercises that soldiers had come to expect, units competed head-to-head in maneuvers, giving their leaders room to get creative.[19] But what I like best are the small anecdotes about Abrams's methods. An example from *Thunderbolt*:

In order to see all the officers together at least once a day, Abrams [as battalion commander] instituted a morning coffee call at which attendance was mandatory. This took place in the officers club, beginning at 10:00 AM, and lasted a strict twenty minutes. It gave Abrams a chance to have a look at people, put out the word on anything he wanted everyone to hear directly from him, and expose them as a group to his personality.

On a given day one of the newest officers in the battalion, a young second lieutenant, arrived late for the coffee call. What is more, he arrived absolutely covered in grease. There was grease on his face, grease in his ears, grease up one side and down the other of him. When he burst through the door, everyone else already assembled, the first person to spot him was his battalion commander.

Abrams stared across the room at his young subordinate, taking in both the hour and his appearance, then shouted, "Look at that! Just look at that!" There was about a three-beat pause while everyone held his breath, expecting the fellow's head to roll the very next moment. "Goddamn it, that's the way a second lieutenant should look at ten o'clock in the morning!" *Abrams finished, elevating the man from culprit to paragon in an instant. It was his familiar technique of making an example in front of the rest of the outfit of someone who was doing what he wanted done.*[20]

And another, dating back to Abrams's command of V Corps in Frankfurt:

Many of the 2nd Armored's soldiers, coming from a post in Texas, had never driven tanks on roads covered with ice and snow and they found it tough going. More than one slid off the high-crowned roads and into the ditches alongside.

One young trooper, having experienced this fate, was trying man-
fully, but unsuccessfully, to get his tank out of a ditch just as Abrams
came by in his jeep. Stopping, Abrams got out and went over to talk to
the tank driver. "Having trouble, son?" he asked. "Yes, sir," said the
soldier disconsolately. "Here, let me show you how," said Abrams. With
that he took the youngster's place in the driver's seat. Gunning the
engine to such a pitch that the crowd which had gathered thought the
transmission would surely be ripped out of the hull, Abrams neatly
popped the tank right out of the ditch and up on the road. "There," he
said. "See how it's done?"

"Yes, sir," said the tank driver. "Think you can do it now?" "Yes,
sir." "Good," said Abrams, and with that he reversed the tank back into
the ditch, climbed out, got into his jeep, and without another word or
a backward glance continued on his way.[21]

In 1949, when my father took over his first company, Abrams
gave him some advice: "Never forget to look in the dark corners of
your organization."[22] Not that the job itself was sinister; his point
was simply that details matter in creating a culture. If you let something slide, that becomes the new standard. Abrams's eldest son,
retired brigadier general Creighton Abrams III, recalls driving
with his father over to the barracks at Nuremberg in the early fif-
ties: "If he saw something amiss—say, if a soldier was out of uniform
or failed to salute—he corrected it on the spot."

Lieutenant General Hobart "Hap" Gay, my grandfather's chief
of staff during and after World War II, told my dad that my grandfather had one major fault. "He had a childlike trust in everybody.
He just could not believe that people were out to get him." Abrams
had a similar faith in people, yet viewed it as a strength. On one
occasion, as head of the 2nd Armored Cavalry Regiment, he went

to bat for a master sergeant—a soldier who had been demoted after twenty-five years of service. "I thought it represented a certain callousness that the military are sometimes accused of, that they don't really have a thorough understanding of human beings and how to motivate them and how to get them back on the track and get them going and make them useful soldiers," Abrams said at the time. He took pains for the man and his family to be moved to his headquarters, where he put him in charge of the movie theater. Ten days later, according to Bob Sorley's book, *Thunderbolt,* the sergeant pocketed the proceeds from the theater and took off. [23]

"My father's comment was not, 'That was a dumb move,'" says Creighton III. "His comment was, 'You've got to bet on people. You've got to believe in them and trust them and let them be all they can be.'"

Abrams also had a knack for politics, something my grandfather—whose frankness constantly provoked the military establishment—famously lacked. Given the extraordinarily turbulent era, Abrams's dexterity and integrity meant everything. While he was working for the chief of staff during the civil rights era, one of his key duties was helping to integrate colleges in the South. Former secretary of defense Melvin Laird praised him for his work at the University of Alabama. "Faced with the same situation that had produced rioting at the University of Mississippi," he said, "Abe had drafted plans for a low-key but highly visible troop presence on the Alabama campus that enabled black students to register without incident."[24]

Soon after, in 1968, Abrams succeeded General William Westmoreland as the head of MACV, American military operations in Vietnam—the third war he'd fought for the United States.[25] It was one of the most draining, reviled, and thankless jobs in Army history. Faced with deepening resentment against the war and the draft at home, he was also hobbled by a lack of reserve forces and increasing drug use among the soldiers. Yet even then, Abrams found a way to move forward: He simply changed tactics. "The mission is not to seek out and destroy the enemy," he proclaimed early on. "The mission is to provide protection for the people of Vietnam."[26]

In the years after his tour with the 63rd Tank Battalion in Germany, my father had worked with Abrams intermittently in Korea, Europe, and at the Pentagon; off duty, they went fishing and hunting together; the general even agreed to be my brother George's godfather. Now Abrams brought my father in to command the 11th Armored Cavalry, the Blackhorse Regiment. Predictably—since my father had been schooled by Abrams and my grandfather— reports soon filtered back to Abrams in Saigon: "Colonel Patton is in places on the battlefield where he shouldn't be as a regimental commander."

"This was coming from George's bosses," says John Abrams, who served two years in Vietnam as a young armor officer. "So the old man flew down; he was concerned. The previous regimental commander that he replaced had been killed," says John. "They had a nice visit, as usual, and as my father was going back to the helicopter that would take him to Saigon, he said, 'You know, everybody's a little bit concerned about where you are on the battlefield. I'm not a very good example to give you a critique on this, but you ought to pay a little bit of attention to that.' George's reaction to him was, from my father's perspective, no discussion, no argument, no justification for it, just 'Yes, sir.' And he moved out."

And so the next set of reports that came back on George was that he was still moving around the battlefield. He'd just added a second helicopter that was providing him machine-gun support and overwatch, and he was more judicious about where he landed. The two officers understood what was going on, what was practical for the roles they were in, and admired each other as colleagues and partners. Likewise, my father provided guidance but almost never interfered with his commanders on the ground. "He would not countermand an order unless something went very much awry," says retired Major General James Dozier, who served on the Black-horse staff. "It was his job to support. And that's exactly what he did."

One afternoon, Abrams dropped by my father's command post and found him in tears. A favorite young sergeant in the regiment had just been killed in action. Abrams's eyes welled up, too. "Don't ever get too fond of them," he said, putting his arm around my father's shoulders. "Believe me, I know what you're going through."

"[He] meant that emotions can't be your guide," my father said later. "You have a mission to accomplish and you can't let your heart rule your head. One must turn his attention to those who are alive and still seeking guidance . . ."

As Abrams directed the eventual withdrawal of U.S. forces in Vietnam, he had to step up the training of South Vietnamese soldiers (the ARVN) to fill the void. This meant cleansing the ranks of racism toward their Vietnamese allies, which was prevalent. Without being preachy, Abrams instituted an inspired new rule: Before any GI did a rotation with the ARVN, he had to have at least four months' combat experience in a rifle company.

"In that four months' time their whole set of human values changes," Abrams explained. "They're no longer interested in what school another fellow went to, no longer interested in what color he is, no longer interested in what city he comes from, or how he

Colonel George Patton and General Abrams in the field, Vietnam, circa 1968–1969.[27]   PHOTOS COURTESY OF THE PATTON FAMILY

speaks the king's English. Those things were no longer important. Their values were about other things: who carried the load when the night was dark—and when the day was long—and when the danger was there all the time. Those were the things that mattered, and that they looked for and saw in others . . . [They] had the experience [to] see people for what they were really worth."[28]

Within the Blackhorse ranks, my father embarked on a similar course. "The 11th was a little bit different from a lot of units over there," says Dozier. "We had a lot of volunteers, and as best I know, within our unit there were no racial tensions to amount to anything, nor was there a lot of drug use. One reason is that we stayed busy: Almost from the day that I joined the regiment until the day I left, we were in combat. And soldiers just don't tolerate soldiers they can't depend on, whether they're black or white."

Shortly after he returned from Vietnam, in June 1972, Abrams was named chief of staff of the Army. I met him shortly afterward, when my family went to visit him and his family at Fort Myer in Arlington, Virginia. I was only seven, and remember Abrams as a big, tough-looking guy with a deep gravelly voice, smoking a cigar and laughing with my dad. Two years later, in 1974, he died of cancer while still in office. My father served as one of his pallbearers in the memorial ceremony at Arlington Cemetery.

The last time they saw each other was in the fall of 1973. It was a low point in my father's career. He'd recently been offered command of a division—the ultimate for an armored officer—but had felt compelled to turn it down. He'd damaged his hip in Germany a few years before and needed reconstructive surgery; by this point, he could barely walk. "That takes guts," Abrams acknowledged. "You may never be offered another division." He offered my father his car and driver to take him directly to Walter Reed Army Medical Center to be evaluated. (A few months later, he underwent hip-replacement surgery at Massachusetts General Hospital.)

After my father recovered, he did get another chance to command a division—and not just any division but the 2nd Armored or "Hell on Wheels," the same unit my grandfather had commanded in 1941, just prior to America's entry into the war. It was the first time in U.S. Army history that a son commanded the same unit as his father. Again, my father followed Abrams's model, passing his lessons down to a new generation. "There was a reputation for the culture that your dad created in an organization," John Abrams told me recently. "I thought for a while that Blackhorse had been an aberration—right-time, right-place, right-people kind of thing. But the same kinds of stories were shared when your father commanded the 2nd Armored in Fort Hood in the midseventies. I was at Leavenworth [at the Command and General Staff College], and it was the number one place that the graduating majors wanted to go."

From there, even more symmetries leapt up. My father became a mentor to John. John later commanded V Corps in Germany—the same unit that *his* father commanded in the early 1960s. When John was promoted to brigadier general in 1991, my father and I attended the small, private ceremony at the Pentagon. Afterward, when we reached John in the receiving line, my father shook his hand, looked him in the eye, and handed him a box containing a pair of my grandfather's stars. Although there was a lot of meaningful jaw clenching, I don't think they spoke more than a few words before my father moved on—it was too emotional for him.

Abrams's legacy rolls on in other ways, too. Not only did all three of his sons become Army generals and all three of his daughters marry soldiers, but Creighton III is also heading up an effort to create a national museum for the U.S. Army.

And then, of course, the M1 main battle tank is named after Abrams. The first model, which rumbled off the Chrysler production line in 1980, was even emblazoned with the word *THUNDER-BOLT* and a streak of red lightning stabbing through a puffy white cloud.

You can see one just a couple of miles from the Patton Museum at Fort Knox. It's parked just outside the main gate.

FOUR

Manfred Rommel

THE 1970 MOVIE *Patton* features a great scene set in the Tunisian desert. The occasion is II Corps' surprise attack on the 10th Panzer Division at El Guettar in March 1943—the Allies' first major win against the Axis tank units. As my grandfather, played by George C. Scott, watches artillery salvos land on a German armored column, he exclaims, "Rommel, you magnificent bastard, I read your book!"

Scott's delivery makes clear the sense of affection George Patton feels for his rival, Field Marshal Erwin Rommel—the great German general known as the Desert Fox. Although no one knows whether that line was actually uttered, Patton indeed admired Rommel's acclaimed book, *Infantry Attacks*—an in-depth examination of his World War I battles in the elite Alpenkorps—and a postwar brotherhood between the two men wouldn't have been at all implausible.[1] "They respected each other," my grandfather's

Manfred and his parents, Erwin and Lucie-Marie Rommel, 1941.

PHOTO COURTESY OF HAUS DER GESCHICHTE BADEN-WÜRTTEMBERG,
SAMMLUNG ROMMEL

biographer, Martin Blumenson, told me. "I think they would have enjoyed being friends after World War II had they both lived."

So maybe it's not surprising that after my grandfather's death in December 1945, his wife, Beatrice Patton, announced that she wanted to meet Rommel's widow. Unfortunately, Beatrice died before she had a chance to pay that visit. But then, in 1958, my father received orders to Germany—where Rommel's family still lived—and followed through on my grandmother's plan.

My father had mixed feelings about U.S. military adversaries. On the one hand, he refused to buy a Japanese car. On the other hand, he once attempted to meet the commander of an opposing

Viet Cong regiment, just because he admired the man's tactical daring. (One can only imagine how that might have flown with Dad's superiors; as it turned out, the VC commander was killed in a B-52 strike before things went any further.) My father's all-time favorite film was *Zulu,* made in 1964. It's based on the true story of 150 ill-equipped British soldiers who—during the Anglo-Zulu War of 1879—successfully withstood a series of withering assaults by four thousand Zulu warriors at the Battle of Rorke's Drift in South Africa. After two days of intense fighting, the Zulus finally retreated. At the end of the movie, the Zulu chief stands alone on the edge of the horizon and salutes the British troops. That's probably how my father imagined himself meeting Rommel's family, albeit from a winner's perspective.

In Germany, too, Erwin Rommel enjoyed broad popularity. He was one of the rare German officers to be regarded as a hero after World War II. Suspected of plotting against Hitler, Rommel had been forced to commit suicide in the fall of 1944. And even though he was a career soldier in the Wehrmacht, which fell under Nazi control, he never abandoned his professional integrity. The forces Rommel commanded in Africa were never charged with any war crimes. In accordance with the Geneva Convention, his troops always treated the Allied soldiers they captured humanely— including Jewish prisoners of war. During his time in France, Rommel also defied Hitler's orders to deport the country's Jewish population. (Other German generals later followed through on the Führer's orders, to horrifying effect.)

"The German people viewed Rommel as a person of honor who'd been drawn into Hitler's war because there was no way around it," says Shirley Fischer Arends, PhD. A close friend of mine for almost twenty years, Arends is a scholar of German history and culture, and is always quick to observe that Rommel wasn't an accidental hero. "He did his duty, and because he did his duty with honor, he had to die," she says.

It's worth noting that Rommel never officially became a Nazi, and always insisted that the military should stay apolitical. This wasn't an uncommon opinion for his generation. In the Weimar Republic—the elected government leading up to Hitler's Third Reich—professional soldiers weren't allowed to vote or join a political party. At home, Rommel confided to his family that he didn't trust the Waffen-SS, the paramilitary force that Hitler created to do most of the Nazis' political dirty work, including running the concentration camps and systematically exterminating millions of Jews.

The first time Rommel led SS divisions was in Italy in 1943. At that point, the SS troops numbered seven hundred thousand. The great majority of them had never seen a concentration camp. While Rommel acknowledged that they were excellent soldiers, the experience only confirmed his suspicions about the SS agenda. According to his son Manfred, Field Marshal Rommel once discovered that an SS officer under his command was collecting stamps in Milan by simply opening the shops and taking what he wanted. When he heard this, Rommel was furious. The officer automatically assumed it was because he wanted a share of the spoils and brought Rommel one of the stolen albums as a gift. Big mistake.

In early 1944, when Rommel's fifteen-year-old son, Manfred, announced plans to volunteer for the 12th SS-Panzer Division of Hitler Youth, Rommel angrily shot down the plan. "My father thought it was a great mistake to create a political army within the army," Manfred Rommel recalls. "He said, 'You'll never know what you might have to do if you're in such a unit. And what you're volunteering for isn't your business—it's mine.'" Drafted a few months later, Manfred entered the regular Army instead.

IT WAS A Sunday afternoon in July 1958 when my parents, George and Joanne Patton, drove to the Rommels' house. Manfred Rommel, then a thirty-year-old lawyer and civil servant, his wife, Lilo, and his mother, Lucie-Marie, lived in a modest two-story cottage in a leafy suburb of Stuttgart.

Before the war, Field Marshal Erwin Rommel had made his family home in Vienna, and Lucie-Marie would have preferred to stay there. But the first thing he did when he came back from Africa in 1943 was to move the household to Herrlingen-Ulm, in south-central Germany. "By 1943, my father knew that a German victory would be impossible," Manfred Rommel told me. "He said, 'The Russians will be in Vienna when the war comes to an end. West Germany near the French border would be safer.' And he was right." (At the time it wasn't easy to find a home in Germany, given that the country was under relentless bombardment by the U.S. and British air forces. Ironically, the home the Rommels eventually rented from the city of Ulm had once been an asylum for Jewish children.)

The Pattons, never ones to let a child miss a historic moment, brought their five-year-old daughter, Margaret, along for their visit to the Rommel family. As they were welcomed into the front hall, my father, a thirty-five-year-old U.S. Army major at the time, ran his eye over all the military artifacts on display and gasped. To him, "it immediately said, 'You're home,'" my mother remembers. Over the next twenty years, my family would return for two more tours of duty in Stuttgart. Meanwhile, Manfred would become the lord mayor of the city (the capital of the German state of Baden-Württemberg and the country's sixth largest metropolis), and his improbable friendship with my father deepened.

My dad and Manfred Rommel shared plenty of common ground. They both admired their fathers and came of age during wartime. They shared the same birthday—Christmas Eve—though my father was five years older. Each lived in the shadow of a national military hero and had to figure out how to live up to the pressure. And while their fathers never actually faced off in battle, the two generals had enjoyed a similar approach: Rommel and Patton famously led from the front, cranking along in visible, aggressive mode. West German diplomat Rüdiger von Wechmar, an Afrika Korps veteran, told me one of his favorite memories of working under Field Marshal Rommel:

"One morning we came to a halt because our commanding officer had stopped the advance when we arrived at a minefield. While the engineers were coming up from the rear, something else also came from the back: a big dust cloud with an armored car in which the Field Marshal was standing. And you could see his angry face. He said, 'Why is this unit stopping the offensive?' And he gave his driver orders to drive straight into the minefield.

"Nothing happened. That was a show of extreme courage—that he, as the commanding officer of the whole army, of the whole Afrika Korps, would take the lead and say, 'We go ahead. I am the first to go.'"

Likewise for my grandfather; as I've heard from many of his troops, they considered him pretty well invincible. "He could have led us to hell and back and we'd have been behind him all the way," a former chief warrant officer named Fred Hose told me at a reunion of Third Army veterans a few years ago. "That's how much confidence we had in the man."

Of course, there were other parallels between Manfred Rommel and my father. War separated them from their fathers for long stretches. Both were young when they lost their fathers, and were forced to grow up quickly. My father was an ocean away when my grandfather died in December 1945. Manfred Rommel, on the other hand, was with his father on the day he was killed, and watched as the guards took him away.

Yet even in the events leading up to that moment, Rommel and Patton history intertwine.

In the spring of 1945, Field Marshal Erwin Rommel had been put in charge of defending the Normandy coastline. Meanwhile, on the Allied side, my grandfather had been benched after his infamous slapping incidents of August 1943. Instead of helping to plan the attack at Normandy, he was used as a decoy to convince the Germans that the long-anticipated Allied landings would take place much farther east, at Calais. A smart move, as it turned out: Hitler held back at least two divisions from Normandy as the invasion unfolded.

"The mistaken assumption of the German commanders—that the main landing would happen in the Pas de Calais—was the result of a well-made strategic deception," observes Manfred Rommel of this turning point. "Patton's troops produced a lot of wireless communications that made the Germans believe that no Allied forces were prepared to cross the Channel. When my father discovered this great error at the end of May, he immediately asked permission from higher-ups to bring two more, well-equipped Panzer divisions to Normandy, along with paratroopers, more artillery, and an anti-aircraft corps. Hitler refused. My father decided to drive to Hitler's headquarters to convince him. But no one there believed German naval intelligence suggesting that the Allied invasion would happen at Normandy. The weather forecast said, 'Landing impossible, sea too rough and poor visibility.' So as D-Day dawned on June 6, the Allied crossed the Channel with six thousand ships and the greatest battle in world history began."

After a month of brutal fighting, in early July, Hitler dispatched Field Marshal Günther von Kluge to France to find out why Rommel had stopped following orders from Berlin. Hitler had been forced to deal with Rommel's insubordination before: During his retreat from El Alamein in November 1942, Field Marshal Rommel had ignored several direct commands to stand and fight—victory or death. "When my father arrived in Tunis, it was almost in disgrace," says Manfred. "Now, during his visit, von Kluge came in as Saul, and left as Paul—converted." At the risk of antagonizing the Führer, von Kluge urged Rommel to write to Hitler directly, laying out his arguments for ending the war. Von Kluge sent a similar letter backing him up.

By this point, Erwin Rommel and a few of his colleagues were already looking for a way to get rid of Hitler and end the war. Ever since Rommel had left Africa, he'd heard secret talk about Nazi atrocities. He asked the then-mayor of Stuttgart, Karl Strolin, as well as the supreme commander in southern France, General Blaskowitz, what it was all about. Both confirmed that Jewish civilians had been murdered. Although Rommel had nothing to do with their massacre, he was already aware of Hitler's paranoid hatred toward the Jews. "Back in 1939, my father had suggested that things would be easier for Germany if Jews could become local party leaders," says Manfred. "Hitler got very upset."

Before the Normandy invasion, Field Marshal Rommel had held out a glimmer of hope that Germany could negotiate peace with conditions. Hitler was already giving up on the idea. "At some point, probably after the German-Italian surrender in Tunisia in 1943, my father asked him if it weren't clear to him that Germany would suffer defeat in the long run," Manfred told me. "Hitler's answer was, 'With me, nobody will make peace.'"

For his part, Rommel wanted to see Hitler arrested and tried for Nazi atrocities. He opposed assassination on the grounds that it was too dangerous and might create a martyr. "My father always said that a dead Hitler could become more dangerous than the living one," Rommel says. At the same time Rommel also told his son that he'd rather let Allied troops march into Berlin than have to stage a last-ditch effort to defend it.

On July 17, 1944, near Normandy, a British fighter strafed Field Marshal Rommel's command car, leaving him with a life-threatening skull fracture. Then, according to his son, just one day after the failed July 20 bomb plot to kill Hitler, the letters from von Kluge and Rommel arrived in Berlin.

The timing spelled doom for both generals. To Hitler, defeatism was already tantamount to mutiny; now his paranoia went into overdrive. A Gestapo firing squad promptly executed Claus von Stauffenberg and two other ringleaders. Other conspirators tried to save themselves and their families from torture and death— fruitlessly, as it turned out—by becoming informers. Two of the names they served up were Rommel and von Kluge. Though exactly what Field Marshal Rommel knew about the plot remains murky, the assumption was that both field marshals had at least been aware of it and had failed to alert headquarters.

Von Kluge, rightly fearing the worst (many of the suspected conspirators had been hanged by piano wire) committed suicide on August 19.[2] At the time, Erwin Rommel was still being treated for his injuries at a military hospital in Bernay, France. But when he returned home to Herrlingen that fall to recuperate, Gestapo guards took up position outside the house, his son remembers. "It was quite obvious that Hitler was suspicious."

Granted leave to visit his father, young Manfred arrived home early on the morning of October 14. Around noon, he remembers, a dark green sedan pulled up and two generals stepped out.

"They asked to speak to my father alone," Manfred Rommel says. "After a while he came out, went to my mother and to me, and said, 'They said I'm charged with high treason and connection with the traitors, and Hitler has offered me to die by poison. I've decided to go with them, and I have only ten minutes to say good-bye.'" Field Marshal Rommel had been assured that nothing would happen to his loved ones if he agreed to the plan; the families of conspirators were generally dispatched to concentration camps. The official announcement—that Rommel had died of a stroke in a military hospital—would be released the next day.

"There was no time for emotion," Rommel says. "My father told my mother and me and his aide-de-camp, 'Never say anything about the real events concerning my death. Otherwise they'll pick you up the next day and you'll disappear.' And when the ten minutes were over, he put on his overcoat, entered their motorcar, and was gone."

Twenty minutes later, the phone rang to inform the family that Rommel had passed away.

For weeks afterward, German magazines and newspapers ran glowing, multipage stories about the field marshal. Their readers, having grown wary of Nazi propaganda, drew their own conclusions about how and why Rommel had died. On November 15, which would have been Erwin Rommel's fifty-third birthday, "Hitler even sent my mother his condolences in a telegram," Rommel told me. "They wanted to stop the rumors about my father's death."

Erwin Rommel, recovering at home with his family, Herrlingen/Ulm, fall 1944.
PHOTO COURTESY OF HAUS DER GESCHICHTE BADEN-WÜRTTEMBERG,
SAMMLUNG ROMMEL

Bitter and morose, he was obliged to go back to the front to rejoin the Wehrmacht after the state funeral. Any loyalty he might have felt for the Führer had evaporated. "I can say honestly that I never did any harm to anybody," says Rommel. "We contributed in shooting down an American bomber and a British bomber, but the crews were saved. And except for that, we did almost nothing except take cover when others threw something from the sky."[3] As soon as he felt sure that his mother, Lucie-Marie, was living safely in an Allied zone of occupation, he deserted and was picked up by General Jean de Lattre de Tassigny's French First Army. Back at home, Lucie-Marie didn't give the freshly arrived U.S. troops any information about her husband's fate. Her reticence cost her their house. It was only after French soldiers brought their young POW back to Herrlingen—trying to confirm that he was truly Rommel's son—that she began to speak.

Manfred Rommel was never cut out to be a soldier. For one thing, he has a lisp, which his late father feared would put him at a disadvantage in the army. The real disqualifier was the younger Rommel's rebellious streak. "When I was fifteen and came to the antiaircraft, I had one sergeant who was especially keen to make me a real soldier," he remembers. "He ordered me to get up before everyone else and bring him fresh water to wash himself with. I urinated in the water and it gave me courage all day long." When he bragged about it to his father, Field Marshal Rommel rolled his eyes. "This is enough," he said. "Please look for another profession."

In the aftermath of the war, becoming a professional soldier wasn't an option for Germans, anyway: The German military no longer existed. So after passing his baccalaureate, Rommel began studying law in Tübingen, earning money by working in a leather-goods factory. As an attorney, he gravitated toward politics, taking a job as a high-ranking civil servant and, eventually, as senior finance minister for the state of Baden-Württemberg.

In 1974, the Oberbürgermeister (lord mayor) of Stuttgart died in office. Recognizing the value of his name, Rommel's political party, the Christian Democrats, urged him to run for the position. Objecting to their motives, he hesitated. But then some of the party members called him a coward, and that was it. "If you want a German to do something, just say, 'You have no courage,'" Rommel jokes.

He won the election, capturing more than half of the vote. And, subsequently, he surprised himself by emerging as a natural fit as a legislator. As he puts it, "I won the first election because of my father—but the next election because of me."

STUTTGART IS ONE of Germany's largest cities and the capital of its most industrialized state. In the years following World War II, it exemplified the country's crumbling and desperate straits. Bombed to the ground, the city was also flooded with refugees—many of them Germans who had been living in Eastern Europe for generations but had returned home, penniless, hoping to find work and escape persecution. By the 1970s, when Manfred Rommel took over as mayor, Germany, with a boost from the Marshall Plan, was already growing into an economic powerhouse; Stuttgart had rebounded, too. But national pride wasn't as easy to rebuild. Just by taking the job of mayor—by stepping into the spotlight, as it were— the younger Rommel began to spin out what would become his greatest legacy.

"He brought back the soul of Germany," Arends says. "He did a lot for every German in the sense that he was a continuity of the old Germany with the new Germany without being damaged by it. People thought his father was an honorable man, and knew how much he and his family had to endure. People loved Manfred, the son, because he was honest and sensible, and because he combined a conscience with a great sense of humor. There was no arrogance, although he was the son of the Desert Fox and old royalty in a sense."

The fact that Manfred chose to stay in local politics surprised some. "He became very famous in Germany and could have run for prime minister," Arends reminded me. "But being prime minister is all about foreign relations. Manfred Rommel wanted to make a difference in his own country—not on the international stage, but to his own German people." For him, working on the lower deck meant a chance to really do something. As he puts it, "Regional and local politics are a discussion of how to solve problems, not an opera-house event."

While it was his family history that initially endeared him to voters, his dry wit and charisma proved more enduring assets. "In local politics, you generally have no majority in your own party," Rommel points out. "You have to get along with everybody." His knack for doing just that wasn't an inherited skill. Field Marshal Erwin Rommel, like my grandfather Patton, commanded respect but wasn't known as the easiest person to work with. Both generals were loved by their men and by the public, yet often infuriated their peers. Manfred Rommel, on the other hand, exudes real warmth and empathy. Soft-spoken and of medium build, he comes across as an original mix of decisive leader and twinkly-eyed intellectual—he jokes often, but is passionate about finding solutions.

I once asked him the secret to his successful diplomacy. He shot back with a short list of things that most men would find impossible:

"Never get excited," he told me. "If you get very angry, it's better to say nothing at all. And if you say something humorous, that's the best thing." Not taking yourself too seriously helps, too: What really works, he added, smiling, is if you're willing to criticize yourself. "Then you say, 'I've learned something from you' . . . This makes people flexible and wins them over." And finally, "at the center of the discussion should always be a decision, and this decision should always be reasonable."

My father had the opposite demeanor. While Manfred Rommel

is disarming and deadpan, Dad tended to be gruff and outgoing, and he commanded attention—the air changed when he walked into a room. Still, as my mother remembers, the two men "seemed to get along seamlessly, and I really think it was because of what they'd shared in life circumstances. Also, they both had a good sense of humor and there was no 'edge' to either one of them. What you saw was genuinely who they were."

IN ROMMEL'S THIRD year in office, a crisis hit that went a long way toward shaping his reputation.

In the late 1960s and early '70s, the Baader-Meinhof Gang—part of the violent left-wing Red Army Faction, which was intent on fostering a socialist revolution—unleashed a wave of brutal attacks. In addition to robbing banks in Germany, they bombed department stores, press offices, U.S. military posts, and other symbols of the new capitalism. They killed and maimed dozens of soldiers and civilians. After a chief justice of West Germany's Supreme Court signed warrants for their arrest, they crippled his wife with a car bomb.

The ringleaders of the group were captured in the summer of 1972. Yet their followers continued the campaign of terror over the next five years. One of their primary demands was the release of a handful of prominent Baader-Meinhof rebels who were being held at Stammheim, Stuttgart's high-security prison. On November 10, 1974, members of the gang shot and killed Günter von Drenkmann, the president of the German Superior Court of Justice. In 1975, they kidnapped Peter Lorenz, candidate for mayor of West Berlin, three days before the elections, and seized the West German embassy in Stockholm. In 1976, they hijacked an Air France

flight from Tel Aviv to Paris, taking hostages. On July 30, 1977, Jür-
gen Ponto, head of Dresdner Bank and a board member of Daimler-
Benz, was gunned to death on his doorstep, and his three police
bodyguards and chauffeur were killed in the process. Baader-
Meinhof took the credit. Shortly afterward, on September 5, 1977,
they kidnapped a national union boss, Hanns-Martin Schleyer.[4]

Whatever public support the gang had enjoyed in its early days
had long since vanished. The mere presence of the Baader-Meinhof
prisoners in Stuttgart prompted many citizens to call for blood.
One day that fall, as Manfred was entering city hall, "a man ran
over to me and said, 'Kill them! You don't have the courage to kill
them!'" he recalls. Rommel, ever amiable, refused to get excited. "I
asked him, 'Can I make a note of your name in case we need somebody to kill them?' The man went away."

On October 5, 1977, three leaders of the Baader-Meinhoff Gang
committed suicide in their cells. A fourth, who was taken to the
hospital with stab wounds to the chest, claimed that they were victims of a murder plot. The stunt was the group's final attempt to
embarrass the German government, and was arguably its most successful: Conspiracy theories flew.

Manfred tried to keep the situation calm—"to stay above the
scenery," as he puts it. But then the father of one of the terrorists
asked if his daughter and two of her collaborators (who had no
known family) could be buried in Stuttgart's public cemetery. The
man was a pastor. "It was a problem because no one wanted the
bodies," Rommel remembers. He approved the burial, and found
the ensuing outcry "almost amusing," he told me. "I got six hundred
letters calling me an idiot." Critics argued that the graves would
become a pilgrimage site and a monument to terrorism. There were
calls to have Rommel removed from office, and from his own polit-

ical party. He held firm. "I felt we needed to demonstrate that we weren't victims of our own excitement," he says. Besides, "in Germany, people have a right to be buried in their home city or village." "I will not accept that there should be first-class and second-class cemeteries," he announced at the time. "All enmity should cease after death." "And," he adds, "after a week, people began to understand that this was the right thing to do."

As it turned out, Field Marshal Erwin Rommel had taught his son two things that proved invaluable to him as a politician. One was to welcome a debate. When the teenage Manfred Rommel disagreed with his father, he remembers, "My mother would get very upset and say, 'How dare you tell your father that he is wrong?' My father would reply, 'Let him say it. It amuses me and I must convince him now.'"

The other lesson: to take the time after a significant experience to mine it for insights. "My father told me, 'After a battle, I always examine my own actions—it's a great source for ideas,'" says Rommel. "I try to do that, too."

The most glaring example: Although horrified by the Holocaust, in order to rebuild the country, the younger Rommel felt that it was important to not just pick up and move on. He felt compelled to revisit the persecution and genocide of the Jews again and again. "We . . . didn't take the Holocaust seriously while it was happening," he admits. "People had every incentive not to believe it. We just didn't believe that the German administration would make the Jews go to camps . . . and then decide who would work and who would die."

This is not to say that Manfred doesn't believe that the Holocaust happened. To the contrary: He can't fathom how anyone could deny it. But as Arends says, "Even as it was taking place, the fact that a modern, civilized country would pull out a group of people from within its society and then exterminate them was past human imagination."

Until 1933, Stuttgart had a thriving Jewish community, full of doctors, lawyers, intellectuals, and artists who helped make the city a special place. Manfred vowed to reestablish it. When the Jewish community's new leader, Meinhard Tenné, first came to see him, "I immediately felt that I was sitting opposite a partner," Tenné told me. "We both thought the same way. He always said that coming generations aren't guilty—they can't be guilty for what happened. But they have to accept their history. And if they do that, it won't happen again."

Together, Manfred and Tenné teamed up with Teddy Kollek, the mayor of Jerusalem, for guidance. Gradually, the city of Stuttgart began inviting its former Jewish citizens back for annual events created in their honor. Many of them eventually returned for good.

For his efforts, in 1987, Manfred was made an honorary Guardian of Jerusalem. "The growing Jewish community in Stuttgart still has problems—and what we've done isn't enough," he admits. Still, it's his proudest achievement. "It's very important because the Jewish people belong to the civilization of Germany," he says. "Some of them have had their families here for five hundred years—longer than America has existed."

Manfred ended up serving three consecutive eight-year terms as lord mayor (winning by a 79 percent landslide in the last election). He finally stepped down in 1996, after reaching the mandatory retirement age.

"Mayor of Stuttgart may not sound like a lot in American terms," Arends told me recently. "But you have famous mayors in America—

in Los Angeles, Chicago, and New York—people who make a big impression." What really stuns is that, in the end, Manfred Rommel deserves a lot of credit for his contributions on the global stage, too. Arends added, "It's fair to say that he has probably done more than any other mayor in Germany to improve U.S.-German relations, by reaching out to the conquerors as the son of the most famous general in the German Wehrmacht. He is clearly a man who understands the importance of building relationships across party lines in Germany, throughout the European community, and around the world." Now in his early eighties, Manfred suffers from Parkinson's disease, something he and my father had in common. He moves and speaks more slowly now. Mentally he's still quite sharp; he's a popular poet in Germany, and has published several best-selling books in his retirement. He and Lilo, his wife of fifty-seven years, live in the same comfortable, unpretentious house that my parents first visited back in 1958.

A few years ago, on one of my last visits with Manfred, I mentioned that I planned to stop by the Friendship Grove, a small arbor on the U.S. Army base in Stuttgart where German and American leaders team up to plant trees in honor of their alliance. On a snowy day in 1979, just before my father returned to the States, he and Manfred had planted two of the first trees there—Christmas evergreens, in a nod to their shared birthday.

As a filmmaker, I was excited by the visual potential of the grove. As a historian, Professor Arends insisted that I look beyond it. "The grove is a symbol that we should all be friends," she told me. "Something not so obvious is that General Patton's granddaughter [my sister Helen] married a German boy and stayed in Germany and is raising her children there. That says a lot about how Manfred

Major General Patton and Lord Mayor Rommel in early 1979.

PHOTO COURTESY OF HAUS DER GESCHICHTE BADEN-WÜRTTEMBERG,
SAMMLUNG ROMMEL

Rommel and your father worked to bring the two countries back together again, on a personal level. It's not just a grove—it's more important than a grove."

Manfred, for his part, encouraged me to go see the grove anyway.

"George Patton and I planted those trees," he reminded me, smiling. "His survived and mine did not and had to be replaced by a healthier tree. But now they stand together."

FIVE

Geasung "Sammy" Choi

I don't measure a man's success by how high he climbs but how high
he bounces when he hits bottom.

GEORGE S. PATTON JR. (*WAR AS I KNEW IT*)

GEASUNG CHOI, born in South Korea in 1938, was eleven years old
when his family members started to vanish. His father was first,
from a bleeding ulcer brought on by alcohol abuse. But Choi's other
relatives disappeared due to something far more sinister: the Communist invasion, which made even less sense to the boy than the
alcoholism did.

On June 25, 1950, the North Korean Army, backed by Chinese
Communist volunteers and the Soviet Union, invaded South Korea.
Their goal was the reunification of the Korean peninsula, which
had been split along the thirty-eighth parallel after the surrender
of Japan in World War II. The size of the force—231,000 soldiers—
ensured victory for the surprise air-land attack. Ill-equipped and
caught off guard, the Republic of South Korea's (ROK) Army was
overrun almost immediately. Within three days, the North Koreans captured the capital city of Seoul, five miles from Choi's affluent neighborhood, which lay just outside the famous East Gate.

The Choi family, circa 1942. Geasung is on the left.

PHOTO COURTESY OF GEASUNG CHOI

His eldest sister's husband, the son of a congressman and a high-ranking official in South Korea's prestigious police investigations unit, disappeared shortly after the invasion. "He'd been hiding in our attic, and the North Korean soldiers came and searched our house until they found him and dragged him out," Choi says. His other brother-in-law, a photographer, soon followed. "The soldiers simply showed up at his house and took him away," says Choi.

At home, amid the cascading political chaos, Choi's beloved older brother was just days away from his high school graduation. Strikingly tall and handsome, Geayoung stood out as an exceptional student, a stalwart of the local ROTC program, and captain of his soccer team. "He was strong, in every sense of the word," says Choi, who shared his brother's good looks but was small and slight for his age. Geayoung was also surrounded by student informers. One of the first moves of the Communists had been to infiltrate the schools.

It remains unclear whether Geayoung or his friends had spoken against the invasion, or if his hometown-hero status suddenly worked against him. "One afternoon, after running an errand for my mother—delivering something to our sister's house—he returned and went to wash up for dinner at the pump in a small courtyard outside the kitchen," Choi remembers.

It was a warm spring evening and still light outside. Choi was inside, having arrived home just ahead of his brother. From the window, he saw two North Korean national policemen walk through the house's outer door and into a small courtyard in the center of the house. "They were wearing their round hats with the red stars and carrying big rifles," he says. "I didn't know why they'd come or what was going on."

The water pump that Geayoung was using stood in a corner of the courtyard on a small concrete patio where the family did laundry. The soldiers reached him immediately. "Everything was so quiet because we were all scared," Choi says. One of his friends happened to stop by at that moment and Choi hurried into the street to get rid of him. When he came back, Geayoung was gone.

It had all happened in a matter of minutes. "My mother was yelling after the soldiers, 'Why are you taking my son?' but they didn't even pay attention," Choi says. "Geayoung didn't have time to say good-bye. We never even knew what he'd been accused of."

The whole next day, Choi waited outside the police station— "across the street, pressed against the wall of a house, so I wouldn't get in trouble"—in case Geayoung came out, in case he hadn't been taken away. In tears, his mother finally came and took Choi home. His father was dead, and both brothers-in-law and Geayoung were gone. The communist invasion had left the economy in turmoil. And there were now six people to support: his mother, his stepmother (his late father's second wife), her daughter, his older sister, his identical twin brother, and a niece. Someone needed to find a job.

"In Korea in 1951, everyone was hustling for work," Choi recalls. Having grown up with two live-in housekeepers, he wasn't accustomed to labor, but managed to land a position as a janitor and stock boy in a shoe factory by the highway, one of the biggest companies in town. After six months, he was promoted to a job in the store out front. There, he says, "I heard people talk about how you could make more money helping the South Korean soldiers"—who by now had retaken Seoul with the UN's assistance—"and of course, I wanted to work for them."

Choi and his friends had already met a first sergeant of the ROK when some officers drove through their neighborhood and pulled over to watch them play ball. "I went to talk to him with some of my friends, and begged him to take me to the front with him," says Choi. The sergeant, a sturdy, fatherly man of about forty, said he wouldn't even consider it: Children weren't allowed past the checkpoints. But a few weeks later, the same sergeant stopped by the shoe store to buy something.

"I walked him out to his jeep and begged him again, 'Please take me with you,'" Choi says. "And then, just as he was leaving, the sergeant suddenly beckoned to me." There were a couple of other soldiers in the jeep, and one of them moved over in back to make room for the boy. When they got near the checkpoint, they hid him under a thick cotton blanket.

"By the time we arrived at the ROK camp that night, it was being blown apart," says Choi. "Though it was dark, so much light was flashing all over the place that I could see everything: men losing legs and arms, the Chinese soldiers' heavy cotton jackets soaked with blood, shells exploding, and people being shot with rifles at close range." The sergeant told Choi to hide inside his small canvas tent and left to join the fighting. "But I was afraid to stay in it, so I walked around it a bit," he says. Barely fourteen, he had no hope of escaping. "I couldn't go farther for fear of getting lost."

The fighting moved toward the mountains the next day. Dazed and exhausted, Choi stayed on, working as a tent boy. He was paid in canned field rations and dense, high-fat crackers that the American troops dubbed "dog biscuits." Eventually, word got back to the camp that Choi's mother was looking for him. The soldiers sent him home.

When Choi entered the house—quietly, intent on surprising everyone—his mother, stepmother, and niece were in the main room doing housework. At the sight of him, they froze. Choi was still in the clothes he'd been wearing when he left home weeks before. He hadn't seen a bar of soap in that time, though he'd done his best to wash himself in a creek near the ROK camp.

His mother jumped up. "Well, who's *this* boy?" she said, stretching the words out for emphasis.

In his teenage myopia, it had never occurred to Choi that his mother might be angry at him for disappearing without warning. But now, as she got closer, she nearly struck him. "Where the hell have you been?" she yelled. "Do you know how much I've worried about you?"

Still, he'd brought back the rations, so she couldn't say much, Choi remembers. "My mother hated never knowing where I was anymore. I reassured myself with the thought that she had a lot of other things to worry about. Anyway, one of us had to do something—we were that close to the edge."

In 1952, Choi scored a job working for a U.S. tank battalion fifteen miles outside of Seoul. The army paid him in cash, which transformed the family fortunes. Not wanting to face his mother's wrath a second time, Choi devised a way to funnel the money home. "I'd go back to my neighborhood and get a friend to find my twin brother, Chang," Choi says. "Then I'd hide—sometimes for hours and hours—until he showed up."

Within a few months, Chang was able to reenter school. "Only one of us could go, and since I was supporting the family, my mother said it had to be him," Choi says. Thinking back on it makes him choke up, even now. Throughout the 1950s, Choi tried to go back to school himself, but the dream slowly fell away. For a teenager with a full-time job and an extended family to support, it simply proved too difficult. Young, steady, and stuck, he would have to be self-taught.

It was at this juncture that the course of Geasung Choi's life changed in ways he couldn't have imagined.

IT WAS NOW 1953; the fighting had moved on and Choi was scrambling for work again. While visiting a relative outside Seoul, he wandered over to a new U.S. army camp. It was a small set-up—about fifteen big GI tents set in a grassy valley with small bushy trees and a creek running through it. A barbed-wire fence ringed the tents. One section of it ran lower than the rest, only about four feet high.

There, Choi found about fifteen hungry Korean boys like him, waiting for the GIs to give out candy. Over the buzz of the camp generators, they told Choi about the terrifying *baek tae gari* ("man with white hair" in Korean). "They said he was very mean and carried a whip and chased everyone away," Choi remembers.[1] "Then, suddenly, he appeared."

My father, George S. Patton, then a thirty-year-old captain whose prematurely gray hair was going white, shouted and cracked his riding crop at the boys. He didn't like them distracting his soldiers. "We scattered like birds," recalls Choi, who went back several times that week to join the boys outside the fence. "Of course, as soon as the man went away, we came back to the fence again. But every time he showed up, we ran for our lives."

Except for the time when Choi didn't. "One day near the end of the week, when the white-haired man came again, I was the last one to move away from the fence," he says. "I walked backward a bit and the man and I stared at each other. And after a minute, he set his whip on his hip and beckoned to me. All the other boys had run away. I was scared, too. 'C'mon, boy,' he said. Somehow, I worked up the nerve to move closer and the man told the guard to let me through the gate."

Captain Patton shared a big tent with a handful of other officers. It had two center poles and just two windows with flaps that rolled down. Nicknamed "Sammy" by the soldiers, Choi slept in a cot in the corner. During the day, he worked hard—making beds, shining shoes, carrying water. At night, he studied English on his own. My father, inspired by the boy's pluck and initiative, began to forge a genuine friendship with him.

"I think it was the first time that an outsider saw him, not as a nameless waif, but as a human being with potential," says my mother, Joanne Patton. "He saw something of value in Sammy and encouraged him."

As a captain commanding 142 men in five tank platoons, my father knew as well as anyone that a little positive reinforcement could be the best motivator.[2] As my grandfather put it back in 1944, "Remember that praise is more valuable than blame."

Five months later, my father was reassigned and the Army camp moved on, leaving Choi behind. He and Dad promised to stay in touch. They exchanged holiday cards for several years. Then, nearly two decades later, in 1972, my father—now a one-star brigadier general and assistant commandant at the Armor School at Fort Knox— got a call from Choi out of the blue. He'd made his way to America and asked if he could come visit.

"On the day of the visit, George spoke to me quite seriously about Sammy," recalls my mother. "He said, 'I don't know what shape he'll be in—he's just a refugee kid and has had a rough time of it. But we have to be wonderful to him because he's very special.' When he arrived and we opened the door, here was this handsome young man looking impeccable in a three-piece suit," she says. He carried a package wrapped in brown paper.

My parents welcomed him inside. "Sammy, how did you ever manage to get here?" Dad asked.

"Well, I work for Miss Book now," Choi replied, drawing out the vowel.

"Miss Book?" said Dad.

By way of explanation, Choi handed him the package. Inside was a stack of books by the writer Pearl S. Buck—winner of the Pulitzer Prize and the first American woman to win the Nobel Prize in literature. Each volume was signed by the author and made out to George S. Patton.

Dad was astonished. How had it ever come about?

Sammy explained: After the U.S. Army camps left, he couldn't find a job for months. A relative told him about Buck's foundation, which ran an orphanage in the countryside about fifteen miles south of Seoul. The author had established the organization "to address poverty and discrimination faced by children in Asian countries"—especially Amerasian children who needed schooling and job skills. Choi had polished his English enough by then to land a position as a translator.

Buck, a tall, handsome woman then in her seventies, came by regularly. On her second visit Choi got to know her. He was struck by Buck's expensive clothes—the sort of outfits he seldom actually saw outside the steps of fancy hotels in Seoul—and her striking gray-green eyes. "Just looking at them, I could feel how sharp she was," he says. "She seemed very quiet and always observing."

Whatever Buck saw in Sammy, she liked it. In short order, he was invited to serve as unofficial butler in her house, which sat on the grounds of the foundation. Soon after, Buck offered him the same position at her estate in the small town of Danby, Vermont, where she lived with her romantic partner, Theodore Harris, an Arthur Murray dance instructor and antiques dealer.

Choi had never traveled more than twenty miles from home. He turned to his mother for advice. "Yes, you have to go," she said. "There's more opportunity for you in America."

Besides, he desperately needed to make money to send home. It was all he thought about.

THE SUBSEQUENT YEARS in Vermont were among the quietest of his life. Always neatly dressed in a dark suit, he served in the dining room when dignitaries came to visit, ran errands, and accompanied Buck on her daily walks (frequently interrupted by people wanting to take her picture). "Mostly, she stayed in the living room, writing and taking notes—that's all she did," Choi remembers. When Buck died from lung cancer in 1973, she left him enough money in her will to open his own antiques shop. Instead, Choi headed for an Army recruitment station.

Still struggling with the language barrier, he flunked the entrance test. Crushed, Choi called my father, who was still at Fort Knox, and told him what had happened. "Sammy, just come on down to Kentucky," Dad said.

A FEW MONTHS earlier, during his visit to my parents, Choi had asked my father about the possibility of coming back to work for him as a house servant someday. "You can't just come work for me," Dad told him. "This is the Army—you'd have to go into the enlisted aide program and learn how to work in official residences."

Now, down in Kentucky, Choi studied hard for the entrance test, passed and began to earn the proper credentials. In the meantime, Dad asked his sergeant major to look out for him.

Soon word came back from Choi's cooking instructor: "He's having a problem with pies." So, to help out, Dad arranged for Sammy to work at our house with my mother on weekends.

"Of course, he was taking orders from me because I was running the house," my mother says. "That wasn't what he'd signed up for. If I criticized anything Sammy did, he'd go into a big funk. And if I did anything wrong—forgot to get something at the commissary, for example—he'd bring it up right away. But he worked so hard to do everything right that it was hard not to admire him."

Over the next few months, Choi's culinary evolution limped along, hobbled by his own paranoid perfectionism. "I remember going out one night when Sammy was supposed to make a cake," says my mother. "There were a whole bunch of cake mixes in the pantry for him to use, and when we got home, we found all these ruined cakes and empty boxes in the trash. On the counter sat the only cake he was satisfied with."

For Choi, the high point of 1973 was becoming an American soldier. At his request, my father administered the oath of office. Choi proudly displays a photo of this moment on the wall in his living room. In the picture, both men are holding their palms up for the swearing in and look very serious—Dad, a one-star general in his uniform, a nervous Choi in his suit. Afterward, they shook hands.

When Dad was reassigned to Germany, Choi was still in training. "We were a little concerned about him when we left Fort Knox," my mother admits. But Choi graduated on time, and at his request, was dispatched back to Korea. Ecstatic to be reunited with his family in Seoul, Choi, now an E4, worked as a first cook at a small Army garrison. If not impressed by his gourmet skills ("I'm not a good cook—I never did like to cook," Choi admits), the Army took note of his sheer hustle and flexibility and hoisted him up the ladder.[3] Still, the next rung, as first cook at Fort Sill, Oklahoma, gave him pause. "I was suddenly responsible for feeding three thousand men at every meal," he says. "When I first got there, I couldn't imagine how we'd even handle the enormous platters and pans." To stir the soup kettles, he had to stand on a stool.

A later posting, in Germany, taught him about racism firsthand. By now, Choi had married Young Suk Park, a part-time fashion model and shoe designer he'd met in Seoul. They'd wake up in their small Frankfurt apartment each morning before four o'clock to drop their sons off with the babysitter before going to work. From there, Choi would gird himself to spend the day in stoic mode. "I had a hard time working over there because of the prejudice," he said. "White, black, Hispanic—they didn't like me, period. I've never been so depressed in my life."

But his hard work paid off. In the summer of 1980, Choi was asked to meet with General Willard W. Scott, the commanding general of V Corps in Frankfurt. Scott, a tall, lanky man with a kind face, was looking for a new aide.

Choi was a long shot for the job and he knew it. "There were a lot of sharp-looking, educated candidates there who had perfect English," he says. He didn't even bother to ask my father for a reference.

FAST-FORWARD TO 1984:

At the invitation of Scott, who'd been named the fifty-second superintendent of the U.S. Military Academy three years earlier, my parents drove to West Point from our farm in Massachusetts to watch a football game. "There was a reception at the superintendent's quarters, and we were going in with lots of other people when General Scott stopped us at the door," says my mother.

"George," he said, "there's someone here you've got to see." From behind him, Sergeant Geasung Choi, Scott's senior enlisted aide, stepped forward with a look of unsuppressed glee. "Goddamn," said my father (his favorite epithet), grinning back at him. "Well, I'll be goddamned."

Not only had Choi won the job back in Frankfurt, but General Scott had also campaigned to take Sammy with him when he moved on. "He kept calling and sending letters asking me to come to West Point," Choi says. "General Paul S. Williams Jr., the incoming commander in Frankfurt, didn't like that. He didn't want me to leave." Having proven himself invaluable in two demanding, high-profile positions, Choi had become a hot property. In the end, Scott pulled rank.

Dad told the story of Sammy Choi many times, and considered him one of the most disciplined, determined, and loyal men he'd ever met—high praise indeed. Choi's family has visited our farm on occasion. When my father died in 2004, Choi flew from Hawaii to Washington, D.C., to attend the funeral at Arlington National Cemetery. The chaplain who presided over the service, Glenn Myers, knew about Sammy and paused in the middle of the service to introduce him to the congregation as a special friend. Choi stood up with his family and bowed. Everyone gave them a round of applause. For my part, I'll never forget watching Choi weave his way through the crush of people at the postfuneral reception to pay his condolences to our family. His two sons were in tow, one in uniform, and he was beaming with pride.

By then, Choi had retired from the Army and was living near the south shore of Oahu, Hawaii. He'd been awarded two honorary medals of service by the president of the United States. He'd put both sons and a nephew through college. (His older son, Ben, is a captain in Army intelligence who has served two combat tours in Afghanistan and one in Iraq; his younger son, Amos, graduated from the University of Michigan and earned his master's degree in computer engineering from Johns Hopkins.) He also brought more than a dozen relatives—"my brother, his two sisters, their children, everyone"—to the United States from Korea. Today, Choi spends his mornings handing out pocket-size Bibles at the beach near his house, and inviting people to join his church.

"Looking back all these years, I feel strongly that God was with me," he says. "Three things helped me to come this far: faith, patience, and self-sacrifice." When asked about his improbable career, Choi gets tears in his eyes. "It makes me so proud, I can't talk about it," he says. "But my family leads a pretty good life. And it all started in 1953, when I took a leap of faith outside an army fence and walked through the gate toward Captain George Patton."

SIX

Julius Becton

ANYONE WHO KNEW my father well might be surprised to see Julius Becton included in my short list of personal heroes. The two men watched each other's career with a cautious eye and ripened into professional rivals. Ultimately, an incident involving Becton triggered the abrupt and regrettable end of my father's military career. Yet it's impossible not to recognize his importance in my father's story. And to see how the two men settled into a quiet respect for each other is to learn a lot about pride, competition, and the value of humility.

In terms of background, they couldn't have been more different. My father, born in 1923, grew up in a privileged family who owned an estate staffed by live-in servants. Becton, born in 1926, spent his childhood in a two-bedroom basement flat in an upscale apartment building, where his father worked as the head janitor. My father was white. Becton is black. My father went to West Point. Becton entered the Army straight out of high school at age seventeen, at a time when the military was still segregated.

Lieutenant Colonel Julius Becton receiving a DFC following the Battle of La Chu, Vietnam, May 1968. [1] PHOTO COURTESY OF J.W. BECTON JR.

Yet Becton went on to outrank my father. By 1978, he had become commanding general of all eighty-eight thousand soldiers in the U.S. VII Corps in Germany—the first black man in the history of the Army to command a corps. After retiring, he went on to become the head of FEMA (the Federal Emergency Management Administration), the president of Prairie View A&M University in Texas, and, finally, superintendent of the Washington, D.C., Public School System.

Today, Becton is in his mideighties and lives in Virginia. Our families are still close: Becton and his wife, Louise, keep in touch with my mother, and I often talk to their son Wes, my closest childhood friend. A few years ago, Becton's children asked me to produce a film about their father as a surprise in honor of his eightieth birthday, which is how I became more acquainted with his remarkable life.

For that short documentary, Colin Powell, the former secretary of state and an early protégé of Becton's, agreed to a rare interview.

"He came to an Army that was still segregated," Powell said of Becton. "He came in at a time when you really, really had to prove yourself, you had to overcome all of this legal discrimination as well as de facto segregation and racism that existed in the Army.

"It was guys like Julius Becton and so many others of his contemporaries—plus black officers going back one hundred years and black soldiers going back two hundred years—that kept serving in the face of this kind of discrimination, serving a nation when that nation wouldn't serve them. So they were pathfinders. They did it. They did it because they knew if they did it, they'd be creating a better path for those of us who came after. They also served because they loved this country and believed in this country. I don't think anyone exemplifies that better than Julius Becton."[2]

To fully understand Becton, you need only to unpack his early years. He grew up in Bryn Mawr, near the center of Philadelphia's Main Line, a string of mostly white, affluent suburbs. The community was largely insulated from the racial struggle that was building across the country, not only because it was in the North, but also because the few African-Americans who lived there worked for the white community in nonthreatening service jobs. Becton's father had a third-grade education; his mother, a housekeeper and laundress, only made it through tenth grade. But they used an obsession with education and old-school discipline to advance their kids.

From kindergarten through seventh grade, Becton missed only two days of class. On weekdays, he and his younger brother did chores around the apartment complex. And always, on Sundays, between religious services and Sunday school and their Baptist youth group, they routinely spent a mandatory, mind-boggling twelve hours at church.

As Becton recollects in his autobiography, the family "stressed constant, habitual respect for other people, especially for women and the elderly . . . From my earliest recollection, Dad hammered that lesson into our heads . . . We were expected to open doors and hold them for women and older people. We were expected to offer up our seats on public transportation. When walking down the street with a female, we were expected to walk on the street side."[3]

SPORTS OFFERED ANOTHER steadying effect. In high school, Becton emerged as a star athlete: the state champion in the long jump, and the only African-American to play on the first string of the football team. His senior year, the team went undefeated. Photos from that time show him looking loose-limbed and confident, with high cheekbones and wide-set eyes. "Athletic teams teach about discipline, loyalty, equality, how to get along with your fellow man, and about your own limitations," he says. "I was the best center and linebacker on my team—that's why I got the job, and it had nothing to do with what I looked like."

In December 1943, he joined the Army Air Corps Enlisted Reserves (figuring that it would give him more control over his career than waiting to be drafted) and was called to active duty in July 1944. He was assigned to an all-black unit in the South. At McDill Army Air Base in Tampa, Florida, the white troops lived in two-story wooden buildings. The black soldiers were housed across the airfield, in tarpaper shacks with corrugated metal roofs. Even the Italian prisoners of war, who ran the laundry and shoe-repair operations on the base, had higher status. "I walked into the shoe-repair place and the white POW behind the counter ignored me until everyone else was served," Becton says. "It made me madder than hell, but there was nothing I could do about it." Instead, he became wary and private; the typical comment about Becton is that he's a man of few words.

In 1945, he entered officer training school at Fort Benning, Georgia. Although the military was still segregated, the officer candidate programs were not. Early on, in one of his most trying moments, Becton's tactical officer, a white lieutenant, approached him and a handful of other black soldiers one day while they were eating lunch. Watermelon was on the menu. The lieutenant, whom Becton describes as "a decent yet ignorant" man, had brought a camera along.

"I want a picture of you eating watermelon," he said. Becton and his tablemates looked at each other uneasily.

"Sir, I don't like watermelon," Becton replied.

"Come on," said the lieutenant. "All you people eat watermelon."

"No, sir, I don't like watermelon," Becton repeated. The lieutenant went to each of the sixteen other black candidates in the company. Each of them said the same thing: "No, sir, I don't like watermelon."

"Later, when some of the other black students and I got together, they congratulated me for standing up to that lieutenant," says Becton. "'But I really *don't* like watermelon,' I told them, and it was true: One time, when I was a youngster, I'd eaten slice after slice and then asked for one more. My father, who thought I was being greedy, said, 'Are you sure? Because if I give it to you, you're gonna eat it.' I felt so sick [afterward] I never wanted watermelon again." As far as

Becton's concerned, that was a good thing, since it handed him an easy response. "I was an eighteen-year-old kid," he said. "I could have easily done something that would have gotten me thrown out of school. But once you lose control, you are no longer in charge.[4] I grew up with that credo. My father was a very proud man.

"My way of dealing with such racist incidents was just to put them out of my mind," says Becton. After leaving the Army in 1946, he became the first African-American to attend Muhlenberg College in Pennsylvania. "I'd decided a long time before then that I wasn't going to let such situations prevent me from accomplishing my goals," he wrote later. "Somebody had to be first, so it might as well be me." Meanwhile, Becton's wife, Louise became the first African-American nurse at Philadelphia General Hospital. Their family mettle would come in handy, since Becton was poised to roll out a whole new set of precedents.

But first he had to learn about the perils of leadership.

RECALLED TO ACTIVE duty in 1948, Becton arrived in Korea in July 1950, as a lieutenant platoon leader of Company L, 3rd Battalion, 9th Infantry Regiment, 2nd Infantry Division. By that time, as Becton later observed on *The Tavis Smiley Show,* "Little had been done to end segregation. I was in an all-black battalion in a white division. However, when our regiment—two white and one black battalion—lost men and needed replacements, it didn't matter if the new soldiers were black or white. Our colonel said to put the men where they were needed."[5]

As September rolled around, his troops had seen a fair amount of action. Still, Becton was grappling with discipline. A turning point came while the platoon, in the midst of a daylight battle just south of the Nakdong River, was attacked by U.S. military aircraft by mistake. Becton's own account of the incident appears in his memoir:

There's not much you can do when planes moving three hundred miles per hour are shooting at you. We just hugged the ground as they strafed us, but some of my soldiers got up and started running when the pilots swung their planes around for a second pass.

[Back in training] I had warned my men in no uncertain terms not to run . . . I had said, "Guys, I'll kill you if you run away from the enemy. [You'd be] putting our entire unit in jeopardy . . ." Now, my men were doing exactly what I had cautioned them not to do, and the new soldiers were in the lead. Of course, the fighter pilots thought they had the enemy on the run.

I had a carbine with thirty rounds in the magazine. I jumped up and unloaded that carbine in front of the running soldiers as they were moving off the hill. Startled, they stopped. They looked at me, looked at the aircraft, and looked back at me: the devil or the deep blue sea. They got back down on the ground.

When the aircraft were on their second pass, my messenger, ignoring the enemy fire still coming from the next hill over, jumped up and ran forward, frantically waving the chartreuse panels that were used to mark our positions. Finally, the pilots realized they were attacking the wrong hill, and after dipping their wings in recognition and apology, they hit the next hill instead.

[Later] my men asked whether I really would have shot them if they hadn't stopped running. "What did I tell you?" I asked. "I was serious. We're alive today, aren't we?"[6]

My grandfather would have approved. Playing him in the movie *Patton,* George C. Scott has a great line: "In about fifteen minutes, we're going to start turning these boys into fanatics—razors. They'll lose their fear of the Germans. I only hope to God they never lose their fear of me." It's a Hollywood moment, but consistent with how my grandfather behaved. He was fanatical about making discipline automatic.

Consider another moment during Becton's tour in Korea: He and his troops had just chased some North Korean soldiers from a small town when they encountered a new kind of dilemma. "On the outskirts of the town we found some caves and heard noises coming from inside—we assumed it was North Koreans," says Becton. "I had my translator, who was a South Korean soldier, repeatedly call them to come out. There was no response. Finally, I told my men to throw some grenades in there. To my chagrin, out came not only North Korean soldiers but also women and children—the North Koreans were known to use them as shields. It wasn't a pretty sight; some were injured and crying. It so happened that my battalion chaplain was with me and saw the whole thing. He said. 'I know what you're thinking, but if you had gone in there . . .' In retrospect, I might have done something differently: I could have sent my soldiers into the cave, which could have been disastrous. I could have gone in with my scout and looked around, which wouldn't have been very smart. I could have ignored it. But I also knew that if I bypassed that area, I might leave enemy soldiers to my rear."

It was another lesson: Sometimes there are no right answers.

Becton, who earned a Silver Star and two Purple Hearts in Korea, received his next big assignment in 1955, as the first black company commander of Company D, a mainly white unit in the 42nd Armored Infantry Battalion in West Germany. As they were training in peacetime, twenty-nine-year-old Captain Becton relied on competitions to motivate his troops. For instance, at their annual physical fitness evaluation, as Becton later recalled, "I told them that anyone with a higher score than mine could have the rest of the day off. I was the first to perform each of the five exercises on the morning of the test, and the entire company stood around to make sure I did each exercise according to the book.

"That afternoon the battalion operations officer . . . came storming into my office demanding to know where my people were. I must have had a good seventy soldiers on pass. When he heard what had happened, he burst out laughing and said, 'That will teach you to challenge soldiers!'"[7]

Becton's company ended up with the highest score in the command.

LIKE MANY OTHER African-Americans, Becton and his wife navigated the civil rights fight on their own terms. When they were assigned to Norfolk, Virginia, in late 1963, their ten-year-old daughter, Joyce, became the first-ever black student at her school. Concerned for her safety, the principal met the bus every morning and saw Joyce safely off each afternoon. Joyce, in her innocence, thought it was because she was special.

Around the same time, other African-Americans were criticizing Becton and some of his fellow black soldiers for not taking part in civil rights demonstrations. Becton countered that there were other ways to move the cause forward. "A lot of folks had the same experience," he says. "We felt we could best serve our country—and the effort to demonstrate our equality—by doing the best we could in our careers."

Back at the office, it was the same story. Like any soldier, but especially as one of the few black officers of the era, Becton had to work to be respected. It's the old rule: People need to see what you're made of if all the stars and bars are going to mean anything. In September 1967, he showed up in Fort Campbell, Kentucky, to lead a unit of airborne-trained parachutists (the 2nd Squadron, 17th Cavalry, 101st Airborne Division). The day after the change of command, the squadron was heading out for its morning run—all airborne groups are required to stay light on their feet—when one of the captains walked up.

"'How far do you want to go, sir?' he asked," recalls Becton. "I said, 'Just do what you normally do.' And I got in the back of the formation of about three hundred soldiers to observe them." Becton was accustomed to jogging a couple of miles a day, but the troops ran double that and more. "And it was hot," says Becton. "I was tired and hurting all over. Some of the soldiers dropped out or were straggling. Still, I knew that if I stopped, I might as well pack my bags and go back to Washington. I couldn't expect my men to respect me. I decided that if I stopped running, it would be because I'd passed out." Three months later, in Vietnam, the men confessed to Becton that they'd run farther that day than they'd ever gone before or since.

The more Becton impressed his superiors, the more challenges they set. Although he'd never commanded a tank unit before, in June 1970 Becton took command of a three-thousand-man brigade in the 2nd Armored Division at Fort Hood, Texas. By the end of the following year, he'd been reassigned to Washington as the armor branch chief.

The job "put me in charge of all armor officer assignments below the grade of colonel for the entire army," Becton wrote later. "I was floored. All my formalized training had been infantry, and I had never been to armor school. I had commanded armor units in combat, but never just armor. Little by little, I began to grasp the significance of my new assignment. The Army had never had a black branch chief. I would be the first, and the armor branch had fewer black officers than any other."[8]

Some purists felt that Becton was unqualified to be armor branch chief. I'm ashamed to report that the most outspoken critic was my father, then–Brigadier General George Patton, who was the assistant commandant of the armor school at Fort Knox. "He made it known to everyone that 'it was a goddamn shame that the branch chief of armor has never been to the armor school,'" Becton noted. Perhaps my father thought that the appointment had been political and took the job away from someone who (in his view) was more qualified? Maybe, as an armor school graduate and former instructor, he was being too much of a traditionalist? Perhaps he'd lobbied for a different candidate for the position? Whatever it was, he wasn't welcoming. "I sent word back," said Becton, "'Sir, you can correct that. Give me an honorary diploma.' I never received a reply."[9]

A year or two later, Becton received an honorary diploma from my father's successor. Afterward, he sent a copy to my father with a note: "Am I qualified now?" Again, no response.

When Becton and my father met up again, in August 1975, events had conspired to put both men in a different mind-set.

My father had just been given command of the 2nd Armored Division—"Hell On Wheels"—at Fort Hood, Texas. My grandfather had led the same division just prior to World War II, making Dad the first officer in U.S. Army history to command the same division as his father.

Becton, meanwhile, had assumed command of the other division at Fort Hood—the 1st Cavalry Division. The outgoing commander of the 2nd Armored had habitually belittled his own troops and disrespected other officers. In comparison, my father struck Becton as a breath of fresh air. "Despite our past differences, I was actually delighted that George would be taking over because I knew he would never abuse his soldiers," he noted in his memoir. "I immediately wrote to George, welcoming him to Fort Hood and offering any assistance I could provide."

The two men proved a good team: They worked well together, the relationship between the two divisions improved dramatically, and our families became good friends.

Still, competition crackled in the air at Fort Hood. The two divisions were pitted against each other in training exercises. Companies within each division fought against each other internally. And their commanding generals competed as well. "He wanted to beat me in everything," says Becton. "And I wanted to beat him. But when it came to beating the bad guy, we were together." You might think that the rivalry would have played itself out by the time my father moved on to his next post, as deputy commander of VII Corps, a unit of eighty-eight thousand men headquartered in Stuttgart, Germany. But in Dad's case, it hadn't.

In October 1978, Becton was named commanding general of the same corps—making him the first black man in the history of the United States to command an Army corps. It was a job that my father, armed with a glowing rating from the outgoing commander Lieutenant General Dave Ott—had fully expected to land. The old competitiveness reared up in him.

"[George] was very proud that the 2nd Armored had come out ahead of the 1st Cav in some kind of a long-standing competition, and he was very proud of himself," says my mother. "As a good commander, he thought that was something of merit that he could stand on. And when he was in Germany and General Ott retired, and the new commander of the VII Corps was named, and it was Julius Becton, [George] felt uncomfortable because, in his heart of hearts, he felt that he had earned seniority.

"He just felt that he was not ready to be a subordinate to somebody that he felt he had bested in military competition. That's the only way I can put it. He decided he was going to ask to be transferred to a different situation."

My mother tried to persuade my father to stay put. She reminded him of his brother-in-law, the late general Johnnie Waters, whose wife—Dad's sister, Bea—died while he was serving in Korea. Waters came home for the funeral. But instead of asking for a compassionate reassignment because he had two little boys, he said, "I go where the Army sends me and I don't ask for special favors." He sent his two little boys to live with his mother-in-law and then stayed on in Korea and finished out his tour.

In my father's own lectures on command, he always insisted, "Once [an] order has been approved . . . and you've had an opportunity to state your case, you execute that order—even though you disagree with it—as if you'd thought of it yourself."[10]

Nonetheless, in this case, he couldn't restrain himself. Less than two months after Becton took over VII Corps, my father stopped by his office and asked to be transferred back to the States.

"I wasn't expecting it," says Becton. "We lived right across the street from each other. Our wives saw each other every day. Our sons were best friends." Besides, he adds, "we were in Germany prepared to fight a war if a real war came, and I was convinced that with George Patton as my deputy commander—responsible for a sizable chunk of the corps—I had the right man in the right position. But I long ago realized that if a person is uncomfortable or unhappy, we will accommodate it."

Politically, it was a disastrous move. "With the times being what they were, race relations were up on the front page, and the secretary of the Army was African-American and so was Julius Becton," says my mother. "So when your husband asks for a transfer, everybody came with an opinion that he didn't want to work for Julius because he was black. That was not in his makeup at all, I can promise you that."

But my father found it hard to deflect the accusation. The truth was that both he and Becton had started off in an army that was practically still under Jim Crow laws, and people were beginning to realize what soldiers like Becton had been through and the sea change he represented.

Before my father left Germany—and before he fully realized the ramifications of his actions—he and Becton worked together on a large maneuver. It was a terrific experience, Becton remembers. "Afterward, George came in to see me and said, 'I like the way you do things. I'd like to stay.'" Becton immediately placed a call on my father's behalf. But it was too late.

In retrospect, it looks like a classic case of hubris. Creighton Abrams, who'd served as a mentor to my father and Becton, had accepted assignments that he felt were beneath him on occasion. So had Becton. My father, in refusing to do so, had sealed his fate. Back in the United States, he found himself placed in what he considered to be a career-ending desk job. He felt compelled to retire from his beloved Army a year later.

"It was always argued in the family: Did he do the right thing?" says my mother. "This is what we've grown up with: You take the king's dollar, you do the king's work. George said, 'No, I feel as though I've earned going to where I can be a leader.' I don't feel that was a schism on racial grounds. I do feel there was a competitive schism there because George, allowed to prevail, knew he was looking at the end and wanted to go out on top."

Becton, for his part, displayed not an iota of schadenfreude. "I didn't consider it to be racism—I would have felt the same way if I'd been in George's shoes," he says. "The Department of the Army chose not to promote him for whatever reason. But I've said this many times: If I went to war, I'd want George Patton by my side."

Interestingly, my father never told anyone that he'd gone to Becton to ask to stay with the VII Corps. Certainly no one in our family had heard about it, so I was shocked when I came across the incident described in Becton's book. But I believe it. And the more I've found out about Becton, the more I realize that he and my father were more similar than they may have wanted to admit.

As it was, the real friendship was left to my mother and the Bectons, and to Wes and me. The night before Mom and I left Germany, a few weeks in advance of my father, the Bectons threw a party for our family. When it was over, we walked outside and discovered that we couldn't pull our car out of the driveway. Wes and a few of my other friends had parked a giant snowball behind it.

If Dad remembered that winter as the beginning of the end of his career, I remember it as the end of my childhood. You can imagine how it would feel to an already self-involved thirteen-year-old: My best friend had just moved in across the street, I played trumpet in the school's traveling band, and we actually had a few female fans. Mostly, I was surrounded by other kids who were also accustomed to the transient nature of Army life, who understood how important it was to make friends. To suddenly have to move back to D.C. and attend a civilian school—to have to break into a teen culture where everyone else seemed to have known one another forever—felt like the bottom dropping out.

On military bases, our family always enjoyed a lot of respect; my father had worked his way through the ranks and was already a lieutenant colonel by the time I was born. At my new school, none of that mattered. There were always a few kids who wanted to beat me up to prove that they could take down the new kid—the fact that my last name was Patton just made me more of a target. Even when I went away to boarding school, things got worse before they got better. So for a long time I resented the fact that my father had requested a transfer from VII Corps so abruptly. It still strikes me as the wrong decision. In the end, I think my father may have thought so, too. But there was no turning back.

SEVEN

Vera Duss—Lady Abbess

On April 21, 1944, thirty-three-year-old Vera Duss, a Benedictine nun known as Mère Benoît (Mother Benedict), received a summons to appear at Gestapo headquarters in Paris. This didn't come as a complete surprise. After the United States entered World War II in December 1941, the Germans required all American citizens in France to declare themselves, just as they'd forced Jews to declare themselves all over Europe. And the Nazis had taken over the U.S. embassy in Paris, so they knew where to look.[1]

A Sorbonne-trained physician, Mother Benedict was living in the Abbaye Notre-Dame de Jouarre, in a small, picturesque French town about forty miles east of the capital. Born in Pennsylvania, she was a dark-haired woman with a high forehead and intense blue eyes. Her American mother (who was recovering from a serious illness) was hiding at the abbey as well.

Mother Benedict had taken some precautions to keep the Nazis from sniffing around. She'd quarantined her mother for a fake case

Vera Duss at twenty-four, Paris, 1934.

of tuberculosis.[2] She'd laid a false trail for herself: a postcard to her abbess saying that she'd left France and was sailing to America from Spain. (A visitor had smuggled it out of the abbey and mailed it back from outside the lines.) Plus, one of the nuns had brothers in the French Resistance who supplied Mother Benedict with an alias and fake identification papers.

Still, the odds that she could fly under the Nazis' radar indefinitely weren't good. First of all, Mother Benedict had an astonishingly high profile for a cloistered nun, because she hadn't been given much of a chance to stay cloistered since the war began. She'd taught at Jouarre's Catholic high school at the bishop's request, run a French Army hospital at the Army's request, and—at the mayor's request—was still treating some villagers, since the other local doctors had all fled when the German tanks rolled in.

Then there was the matter of the thirty or so German soldiers who had set up camp in part of the abbey and shared its communal kitchen. (They insisted on doing their own cooking for fear of being poisoned.[3] Such was their opinion of French nuns.)

When the summons from the Gestapo arrived despite Mother Benedict's best efforts, she panicked. The notice stated that if Mother Benedict didn't appear at the Nazis' Rue de Saussaies headquarters at an appointed time, German soldiers would head to the abbey to arrest her.

Mother Benedict and her friend Mother Mary Aline Trilles de Warren, a beautiful, wellborn French nun with a flair for the dramatic, quickly hatched a plan. Wrapping Mother Benedict's head in a cloth for a supposed sinus infection, they worked their way to a train station in another town (where no one would recognize them) and set off for Paris.

Complications set in: A sudden bombardment showered debris on the tracks, forcing their train to divert to a freight station on the outskirts of the city. It finally arrived hours later, around 2 a.m. Mother Benedict recognized the neighborhood, which lay about three miles from her cousin's apartment in Saint-Germain-des-Prés. Waiting around the station till daylight was too risky; they couldn't risk having Mother Benedict's forged identification papers examined by Gestapo patrollers. Ignoring the stationmaster's warnings, they picked up their suitcases and set off on foot in the dark.

It was a moonless night, cool for late April. Feeling their way, the two women crept along the Left Bank of the Seine. Over an hour into their trek, they passed the Cathedral of Notre Dame—and in the next instant, they saw a Nazi patrol car headed toward them, floodlights blazing. There was nowhere to run: High walls edged the river on both sides.

The nuns' veils and habits were black. To hide the white wimples covering their heads and shoulders, they instinctively turned to the wall and pressed up against it. The patrol car grew nearer and slowed down, sweeping its lights along the high wall as the women prayed.

The floodlights slid closer. At precisely the moment when they reached the nuns, the beams hovered just two inches above their heads before moving on. Eventually, the patrol car pulled away and—awash with relief—the women felt free to move again, whereupon they hurried to Mother Benedict's cousin's apartment and practically scared him to death. (He'd taken in a Jewish couple the night before and assumed that it was Nazis ringing the bell.)[4]

The abbess of Jouarre had advised the nuns to go to the Benedictine monastery in Saint-Germain-des-Prés. They were there that afternoon, unpacking, when the prioress brought news from her ecclesiastical superior, the reverend father: Mother Mary Aline could stay but the American nun would have to go. And another thing: She should do away with the habit and dress like a laywoman.

Mother Benedict, horrified, picked up the phone and called a doctor friend from her Sorbonne days, Françoise Bonnenfant. In short order, Mother Benedict and Mother Mary Aline, veils and habits firmly in place, were staying with Bonnenfant on Rue Freycinet in the heart of Paris. What they found there bowled them over. A member of the French Resistance who thought it safest to hide in plain sight, Bonnenfant lived in a building teeming with Gestapo. She even went so far as to hide the code of the underground—the key to identifying her collaborators in the Resistance—in the elevator, under the mat.[5]

Mother Mary Aline now faced her biggest challenge. With Mother Benedict's bogus postcard about sailing to America in hand, she headed to Nazi headquarters to keep the appointment listed on the summons. The female German official who met with her might have come straight from central casting: pale blond, trim, stunning, with two SS officers by her side. Drawing on her acting background, Mother Mary Aline gave the performance of her life, insisting that Mother Benedict had left Europe and that there was no point in sending soldiers to the abbey. The Nazis bought the story and closed her file.

You'd think that the two nuns would get a breather at this point, but no: With the prospect of an Allied invasion looming over Paris, Mother Benedict's friends decided it was too dangerous for her to stay in the city. By the end of May, she and Mother Mary Aline had been spirited back to Jouarre and were tucked away in the abbey in the middle of the night.

Over the next twelve weeks, Mother Benedict was allowed no visitors. During that time, she contracted hepatitis and nearly died. She felt totally isolated and in despair. And then, on a gorgeous August day when the Allied troops were closing in and the Germans had finally cleared out of Jouarre, on a day when Mother Benedict was sitting amid the riot of flowers in the garden, trying to rebuild her strength, things really started to heat up.

IT WAS A Sunday, August 27, 1944. All weekend, air-raid sirens and machine gun blasts had been ringing out from the southwest. By late afternoon, near the end of Vespers, the nuns could hear heavy equipment rumbling through the streets. They huddled near the door of the church, listening, as the sounds became more pronounced.

A younger nun ducked her head outside to investigate. "One of the Lay Sisters said that the British are here!" she exclaimed. Another voice piped up: "Let's go to the tower and watch!"

Mother Benedict still felt weak and exhausted. Just walking to Vespers had worn her out. Nonetheless, she led the way, struggling up the narrow staircase of the abbey's eleventh-century bell tower. When she reached the third-floor attic, she walked toward a blown-out window and looked out.

Below, the street was jammed with jeeps and tanks. Around them, the townspeople of Jouarre were milling around, waving and crying with joy.

One of the other nuns hurried up beside Mother Benedict. "This is the French underground!" she said.

Caught up in the tide of emotion, Mother Benedict gazed in grateful recognition at the white stars crowning each jeep. "My eye!" she said in French. "Those are the Americans." In fact, as she would find out later, the men were from George S. Patton's Third Army.

Looking at the soldiers, her compatriots, "hit me really hard," she said later. "They were naked to the waist, dark brown from head to foot. They were just so sunburned and so exhausted, and their khaki uniforms were dust covered. It was just terribly moving to see them." [6]

A giant American flag was unfurled. Mother Benedict, riveted, was almost falling out of the window at this point. The other nuns clutched her scapular to pull her back.

Suddenly Mother Benedict turned and saw the abbess, and another, more powerful, revelation hit her like a lightning bolt: She needed to do something to pay back these men and the other soldiers who had died for Europe's freedom. "I had this image of monastic life planted in America and the knowledge that it would involve me in a very special way," she said. "It was so totally unexpected and yet so absolutely evident." She'd never imagined leaving Jouarre; now she saw nothing else.

Mother Benedict headed to the infirmary to rest and think. The doctor in her suspected that what she was feeling might just be exhaustion. After a while another nun rushed in with a roll of Life Savers, a gift from some of the soldiers, and asked Mother Benedict if she would give her a message to take back to them.

"I looked around," Mother Benedict said, "and there were two roses in a vase, one already drooping but one still beautiful, a very pale pinkish yellow. I took the rose, gave it to her, and I told her this was my message.

"She came back later to tell me she gave a soldier the rose, saying, 'This is from an American nun,' [and] he burst into tears."[7]

Mother Benedict took the moment as an endorsement for her mission. No more doubts.

SHE HAD HER work cut out for her. As a rule, an abbey—not an individual nun—could start a foundation.[8] Even then, it was usually at the invitation of the bishop in the diocese where the new foundation would be built. Mother Benedict went a different route. She was flying solo and had no money. She didn't even know an American bishop. Just about the only thing she did have, by the time the war ended in the spring of 1945, was the grudging approval of her abbess, who agreed to let Mother Benedict pitch her idea to some higher-ups.

Mother Benedict spent the next few months meeting with church officials in France. She wrote letters to Rome that went unanswered. She got appendicitis. Then, in rapid succession, she caught two lucky breaks. First, in May 1946, she landed the support of the nuncio, the influential Vatican representative in Paris (and future Pope John XXIII). Second, she chanced upon a well-timed gift of cash from a childhood friend, enough to bankroll a trip to Rome.

Armed with letters of introduction from the nuncio and from her abbess, Mother Benedict enlisted senior Vatican dignitaries in her cause. With their help, she also refined the concept for her American abbey and wrote it into a proposal: It would be a contemplative, self-supporting community built on farming and manual labor—Benedictine themes sure to catch on in the Puritan-driven New World. And then the radical leap: It would be run by educated nuns, as accomplished in their respective fields as Mother Benedict herself. That model of self-discovery and connection with the world offered something that American women could embrace, too: Mother Benedict and her advisers sensed that the centuries-old European model of contemplative life—still in place in 1946— needed to take a more inviting shape across the pond.

Toward the end of her visit in Rome, in early June, nearly two years after she first began her campaign, Mother Benedict reached what should have been her victory lap: an audience with Pope Pius XII himself. Excitedly, she told him why she had come to Rome. In addition, according to Vatican protocol, she handed him the hard-won letter that authorized her mission and would serve as her calling card to American bishops.

"Very interesting," said the pope, a slender man with pointed features and tiny round spectacles. "I give you all my blessings."[9] And then, in perhaps Mother Benedict's most heart-wrenching moment yet, he held on to the letter, as it was addressed to "Most Holy Father," and refused to give it back.

Afterward, one of the Pope's aides, a monsignor wearing a fuchsia cape and an air of exasperation, explained the situation to

Mother Benedict, who was suppressing an urge to scream: Once the Sacred Hand of His Holiness had touched a document, it could never be returned. And to confirm her sinking opinion of the bureaucratic red tape, she couldn't even get a copy of it.

Undaunted, Mother Benedict retraced her steps and eventually secured new (albeit inferior) documents to take to America. She found a French benefactress who not only agreed to pay for Mother Benedict and Mother Mary Aline to sail to the United States on an abbey reconnaissance mission, but also put them in touch with someone who could help on the other side: Lauren Ford, an American artist based in Bethlehem, Connecticut. An angular woman with short, wavy brown hair and a quaint sense of fashion, Ford had connections. Her inspirational paintings were featured in *Life* magazine and on countless Christmas cards, and her father built hotels.

When the two nuns stepped off the boat in New York on August 24, 1946, Mother Benedict had exactly fifty dollars in her wallet. Ford and an artist friend met them and took them straight to lunch in midtown. When the bill arrived, the two artists confessed that they'd spent all their money on new handbags while waiting for the ship. After footing the bill, Mother Benedict was left with a mere $7.53. The women set off for Connecticut. As if Mother Benedict needed further proof that life is a test of endurance, their car broke down on the way and had to be towed. The repair bill came to $7.50.

So, armed with the princely sum of three cents, Mother Benedict prepared to launch her foundation.

Fast-forward to the early 1970s. My father rang the bell at Regina Laudis Monastery, whose Latin name means "Queen of Praise." Founded by Mother Benedict in 1947, it sits on a hill within a lush, wooded, 450-acre plot in Bethlehem, a small town in Litch-field County, Connecticut. True to Mother Benedict's word, the monastery stays connected to society by operating like a sort of monastic brain trust: Nowadays, several of the nuns are former lawyers and investment bankers. The librarian, Mother Lucia, has a doctorate in literature from Yale. Mother Noella Marcellino, an artisanal cheese maker and Fulbright scholar, has studied the microbiology of cheese in France and been the subject of a PBS documentary, *The Cheese Nun*. The abbey's resident sculptor, Mother Praxedes, has worked with Alexander Calder's technician. The nuns have raised their own food for decades; to keep up-to-date with advances in farming, at least three nuns have earned PhDs in agricultural studies.

The visitors' entranceway is a tiny, dimly lit room with stained wood paneling, dark even at high noon. On the day that my father and my sister Margaret arrived, one of the nuns appeared through the grille in the interior door. After greeting them, she went to announce their arrival to Mother Benedict. Margaret, then in her early twenties, was thinking about entering the monastery. My father, whose express aim was to shut down the plan, had come along to gather intelligence. He loved Margaret more than he could say, and would have had her join the circus before becoming a clois-tered nun. To him, it seemed too isolating, a way of life designed to cut Margaret off from her family and the world.

One thing Dad always emphasized to his soldiers was the value of what he called "cultural empathy"—understanding the motiva-tions and habits of one's enemy before going to war. As the minutes ticked by in the dark vestibule, he was already finding common ground.

"Well, I do this, too, you know," he said, blinking in the darkness.

"What's that?" Margaret asked.

"Keep people waiting," he said.

Growing up, I really didn't know Margaret very well. She's twelve years older than I am and left for school when I was a toddler. Now she's one of my closest friends. But at the time, based on my limited sense of her, Margaret was the last person I'd have pictured as nun material.

First of all, my sister wasn't Catholic. She wasn't even a very devout Episcopalian. A pretty brunette with hazel eyes and an expressive face, she had no shortage of male admirers. What's more, she had a major restless streak. She got kicked out of high school for smoking pot. She attended a protest against the Vietnam War, even as Dad despaired that it would be used as propaganda against his men. By choice, she spent her college years hopscotching from Bennington to Germany to Dartmouth to Italy to Wesleyan. Margaret was always searching. Actually, as I look back, it makes absolute sense that she became a nun. But at the time it seemed to make no sense at all.

In fairness, Margaret was probably more surprised than anyone by her calling. "I often thought I'd marry into the Army and have a bunch of kids and travel," she says. But as an eighteen-year-old freshman at Bennington, she had a roommate who was starting Catholic instruction at the monastery. One spring weekend, out of curiosity, Margaret tagged along. Soon she returned for a longer stay. This time, Mother Benedict asked to meet her.

"We're having a ceremony tomorrow, August twenty-seventh," Mother Benedict said through the grille at the visitors' entrance.

Margaret Patton, circa 1975. PHOTO COURTESY OF SISTER MARY CONNORS, FSE

"It's to celebrate the anniversary of the liberation of Jouarre, the abbey out of which Regina Laudis was founded. We want you to raise the flag."

"Um, I don't think you have the right person," said Margaret. She was definitely not making public that she was General Patton's granddaughter.

Mother Benedict refused to be put off. "I really do have the right person," she said. "You don't know this, but our foundation owes its life to your family. Your grandfather preceded you here, via our parent abbey in France, and we wouldn't be here without him."

So, the next day, Margaret raised the flag. "I remember the day as kind of riveting," she says. "I couldn't put it together: Here was this monastery that I responded to, deeply, and it had an American flag stuck in the middle of the property, which to me seemed nationalistic." Ultimately, she saw it for what it was, "a place of peace that had come out of a war situation. That led to a reckoning with my genealogy," Margaret continues. "So much of our family history was about war and killing: Where is that in me? How does that energy get channeled and used?"

In short, "I really fell in love," she says. "It's hard to explain, except that that's how it was for me. Even my mother was crestfallen because she's a very devout Episcopalian. She said, 'Well, Margaret, couldn't you at least visit one of the Episcopalian monasteries? Because we have them.' But there was no point to that for me. I knew I was going to end up here, I just didn't know when."

OUR DAD HAD fought a lot of battles before, but never against nuns. "We went through a whole routine all the time," says Mother Placid Dempsey. "Sometimes he would try to flatter me, sometimes he would try to cajole me, and other times he would ask me serious questions. It was fun, kind of like 'Who's gonna win this argument?' One time he told me, 'You know, a lot of nuns have left the Catholic Church.' I said, 'General, remarkable though your daughter is, she cannot fill in for about a hundred nuns who've left the monastic life.' You know, forget it. He was afraid that we were going to pressure Margaret to enter the monastery, and of course we weren't going to do any such thing." (In fact, it generally takes several years to enter—as it turned out in Margaret's case, almost ten. Mother Benedict kept telling her to go back out, date, get her degrees, and achieve some professional success, because living in community is a radical way of life: You take vows of obedience, stability (which means you rarely leave the premises except on mission), and *conversatio morum* or conversion of life (which encompasses poverty and chastity). You also attend religious services and sing Gregorian chants for several hours a day.

Over time, Mother Benedict, who was elected lady abbess in 1976,[10] became one of my father's favorite sparring partners. And gradually, once he started to relax a bit, they grew to be close friends. He admired her perseverance and how much she had accomplished, and they bonded over lots of things: my grandfather's role in liberating Europe, the fact that Dad and the abbess had both known war, and their love for Margaret. Dad also saw some of his leadership tactics in Lady Abbess. They both knew how to set a pace.

For example, Margaret remembers helping Lady Abbess cut lilies one morning. The abbess wanted to place them directly into cold water. She dipped her finger in one of the buckets.

"'This is tepid,' Lady Abbess said.

"I said, 'I know, Lady Abbess, but I have cold water for you in the vases,'" says Margaret. "Talking back to an elder was not monastic and kind of bratty. But I was thinking, Oh, come on." They went back and forth for a minute. Finally, the abbess hauled off and kicked the bucket over. "'Sister, do I make myself clear?' she asked. Of course, that was a feminine expression of something that I knew perfectly well from the way we were brought up," Margaret says. "Our father could be extremely severe when he felt you weren't being honest or doing your best."

And the water was cold after that.

I guess the thing that won my father over to the nuns in the end was that he truly understood what it meant to have a calling. Our grandfather tried to make sure that Dad's decision to go into the military was his own. He gave him every opportunity to choose another path. He didn't send him to a military high school, for instance, and he encouraged my father to spend a lot of time on the Parker Ranch in Hawaii when they were stationed there so that he could see another way of life. But really, there was nothing else for Dad from the very beginning. So even if he didn't understand Margaret's vocation, he respected it. And he made it a point to stay involved.

On the weekend she was supposed to graduate from Dartmouth, Margaret made plans to go on a Regina Laudis retreat instead. That was a bad idea, because Dad simply gathered up whatever family members were at home and drove up to the abbey and re-created the graduation ceremony right in the middle of the retreat, complete with a photo for the Christmas card. Another time, he was asked to give a lecture on guerrilla warfare to the nuns, Margaret included. Dad flew in by helicopter and set down on the abbey's parking lot.

"It was kind of like, 'Oh my God, here comes Dad,'" says Margaret. "I was going with it, but it was awkward. I remember the first thing he said was, 'Who's in charge here?' He wanted to know who was running it. In the end, I felt proud of him. He gave a great lecture."

If you want to get philosophical about it, there are a million similarities between my father's military life and Margaret's monastic one: duty, honor, discipline, patience, teamwork, intensity, the good of the group, rituals, and a clear structure. (There's even a passage in *The Rule of Saint Benedict* about the importance of "cleaning the tools," i.e., taking care of your gear.)[11] The abbey actually drew them closer. Also, Dad was all about results: In her midtwenties, motivated by her experience at the monastery, Margaret founded a Montessori school. It was hard to argue with that. And despite the fact that my father would very regularly say to Margaret, "It's time to go to Lady Abbess and tell her thank you very much but you're done," the nuns all adored him.

The five-pointed star held many associations for Lady Abbess: She had been baptized on the Epiphany and made her first vows in Epiphanytide; she had been led to make her foundation in the town of Bethlehem; and, besides, the star was the insignia on the American vehicles that had liberated Jouarre. The shape was scattered all over the abbey—in the architecture and the iron grillwork in the chapel. On one occasion, Lady Abbess requested a memento of General George S. Patton Jr., in order to have something at the abbey that had belonged to him, as a way to keep him present in prayer. My father's sister, Ruth Ellen Patton Totten, who by that time also knew Lady Abbess, offered one of the silver stars her father had worn on his uniform. Amazed that the memento chosen would be a star, Lady Abbess had it mounted onto a tulipwood cross that she often wore around her neck.

For Dad, it was an emotional thing, and you could tell Lady Abbess felt the same way. She was buried wearing my grandfather's star.

MY MOTHER DIDN'T attend the ceremony the night that Margaret officially entered the abbey. I don't think she could bear it at the time. The rest of our family was doing other things. I was a junior in high school filling out college applications and felt like Margaret was part of some completely different world, which I guess she was. But my father felt it was his duty to be present.

It was New Year's Eve 1981. Dad took Margaret out to dinner (where the maître d' begged her to rethink things) and a dance, and then they left to go to midnight Mass at the abbey. "The ground was covered with snow that night and the sky was full of stars," says Margaret.

She entered one of the farmhouse residences on the property and changed into her postulant's black tunic and headscarf. Dad was sitting in the living room reading Scripture when she came out.

"He looked me up and down and said, 'So, that's the uniform, huh?'" says Margaret. "That was really the tenor of how he took it." After Mass, she and Dad walked through the snow down to the enormous, arched wooden gate that leads to the abbey's enclosed gardens, which are surrounded by a tall, solid wooden fence that's like a wall.

The tradition is that the woman asking to enter knocks at the grille in the gate and tells the abbess inside what she's seeking. For Margaret, it was, "I want to enter this standing army of women."

What was supposed to happen at this point was that Dad would offer some prayers. Then Margaret was supposed to cross through the gigantic gate. Then Dad was supposed to go back to the Mayflower Hotel. But what actually happened, because the nuns loved Dad and had been worrying about him, was a little different.

One of the worriers was Mother Dolores Hart. A former actress who had starred in such films as *Loving You* and *Where the Boys Are* with people like Elvis Presley and Montgomery Clift in the late 1950s and '60s, she was still breathtaking in a Grace Kelly way. "I knew that the general thought that he was losing Margaret to something dull and tomblike and totally other," she says. "I mean, this wasn't different than it is for most parents, except for him it seemed even worse. I kept asking myself how we could make this a vibrant experience, an awakening for him." The abbey had been having some trouble with trespassers, so Mother Dolores had been working on target practice with a friend. "A few days before Margaret's ceremony, I asked to borrow his .38 revolver so I could get in some extra practice time," she says, smiling. She actually had something else in mind.

In the meantime, Lady Abbess and some of the other nuns had arranged an impromptu cheese-and-cracker reception for Dad after the ceremony. To host it, they recruited Catherine Lamb, a new postulant who had run the Cardinal Spellman Servicemen's Club in New York.[12] And they managed to get a bottle of cognac, too, which was a big deal—alcohol is reserved for special occasions at the abbey.

Anyway, after Dad said the prayers, right as Margaret was about to cross the threshold, there was a huge bang and a volley of gunshots ripped through the air. All courtesy of Mother Dolores, who was hiding nearby, in the bushes by the carpentry shop. Dad and Margaret jumped about a mile. Mother Dolores, satisfied, slipped the gun back into its holster. "It made for a very memorable moment," she says. "At least the general would know that his daughter wasn't entering into something dull."

Margaret, exhilarated, walked inside and the gate closed behind her. The moment marked the first phase of her monastic life, known as postulancy, during which she would begin to find out whether she could persevere to the point of asking to become a novice. If so, that would mean no phone calls or visits from friends or family for twelve months.

"Good luck, Margaret!" Dad shouted over the enclosure wall.

"Thanks, Dad," Margaret called back. "I'll need it."

Afterward, at a private reception, Catherine Lamb handed Dad a glass of cognac. "Are you going far tonight, General?" she asked when he finished his drink.

"No," he replied.

"Well, you seem pretty low, sir."

"Yeah," Dad admitted. "I am pretty low."

She poured another glass. "General, have another."

And then it was the New Year.

All the knotted connections between Lady Abbess's family and mine add up to a flawless study of unlikelihoods:

That my Episcopalian grandfather, with his out-there beliefs in reincarnation, had been involved in something that would prompt a nun to start a monastery in America.

That the abbess managed to overcome countless setbacks to make it happen.

And that, against all odds, Margaret found her way there.

Strange to say, two other weird coincidences make it seem like a kind of grand, awesome destiny.

First off, when my father died in 2004 (just a year before Lady Abbess passed away), Arlington Cemetery just happened to schedule his memorial service for August 27—the anniversary of the liberation of Jouarre.

Then there was the time that my mother visited the abbey and, in the gift shop, spotted something that stopped her in her tracks. It was a big painting of a little blond girl walking on a path through a forest, with rays of light sifting down through the trees and a large guardian angel behind her, guiding her steps.

"How on earth did they get that?" Mom asked Margaret.

As a child, Margaret had a print of that exact painting, *The Guardian Angel,* hanging over her bed.

Lady Abbess, Mother Margaret Georgina, and me visiting a small abbey garden I'd planted, spring 1995.

And the artist was Lauren Ford, the very woman who had helped Mother Benedict and Mother Mary Aline get to Bethlehem, Connecticut.

WHEN I WAS twenty-nine, on the verge of attending business school in Switzerland, I went to visit the abbey. I arrived around noon and immediately set to work helping Margaret, who was responsible for several gardens, plant bulbs near the cemetery. By dinnertime, I had such an epic case of poison ivy that I could barely walk. (Forget the telltale three-leafed sprigs that identify it. The leafless poison ivy vines of winter are much more potent.) As a result, instead of staying one or two nights as planned, I had to spend nearly a week convalescing in the abbey's guesthouse. And I started to question exactly why I was going to business school in the first place. Was it for me, for Dad, or because I felt a need to validate my decision not to enter the family business?

Given what our father and grandfather had achieved, expectations for all the Patton children ran ridiculously high. On countless occasions, my brothers and sisters and I were all dressed up and taken places to represent our grandfather. At the same time we were raised with a strong consciousness that we'd done nothing to earn our time in the spotlight. People simply needed to say thank you and we were there—even if there were more deserving people left in the shadows. I think that's something we've all paid for in different ways. For me, at least, it meant a struggle to feel authentic and make decisions without the burden of perfection. All I knew was that at that particular moment, going to business school felt utterly wrong.

There's a saying that the biggest turns in your life happen when you're not there. Or in my case, when you're laid up and slathered in calamine lotion. The longer I stayed at the abbey, the more it struck me as a place where I could explore a few things and maybe even figure out what I wanted to do with my life. I ended up staying a year.

That happened to be the time commitment that Lady Abbess required from each participant in what was then called the Land Program. One of her bedrock tenets was that it's important to stay connected to the full cycle of creation—the calving and the slaughter, the planting and the harvest. The nuns trained me to take charge of the cattle—about fifty Jerseys and whiteface Herefords—as well as the fruit orchards, which were filled with apple, pear, and plum trees.

Each morning I'd get up at about six-thirty and feed hay to the cattle. After breakfast, I'd go back to the barn and shovel massive amounts of mucked-out manure into the compost heap. Or, depending on the season, I'd get to work planting, pruning or spraying the trees, harvesting fruit, planting bulbs, or, as it happened on one occasion, defrosting a newborn calf in the abbey's boiler room. In the fall, Mother Augusta, dressed in her denim work habit, taught me how to use the hay baler. In the spring lambing seasons, we took shifts to watch over the sheep and make sure the newborns, wet from delivery, didn't freeze.

The nuns attend eight—yes, eight—religious services (known as offices) throughout the day, every day—some ten minutes long, some almost two hours long. I'm not Catholic, but I tried to attend at least the morning Mass and Vespers, because it helped me learn the rhythm of the place. Also, it was a chance to catch my breath and think.

At six-thirty each night, I'd have dinner in the little red farmhouse that I shared with the other male visitors to the abbey. A big social highlight would be taking the resident abbot to dinner and a movie. (The first few months, I'd been regularly sneaking off to a nearby diner for breakfast, but the place had pretty waitresses and the nuns felt that it wasn't helping my journey, so I cut back.) Most nights, I was wiped and sound asleep by eight-thirty. I've never been more fit in my life.

On weekends, I taught Sunday school with one of the sisters and took part in group work activities: baling hay or making apple cider with Mother Augusta, thinning a forest with chain saws alongside

Sister Ozanne, chipping brush with Sister Jadwiga. (The nuns were big on their wood chipper, which they called Saint Ignatius of Antioch after the Christian martyr who was eaten by lions in the Colosseum.) I worked holidays, too. Christmas and Easter were the most important days for the nuns—I couldn't in clear conscience ask for those days off—so at Christmas my parents brought my brother George up to the abbey to celebrate.

My sister Helen, who'd interned at the abbey two years earlier, had warned me that living on Lady Abbess's terms would come as a gigantic shock. Her exact words were, "The abbey experience is like living in a hall of mirrors. You have to face yourself every day. If you're willing to risk that, then you'll grow." I didn't appreciate precisely what she meant by that until I was in my second week of shoveling shit and literally working for my food. By then, the novelty had worn off. Forget my privileged background and famous name: When it comes to forming your identity, there's nothing like subsistence living.

For openers, I had to learn to shut up. The Benedictines teach that it's more important to understand than to be understood. Lady Abbess herself, then in her eighties, was a consummate listener. I worked with her in her rose garden and had dinner with her from time to time, and even though I know she liked me, she never said much. When she did speak, it was usually to ask me a question or to say something so profound that I could never actually re-create it in my diary later. And that level of attentive listening is a corollary of something else I learned at the abbey: focus.

The nuns' professional objective is to be "equal to or surpassing" anyone else in their field.[13] But not as a competitive thing: The pursuit of excellence is a way of expressing a Benedictine commitment to transform yourself, work toward the common good, and find transcendence in the everyday. The goal, as I saw it, was to achieve such a level of focus on your work that the very act of working itself becomes a form of prayer. I remember walking by the bookbinding studio one morning shortly after I arrived. Inside, facing a window in the tiny cabin, Sister Simonetta, whom I'd recently met, sat at her workbench. I stood in front of the window and waved hello to her. I kept waving. She never noticed me. That was my first lightbulb moment.

I'm sorry to report that I'm naturally not the most patient or focused person—I live in Manhattan and I have mild ADD. But at the abbey, a lot of lessons that my father gave me growing up started to take hold. He always told me, "If you can bring your vocation and avocation together, you'll never work again." (His love of soldiering was certainly proof of that.) And: "Whatever you do, be an expert at it." Now, though it had taken me a long time, I started to get the connection.

I also had to learn to stop being so hard on myself. For a long time I'd been beating myself up for not having more direction, and often wondered if I should have gone into the military. I'd always secretly envied my father's calling to be a soldier, Margaret's calling to faith, Helen's call to the theater, my brother Bob's calling to be a writer. Even my developmentally challenged brother George has known since his teens that he was meant to be a horseman. But as the months went by, I began to understand my father better and how hard he must have had it.

Think about it: He couldn't imagine being anything but a soldier, even though it meant working in the immediate shadow of a legendary war hero. It's inspirational, but the reality must have been pretty tough to deal with at times.

And there was Margaret: Before my stay at the abbey, I think

I'd always suspected that becoming a cloistered nun was, on some level, a form of escape. You'd think that it would be totally peaceful to be surrounded by people who believe the same thing you do and share all the same goals. But if anything, it was like real life in a more concentrated form. That's another Benedictine tenet: You define who you are through your relationships with others. Mother Dorcas, a research scientist and MD who'd become the abbey's baker, noted that back in the day, Christians did penance by strapping their backs or wearing hair shirts and were occasionally thrown to the lions. Now you just make them live in community.

The third lesson: It turns out that living in a microcosm of society really does make you live in a more conscious way. In my case, at least, I began to feel less judgmental and more connected to the people around me—to Lady Abbess, to my sister, to the nuns I worked with every day. Once you really begin to understand it, a monastic community is not unlike the tribal clan in the movie *Avatar*. Everyone there is part of an organism. The nuns are all devoted to one another, even if some of them don't always see eye to eye. The members of the group need one another to succeed, not unlike soldiers in a military unit.

In August, when the community celebrated the anniversary of the liberation of the abbey in Jouarre, Lady Abbess chose me to give the presentation. I stood on the lawn in front of the flag and talked about the history of the abbey and my family. And when I left the abbey, amazingly, I tumbled into a career that eventually enabled me to combine all of my gifts and interests—filmmaking, teaching kids, and working with veterans. That's one of the most rewarding things I took from my year out: It was possible—in a healthy, proactive way, and on my own terms—to engage with the very legacy I both revered and felt overwhelmed by as an adolescent.

When I was younger, my father often worried that I hadn't found my path or become an expert at anything. Yet I'd like to think if he were still alive, he'd be proud of the work I'm doing now. I think it was my sister Mother Margaret Georgina who pointed out to me that some relationships can only go so far in life; they have to continue after death. I get that now, too.

As I'm writing this, I'm in the midst of my second divorce, so I obviously have a lot more transforming to do. (My friends joke that I found it easier to live with forty complicated women than just one.) About all I can do is to keep trying to figure out what I did wrong and try not to repeat it. Otherwise, I don't dwell. The Benedictine way is to process the good and the bad honestly, always strive to remain self-aware, and keep moving forward.

I'll never forget ringing the abbey doorbell during a weekend visit. Mother Dolores, the former movie star, answered. At the time, I was in the midst of a difficult falling-out with a mutual friend. She asked me how I was coping with it all, and I said, "Well, there have been some hits and some misses, as I'm sure you're aware."

To which she replied, "Certainly, but you must remember to only count the hits."

PART THREE

THE YOUNG
COMMANDERS

An Army is a team; lives, sleeps, eats, fights as a team.
This individual heroic stuff is a lot of horse shit.

—GEORGE S. PATTON JR., MAY 1944[1]

I WANT TO begin by saying that I didn't originally intend for this group of heroes to appear right in the middle of this book, but it actually makes perfect sense: To me, they're the heart of it. Each of them served under my father as a young commander in Vietnam in the late 1960s or in Fort Hood, Texas, in the 1970s—some, in both places. From then on, they started a tradition of getting together every year.

In 2000, they held their annual reunion at my parents' farm in Massachusetts. I just happened to come home that weekend. My father was fading rapidly that fall, and in the way of any child faced with losing a parent, I suddenly found myself thinking of all the conversations I'd meant to have with him—conversations that wouldn't be happening now.

At the same time, watching them at close range over dinner and card games, I was electrified by the loyalty of our visitors. They were all protégés of my father and had become some of his closest friends. And yet the time they'd served with him was brief—only two years, in some cases. I couldn't help wondering: What was it about these men that my father admired so much? And what was it that kept them coming back each year?

Years later, still puzzling the question, I decided an exploration was in order. So I turned to the members of the group I knew best.

EIGHT

Jim Dozier

At 5:30 P.M. on December 17, 1981, the doorbell rang at Major General James Dozier's penthouse apartment in Verona, Italy. This was unusual—visitors were supposed to call up from the street entrance before gaining entrance to the building. And Dozier, as one of three U.S. generals stationed in northern Italy at the time, was supposed to be careful about security.

Judy, Dozier's wife of twenty-five years, had just gotten dinner started. She was sitting at the table with him, drinking a glass of red wine, when they heard the bell.

"This makes me uncomfortable," she said. "Maybe you shouldn't."

But Dozier was already on his feet. A West Point graduate, he'd survived a year in Vietnam and had the bullet wounds to show for it. After that, it was easy to shrug off fear. Besides, as he frequently pointed out, he was an unlikely target. That wasn't just simple modesty talking. As a senior official at NATO, Dozier had nothing to do with the solely American nuclear arsenal that had stacked up

Major Jim Dozier in Vietnam, 1969.

across Europe during the cold war. Even within NATO's Verona headquarters, he played a quiet, administrative role. Plus, the terrorist violence that had rocked Italy for more than a decade hadn't jumped to Verona. The city, with its romantic *Romeo and Juliet* overtones, was considered a safe zone.

Picture the contrast: The top U.S. Army general, George McFadden, who lived twenty-eight miles east in Vicenza, wore a bulletproof vest to work, rode around town in a customized armored limousine, and switched up his schedule every day to throw off assassins. Meanwhile, NATO Security allowed Dozier, a clean-cut, five-foot, nine-inch fitness nut, to jog several miles a day through Verona's cobbled streets.[1]

Now Dozier walked to the door and, without opening it, asked, *"Chi è?"*

There's a leak in the building, came the reply. Dozier relaxed. The building was about seventy years old and something was always in need of repair.

He opened the door. The plumbers were young, bearded, and carrying toolboxes. Dozier led them toward the laundry room, where he knelt down and peered under the washing machine. No leak.

"Il termosifone?" the men asked. Dozier's Italian was good, but not so good that he recognized the word for radiator. He got up and then followed Judy back down the hallway into the kitchen to get the dictionary. It was as he was flipping through it that one of the men—Pietro Vanzi, a member of the Red Brigades terrorist group—seized Dozier from behind.

At the same time, Vanzi's partner, twenty-six-year-old Antonio Savasta, pulled out a Beretta pistol and pointed it at the general's head. Defiant, Dozier lunged at him anyway. The fight tumbled into the hallway. After a long struggle—the general was in fighting shape, even for a fifty-year-old—Vanzi finally knocked him unconscious.

Back in the kitchen, Savasta hurled Judy to the kitchen floor. After taping her mouth shut, he began chaining her wrists and ankles together. Meanwhile, a second team of insurgents arrived, pushing a dolly. On it sat a steamer trunk disguised as a refrigerator packing crate. A few of the insurgents began ransacking the apartment for evidence. The others wedged Dozier inside the trunk, hoisted it back onto the dolly, and rolled it out to the elevator.

The rebels later admitted that if Dozier hadn't opened the door, their backup plan had been to kill him by shooting straight through it. [2]

. . .

Two HOURS LATER, Savasta and two other kidnappers flung Dozier onto a metal cot, ripped off his blindfold, removed his earplugs, and cut the plastic packing tape from his mouth. Working methodically, they chained his right wrist and left foot to the frame of the cot. Dozier looked around. The cot sat in a sky-blue canvas tent. The tent, in turn, was set up inside a room on what Dozier—based on his journey inside the steamer trunk—correctly guessed was a low floor in a building about ninety minutes outside of Verona.

The rebels were dressed in tracksuits and wore ski masks to hide their faces. By the time they had Dozier secured and Savasta was ready to speak, a fourth rebel—a woman, also masked—had squeezed herself into the tent.

"The rebels had done what they set out to do, and they were on an emotional high, waving loaded pistols around," Dozier recalls. "Every time I flinched they reacted violently, pointing their guns at me."

He had virtually no prisoner-of-war training. Yet instinctively, Dozier did a few things right.

First, he asked about his wife. "The last time I'd seen her, she had a pistol at her head," he remembers. "It sounds like a small thing, but that started a dialogue that got the rebels looking at me as a human being."

(In fact, Judy, hog-tied, gagged and blindfolded back in their Verona apartment, had managed to open the padlock to the chains that linked her wrists to her ankles. Slowly, she'd wriggled across the floor to the laundry area—and from there, slammed her knees against the washing machine until her downstairs neighbors came to investigate.)

Once he felt assured that Judy was okay, Dozier could focus on his own survival. As he well knew, Italian terrorists had executed hundreds of people over the previous decade. The turbulence in Western Europe first erupted in a wave of student riots in 1968—a sharp backlash against the Italian economic crisis, rocketing oil prices, and growing resentment toward the Vietnam War. In its wake, leftist rebels kicked off a surge of terror designed to upend the country's right-leaning government. They conducted thirteen thousand acts of sabotage, often funding their campaigns through kidnappings. Unless their captives agreed to denounce the government and become propaganda tools for the terrorists, they were usually murdered. Just three years earlier, in 1978, the Red Brigades had kidnapped and brutally assassinated Aldo Moro, the former Italian prime minister.

Savasta fitted Dozier with a pair of heavy-duty padded earphones. Attached to a portable tape recorder outside the tent, they blasted hard rock and heavy metal round the clock. Repeatedly, Dozier begged the rebels to turn down the volume, but they refused.

Dozier adapted. The second thing he did intuitively was to make himself into a polite, predictable prisoner. He went to great lengths to make sure that he did the same thing at the same time every day. The effort bought him a measure of freedom. "After about a week the guard stopped paying as much attention to me and I was able to sneak the headset off for short periods," says Dozier. "That way, I could listen to what was going on outside the building—the morning buildup of traffic and things—so I knew that I was in an urban area."

His West Point training had taught him to stay calm by focusing on the things he could control. He started by leaving a trail: clear fingerprint impressions on his cot and the tent for the police to find, his name scratched in the tent's plastic floor. He found a

scrap of cardboard under his cot and made a mark on it each morning to keep track of the passing days.

From what Dozier had read about POWs in World War II,
Korea, and Vietnam, he also knew that it was important to stay as
mentally and physically alert as possible. Despite the fact that he
remained chained to the bed, he followed a strict regimen of sit-
ups, deep knee bends, and isometric exercises to keep in shape. He
devised a way to play one-handed bridge without cheating too
badly. He played a lot of solitaire. When one of the rebels gave him
a pencil and paper to record his scores (Dozier had been scratching
them into a corrugated box top with a fingernail), he used an alpha-
numeric code to keep a diary.

He'd learned from his time in combat that it was important to
eat and rest whenever you got the chance. Luckily, the food his kidnappers gave him was simple but adequate. And even through the
booming, bass-heavy din from the headphones, Dozier willed himself to sleep.

Two years earlier, when he was first promoted to brigadier general, Dozier had been ordered to attend a weeklong course at the
Army's Center for Creative Leadership. It had been a humbling
exercise, all about learning how to view oneself through the eyes of
others. "It really brought home that what you see in the mirror isn't
necessarily what other people see," Dozier says. The experience
would prove invaluable to him as a prisoner.

Looking at himself through the hostile eyes of the Red Brigades,
Dozier must have felt tempted to do some image control. But he
refused to try to charm his captors by pretending to be something

he wasn't. In the days and weeks after he was abducted, the rebels put him on trial as a war criminal in a people's court. "One of the things I told them when they first started quizzing me was, 'I'm not going to lie to you, but I'm not going to give you any sensitive material either,'" Dozier says.

Back at the headquarters of the Southern European Task Force, Dozier's Army colleagues were praying that the terrorists wouldn't try to break him with torture, since they knew what he could give away.

"The general knew as much as anyone about NATO's wartime strategy," wrote Richard Oliver Collin and Gordon L. Freedman in their book about the kidnapping, *Winter of Fire*. "He was an expert in tank warfare and in the employment of tactical nuclear weapons. He was familiar with the nation's intelligence system and had been receiving regular briefings at the supersecret code word level, which meant that he understood spy satellites and communications intercepts and aerial photography. There was only one conclusion: a detailed and successful debriefing of Dozier would constitute a major national security disaster for the United States."[3]

Yet the kidnappers were no Soviet-trained interrogation experts. They didn't believe in torture or see any propaganda value in it. Most of their evidence against Dozier revolved around his service in Vietnam. In fact, it soon grew on Dozier that the questions were coming directly out of material, particularly his military honors, that the rebels must have seized from his apartment on the night of the kidnapping. He came to rue the day the military started inflating award citations.

"Did you kill people in Vietnam?" the rebels asked.

"Of course I killed people," Dozier replied.

Did he feel any remorse? He'd been fighting communism, for a people he believed could be rescued. He'd played by the rules. War could be savage. The short answer: no.

Repentance was important to the rebels. Dozier showed no sign of being converted. One of the terrorists finally sat down with him and painstakingly translated the Red Brigades' ten-page manifesto. "Their rhetoric was just ridiculous," Dozier says. In fact, the rebels struck him as more and more bizarre. "At one point in the questioning, they wanted to know what the overall U.S. plan was for the subjugation of Italy. I said, 'There is no such plan, and even if there were one, I wouldn't know what it was. Give me an example of what you're talking about.' They brought up the Marshall Plan [the American effort to rebuild European countries after World War II], which they thought was a U.S. plot to subjugate Europe."

Dozier's abduction was part of a larger Red Brigades campaign, code-named Winter of Fire, that was designed to create political turmoil and undermine the American presence in Italy. The rebels' agenda—ransom Dozier for money, embarrass the Italian security agencies who were responsible for protecting NATO officials, and destabilize the government in the process—seems bumbling on every level. The Italian government refused to negotiate with terrorists, much less bankroll them.

As Dozier eventually learned, the kidnapping itself was amateur hour right out of the box. "My picture was in the papers, but to make sure they got the right guy, the rebels staked out a coffee shop near NATO headquarters," he says. "After mistakenly following two other guys, they finally went to a store that specialized in toy soldiers and got hold of an instructional booklet that showed how to decorate a general's uniform. They were just that naive."

Later, the kidnappers admitted that they didn't like Dozier, but that he'd acted like a general—disciplined, proud, and honorable. That earned their respect and, in the end, was what would keep him alive.

For the time being, Dozier tried not to plan too far ahead and take care of himself as best he could. He thought about his family and friends. His former commander—my father, George S. Patton IV—appeared often in Dozier's dreams. "It helped to know that people like him were out there moving heaven and earth to get me free," Dozier remembers.

Soon after the kidnapping, Judy Dozier called our house in Massachusetts. I was home for winter break at the time and answered the phone. My father immediately got on the line and offered to fly to Italy and join the frantic hunt. Unbeknownst to them at the time, the answering machine on our home phone recorded the conversation. Later, since he saved everything, my father saved the tape. "The guy's like a younger brother to me," you can hear my father saying to Judy. "And you know, when you fight a war with a guy you get kinda close to him."

DOZIER FIRST MET my father in 1956 during his first class (senior) year at West Point, where Dad, age thirty-three, was serving on the faculty as a tactical officer. They met again briefly in Germany. And then, in 1968, Dozier surfaced in Vietnam as the operations officer of the 11th Armored Cavalry Regiment, known as "Blackhorse." My father was the regimental commander.

The regiment covered three sectors: The western third consisted of rice paddies and arable land. In the middle lay rubber plantations that hadn't been tended in years; they were heavily overgrown and almost impossible to navigate. The eastern third was jungle with a dense canopy of trees as high as two hundred feet and very little undergrowth.

It was Dozier's first time in a combat zone. My father spotted something in the tough, sandy-haired officer early on. "Articulate, tough, smart, and loves to soldier. Stays in the field. Strong disciplinarian. Very honest. Admits when he screws up," he would later write about Dozier in an internal memo recommending him for promotion to brigadier general. Dozier was quirky, too—he wore his hair even shorter than regulations required. But mostly, as Dozier himself was surprised to discover, he had a talent for staying focused in the heat of battle.

"I often got so involved in what I was doing and getting it right that the fear stayed in the back of my mind," he admits. "I sort of liken it to a professional quarterback. The guy's well trained, he knows what he's got to do and is good at doing it. He knows he might get creamed, but that's secondary. The main thing is to get rid of the ball and keep the game going."

Mobile warfare lends itself to innovation. Tanks move much more rapidly than foot soldiers, making it easier to take advantage of opportunities and change strategy abruptly. Working that way cultivates a different kind of mind-set—something that appealed to Dozier.

My father relied on Dozier for his ability to keep a cool head in combat. "To find the bastards," as he put it, he turned to another of his favorite commanders, John C. "Doc" Bahnsen. Bahnsen, a major whom Dad handpicked to run the regiment's Air Cavalry Troop, was a rebel and inveterate ladies' man but had an intuitive ability to visualize a battle. He was known throughout the unit and throughout his career as a legendary, fearless fighter.

"I was George Patton's prodigal son, so to speak," Bahnsen says. "He was very proud of me and called me his 'bona fide killer.' He used to say, 'You're a son of a bitch, Bahnsen, but you're my son of a bitch.' He meant it affectionately."

One day, Bahnsen remembers, my father called him into his command truck and said, "Doc, I want you to form a little committee: We need some variety, imagination, and boldness in our operations."

"Right. We need a VIB committee," Bahnsen replied.

"A what?" my father asked.

"A Variety, Imagination, and Boldness Committee," said Bahnsen. He gathered Dozier and Andy O'Meara, the regimental intelligence officer; Glenn Finkbiner, the logistics officer; and a few other trusted peers. After the evening briefing, the group frequently got together to solve the more intractable problems facing the regiment.

My father valued instinct. For Dozier, something clicked. "It's amazing what a group of people who are creative and can concentrate on a problem can accomplish," he says. "The program paid tremendous dividends. The lessons I learned in the 11th I used my entire career."

At the time, the greatest frustration for the U.S. military was the slipperiness of the enemy. The Blackhorse Regiment initially found itself surrounded by villages that were heavily Viet Cong. Later, even after the Viet Cong were largely routed from the area, most of the hamlets still supported the North Vietnamese Army. None of the Communist guerrillas could be found in the villages during the daytime. They were all hiding in the jungle nearby. "They're just like ants," my father said in one of the tapes he sent home to my mom in the summer of '68. "The place is just crawling with VC, but they're not in any big unit configuration where you can tie into them."[4]

What the VIB Committee did know was that the guerrillas periodically tried to sneak back into the hamlets at dusk.

"You know, the VC could read us pretty good," says O'Meara. "They knew that we flew chow in at about 1700 hours, before our soldiers prepared their night defensive positions. While our soldiers were feeding, nobody was out on reconnaissance, and there was very little activity on the part of the Americans. So the Communists used our downtime to take care of their own administrative needs. They'd leave their fortified positions to get rice from a village, or send out couriers. They ran through our areas along the creek lines."

The committee's solution was to deploy helicopters on late-afternoon reconnaissance missions. My father nicknamed almost everything: He dubbed the plan "The Children's Hour," after the Longfellow poem:

Between the dark and the daylight,
When the night is beginning to lower,
Comes a pause in the day's occupations,
That is known as the Children's Hour . . . ![5]

My father, in another move that would have made his superiors cringe, insisted on playing a lead role in the missions. "We'd get in the Huey and run these creek lines where we knew the enemy troops were moving," O'Meara recalls. "I sat on the left door and Colonel Patton sat on the right. He liked to use an M79 that fired fragmentation grenades—they were very lethal. I had an M16 and the door gunners were firing with M60 machine guns. Meanwhile, Dozier would be sitting across from me, watching what was going on and managing the troop movements by radio. We weren't flying at a high altitude. It was sort of sporting; I mean, you could blow yourself out of the sky if you weren't careful."

A few of the VC escaped through underwater tunnels: "They'd dive down and go back up into what amounted to an air lock," says O'Meara. Yet the effort killed, wounded, or captured a significant number of enemy soldiers. "We'd both shoot them and capture them," says Dozier. "That is to say, we tried to capture them without shooting. But sometimes they made that difficult."

Another vexing wrinkle: the Viet Cong unit that hemmed in the Song Be River. At this point, the whole game for the U.S. military was getting the enemy to fire and reveal their positions. So the VIB Committee sandbagged the interiors of metal engineer boats, manned them with soldiers wearing night-vision goggles, and ran them down the river. If the boats drew fire, all hell broke loose.

"George was a firm believer in what came to be known as pile-on tactics," says Dozier. "We'd pile on artillery, people, helicopters . . . it was sort of like attacking a fly with a sledgehammer." My father's expression—"Find the bastards and then pile on"—became the motto of the regiment.

Within weeks, there were no more Viet Cong on that stretch of the Song Be.

Above all, officers in Blackhorse were supposed to deliver a steady stream of fresh intelligence. The regiment got so much pressure from headquarters to score insider tip-offs that my father brought some VIB into that, too. Dozier recounts one late-afternoon firefight, when my father's unit captured a young Viet Cong lieutenant.

"The man wasn't wounded," says Dozier. "George looked at him and said, 'This is too good of an opportunity to pass up.' So we put the guy in the command control helicopter—he was scared to death—and flew up to 1st Infantry Division headquarters, to which Blackhorse was attached, just in time for the evening briefing. George marched him past the guards at the command post, into the briefing room, and held him out to General Talbott, the division commander. "General, you asked for fresh intelligence," he said. "This is as fresh as it gets.'

"It really woke up the briefing," Dozier adds. "I thought Talbott would have a stroke. But doing unconventional things was part of George's personality, and also the type of instinctive thing that made us very effective, even within the bureaucratic spiderweb. We thought it was great." (In fact, Talbott would be instrumental in helping my father get his first star.[6])

Dozier came home from Vietnam with a Silver Star and a Purple Heart, both earned while serving under my father in combat. In 1976, the year after my father became commander of the 2nd Armored Division at Fort Hood, he tapped Dozier to head up one of his brigades. There, in flat, middle-of-nowhere central Texas, they had to find creative solutions to a whole new set of problems.

The division casualty list was filled with victims of drug and alcohol abuse. It was common for younger soldiers to drive hundreds of miles on weekends looking for fun. Throw in drinking or the influence of some kind of pharmaceutical, and the highway sprees often turned deadly. My father had always insisted on being called immediately if one of his soldiers was killed, even if it was in the middle of the night. He couldn't get over the number of deaths—and this was peacetime. Soon "we had a full-court press against DUIs, with signs all over the place," Dozier recalls. As a stark warning, my father had several of the totaled cars piled up at the entrance of the base, and wreathed them in white cemetery crosses—one for each fatality.

Dozier and Joe Maupin, my father's beloved division chief of staff, became part of a team charged with designing activities to keep the men on the post. One of their more memorable efforts was a Willie Nelson concert in late summer of 1976. It was supposed to be an all-day affair, and men starting arriving—and drinking— around 10 a.m. Soon, the stands at the football field were full of soldiers, the roadies were all set up, and it was time for the concert. But by 10 p.m., still no Willie.

Finally, my father climbed out of the stands and marched over to Nelson's tour bus. "He was furious," recalls Maupin, who went with him. "When we opened the door, a cloud of smoke came out. The driver was slumped over the wheel, drunk and doped. George stepped over someone on the floor, headed to the back of the bus, and found Willie Nelson, who was gaga-eyed, and said, 'You get your goddamn ass out there right now.' Willie kind of teetered up and saluted. And then gave a hell of a show."

"I don't remember the incident, but the story sounds about accurate," says Nelson's longtime harmonica player, Mickey Raphael. "Actually, I might have been the guy on the floor."

I was about eleven at the time, and one of my favorite memories of Fort Hood is the way my father often took me to work. I especially loved accompanying him on unannounced dawn "drop-ins" at the various mess halls on post. It surprised the heck out of everyone to see CO Patton in line for grits and "SOS" goop, just like everyone else. My dad said there were two reasons behind the drop-ins: First, unsanitary or poorly serviced facilities shaped up in a hurry when the division commander started showing up on any given morning. Second, it boosted the soldiers' morale to know that he cared enough to spend time with them, and even eat the same chow. It meant a lot to me, too: As the youngest son of "Powerhouse Six" (my dad's radio call sign in the division), I even had my own handle: "Little Six."

Once, my father woke me up at midnight to see several troop carrier jets landing at the airfield. They were delivering elements of a brigade rotating back from an extended training exercise in Europe, and the jets were huge: Lockheed C-141 Starlifters, one of the largest cargo jets made at that time. Dozier and a few other officers were there, and stood smoking cigarettes with my father as the jets roared in with their white landing lights blazing. At some point Dozier made a joke and Dad laughed and said, "Aw, shit." It was the first time I ever heard my father curse, and I'll always remember how it felt to be included among his men in that way.

Looking back, Dozier considered his years at Fort Hood as a highlight of his career. During that time, he and my father's other commanders forged an enduring friendship, remarkably strong even by military standards.

"I think all good leaders are mentors in one way or another," says Dozier. "We all learned from him."

As A CAPTIVE, Dozier knew that survival meant waiting to be rescued—or for the terrorists to make a mistake. In the end, he got both.

Just after midnight on January 27, 1982, the Italian police got a tip from a Red Brigades member who'd participated in the kidnapping, Ruggiero Volinia. They'd captured him while raiding the apartments of a dozen suspected terrorist sympathizers—a pile-on tactic that had netted several girlfriends, boyfriends, and visiting relatives.[7] Volinia wasn't even suspected of anything. But as the inspector later admitted, "I was doing my 'we-know-everything-so-you-might-as-well-confess' routine," and Volinia caved.[8] Thinking he was saving his girlfriend, who'd also been apprehended in the raid, he led the police to a Red Brigades weapons arsenal. And then to the place where Dozier was being held.

Just twelve hours later, on his forty-second day of imprisonment, an NOCS unit (Italy's version of a national police SWAT team) swarmed the rebels' second-floor apartment in Padua. It was fifty miles from Verona—just about what Dozier had calculated when he was transported there in the refrigerator crate. Snipers trained their rifles on the building. With a shoulder lunge, a commando broke down the door.

Inside the bedroom, Dozier was sitting on the bunk reading George Orwell's *1984* for the second time. "I noticed the walls of the tent billow, which is what happened when anyone opened the door to the room," he remembers. "Then I saw an arm reach through the outer flap of the tent and hand my guard a pistol." Dozier tugged off his earphones and stood up. The guard didn't even have a second to hesitate before the police burst through the door.

"Up till then, the intelligence we were getting was that Jim would be executed shortly—that the rebels had gotten whatever they wanted out of him," recalls Dave Palmer, who was then a brigadier general in Baumholder, Germany. "Judy Dozier had come up to Frankfurt to stay with friends, and our wives took turns staying with her. We wanted to make sure that she wouldn't be alone when the word came."

At around the precise moment that Dozier's rescue was underway, Judy was coming downstairs to breakfast. "For some inexplicable reason, I feel more optimistic this morning than I ever have," she said to a friend. Just before noon, as Judy arrived at a lunch party, the call came through with the good news. Everyone was screaming and crying and hugging, remembers Sherry Brown, who was with Judy at the time.[9] Within two hours, Jim Dozier, back in the emergency room in the Vicenza hospital, was able to talk to his wife. "That was his first request," Brown says. "His second, we all had guessed—those of us who knew him so well—was for [a] shave and haircut."[10]

When Judy arrived at the Abrams building in Frankfurt for a press conference later that day, she looked up. "There were hundreds of folks pressed against the windows, waiting and cheering," Brown says. "When we entered the building, spontaneous applause rose from the crowd. Of course, that put us all back in tears again."

After the call from President Reagan, after the weeks of Army debriefings, and after the newspaper and TV interviews, the Doziers flew back to Washington. James Dozier didn't do much those first few days except visit a local veterans' hospital. But it wasn't long before the Doziers came to celebrate at my parents' farm. At the end of church that Sunday, my father stood up and introduced Dozier to the congregation, extolling his merits and bravery for so long that Dozier sank down in the pew and prayed for him to stop.

Their final visit came eighteen years later, in September 2000. By then, my father was in late-stage Parkinson's. He was lucid only half the time and too frail to stand. So, at my mother's request, Dozier, Maupin, and a few other friends—all part of a tight-knit group made up of my father's former commanders and senior officers—held their annual get-together at my parents' house.

Of all of them, Dozier struck me as the most like my father, at least in the way they talked about combat. Dozier always described my father as having battle sense, and the way Dad spoke about

Dozier, you knew he felt the same way about him. And the point I want to make is that their friendship was a symbol of how mentoring really can work both ways. My father never had a brother. Also, to his occasional regret, none of his children followed him into the military. Yet in Dozier he found someone as fanatical about soldiering and personal integrity as he was. When I mentioned this to Maupin, he laughed. "Yeah, I think of them both as real kill-'em-all-and-sort-'em-out-on-the-ground types," he said. "Dozier would have made a terrible secretary of state but a great secretary of defense. And, you know, you need those types, too."

At the time of the reunion, Dozier's wife, Judy, was losing her own fight against Parkinson's and was hunched in a wheelchair. Dozier found the challenge of being a caretaker far more wrenching than being kidnapped ever was. "Your emotions run the gamut there," he told me.

He must have felt horrified to see my father so diminished—a clear map of where Judy was headed. Yet when I called to ask him about it, Dozier remembered the visit like I did: as a happy occasion. "The mood was pretty festive," he said. "We played poker. We went for walks. We joked around. It was almost like a family relationship—at least, that's how it felt to me."

It seemed like a nice way to say good-bye, he added. "It's a soldier thing, I guess. You live with people and you watch them die and you make the most of the middle."

NINE

Dave Palmer

In 1961, Dave Palmer, a tall, blue-eyed twenty-seven-year-old with perfect posture, assumed command of a tank company of about a hundred soldiers at Fort Hood, Texas. He was only a few weeks into the job when the Army took on a fund drive for the United Way. The battalion commander, a short, middle-aged lieutenant colonel, assigned a quota of two hundred dollars per company.

At their next formation, Palmer recalls, "I told my men, if you contribute once, I won't ask you to contribute again. So we all met our quota and sent it in." But a few days later, his commander announced that they'd come up short at headquarters. He wanted Palmer to go back to his company and scrape up another hundred dollars.

"That was a lot of money then," Palmer says. "My mortgage payment was eighty-seven dollars, to give you some idea. I walked outside and thought about what it would be like to ask my men to give again, when I'd told them they didn't have to give any more."

Captain Dave Palmer, whose unit was recognized as the top armored company in the 1st Armored Division, Fort Hood, Texas, 1961.

Then he went home, to the little one-story brick house he shared with his wife, and wrote a check for one hundred dollars—a fourth of his monthly income. Shortly thereafter, it landed on the desk of the brigade commander. "Why is this captain giving a hundred dollars extra, when everyone is giving one or five?" he barked.

The battalion commander summoned Palmer to his office. "What are you doing here?" he demanded, shaking the check at him.

"Well, you said you wanted another hundred dollars from my company, but I'd already promised my men that if we raised two hundred, that would be it," Palmer replied.

"Yes, but I don't want *you* to pay it," said the battalion commander. "I want your men to pay it. Take this check back and rip it up."

"Okay," said Palmer. "But if I do there won't be any more money from my company. That's it."

The battalion commander's mouth hardened. "Well then, you may not have any company to command," he said, handing him the check. "Dismissed." To be relieved of command would have meant the end of Palmer's career—"I figured I might as well go sell insurance," he says. Yet the ax never fell. In fact, the matter was never mentioned again.

"And I did have to rip up the check in the end," Palmer adds. "Higher headquarters wouldn't accept it."

My father always said that there were two kinds of leaders: obtrusive and persuasive. He unabashedly identified with the former group—colorful types like Douglas MacArthur, Horatio Nelson, and his own father, who could lead by sheer force of personality and, when necessary, switch on the bull-in-the-china-shop act. By persuasive leaders, he meant cerebral consensus builders like Dwight Eisenhower, Robert E. Lee, and George Washington—men who worked to persuade people to their point of view rather than simply run them over. The goal was the same, just the way of getting there differed.

When my father and Dave Palmer met at West Point back in 1954—Dad a tactical officer, Palmer a fledgling cadet—their personalities were already a mismatch. My father swore, and often. He was theatrical, the kind of guy who could suck the air out of a room. Palmer is soft-spoken, coolheaded, reserved. Few people have ever heard him swear. Yet, right away, something clicked between him and my father.

They had some personality traits—especially guts and honesty—

in common. At a young age, they were both willing to risk their careers where their men were concerned.

Consider my father in 1953: Near the end of the Korean War, at the age of twenty-nine, he'd assumed command of A Company, 140th Tank Battalion. After months of fighting, he was moved to the Punch Bowl, which he described years later as "a lovely little place." (He was being sarcastic—it was the site of an extinct volcano almost two miles above sea level.) One day early that summer, they learned that the Army chief of staff, General Maxwell D. Taylor, would be arriving the next morning to inspect the troops.

By this point, my father's tanks were smothered in mud and dirt, but the troops had very little water as it was; washing tanks was out of the question. The division adviser, a colonel who was a staff officer from Seoul, informed my father that he wanted all of the tanks shined up immediately. Here's how my father described the scene to me years later:

"The colonel told me that he was arranging to get me some diesel oil and I was to wipe down all the tanks, get the dust off," my father remembered.

"I said, 'No, Colonel, sir.' He was a full bird, you know; I just got a couple of railroad tracks on. I said, 'I can't do that.' "[1] The Chinese were using a lot of white phosphorus in the area; if a round had hit a tank greased in diesel fuel, it would have gone up like a torch. The colonel replied, "Well, I'm going to the division commander and request that you be relieved."

"I told him that was certainly his privilege but that I, too, would take my case to Major General Gaither, the division commander," my father continued. "The colonel was furious and shouted, 'You better not go down there!'

"I replied, 'I'm going, sir, and I'm leaving now.' "[2]

By the time my father reached division headquarters almost two hours later, the colonel had already called in and reported him for disobeying orders. Fortunately, Gaither supported Dad's decision. Yet my father remembered this pivotal moment—the first time he refused a command, on principle, as a terrifying experience.

Dave Palmer came from a civilian background; his mother, a divorcee, worked in a munitions factory in a small Texas town. Everything he learned about the military, he learned at West Point. During his first year at the Academy, my father gave the cadets lectures on armor and got people to listen: "He was responsible for many of us choosing to go into that branch of the military," Palmer remembers. "George was distinctive-looking and colorful, aggressive, a real warrior type. I remember thinking, if that's the kind of guy who's in armor, sign me up."

The admiration cut both ways. In my father's papers, I found a memo he'd written, recommending two men for promotion to brigadier general. One was Palmer. The other was Jim Dozier, an obtrusive leader all the way.

DURING THE VIETNAM era, one of the biggest issues facing the army was readiness—or, more specifically, the lack of it. President Lyndon Johnson's administration had opted to wage war in Southeast Asia without calling up the reserves. Thus, readiness for units not actually in Vietnam posed a major problem. First call for support—people, equipment, supplies, money, parts, ammunition—went to the war zone, leaving other areas often short. This, in turn, had a negative impact on their ability to reach out and maintain a ready state.

In 1969, Palmer was assigned to command a tank battalion in Germany: the 2nd Battalion, 33rd Armor, 3rd Armored Division.

"We were quite short on men, only about 80 percent strength," he says. "Moreover, the men we did have were very new—there weren't a lot of officers—and there were very few parts to go around." As a result, it was impossible to keep all of the battalion's equipment operating. "A tank would break down and we wouldn't have the gizmo to fix it for three weeks," Palmer remembers. "The situation looked pretty bleak. And this was going on all over Europe."

Every month, the commanders were required to fill out pre-printed reports on their readiness: how many men they had, how many tanks were working, etc. They were judged against their peers. Did the system encourage people to cheat to make themselves look better? Of course it did, recalls Palmer. A lot of officers managed by statistics, he says. "For example, they might have one tank with a broken carburetor and another with a broken engine that could theoretically be pieced together into one working vehicle. So they'd say they had one tank down instead of two."

Yet Palmer stuck with total accuracy on his readiness reports. As a result, the scores for his battalion were always low. Taking note of his numbers, the brigade commander spoke to Palmer privately in his office. "He said, 'You know, Dave, the others are finding ways to get around this,'" Palmer remembers.

Still, Palmer refused to go along. "The brigade commander thought I was being foolish," he says. "But I felt that the government should know what state we were in. I couldn't say that I had an extra cook and that he could run a tank—he wouldn't have the slightest clue how to do that."

This went on until one snowy morning in midwinter, when the brigade was treated to a surprise inspection. All of the battalions were ordered to move their tanks into holding areas, which lay in the woods in the German countryside. Upon his arrival, the inspector general called the battalion's three commanders, including Palmer, to the area to check their readiness.

"He looked at my report and it said that out of fifty-four tanks, I had ten that weren't working," says Palmer. "Ten hadn't moved out." The inspector looked at the report of the second battalion commander. "This says you have five tanks that don't work, but there are really fifteen," he observed.

The 3rd battalion commander's report showed a similar disconnect. "You can go," the inspector general told Palmer. The other two commanders had to stay and demonstrate why their reports weren't accurate.

"That was embarrassing to them, to say the least," Palmer told me. "I don't know what went into their records, but by being honest, I came off just fine."

Looking back, it's interesting to see how Palmer handled the issue of readiness honesty in his low-key way, while my father addressed it in a grand gesture.

When Dad assumed command of the 2nd Armored Division at Fort Hood in 1975, the outgoing commander, Major General Bob Fair, and his staff gave him a briefing on the state of the division. Joe Maupin, then a lieutenant colonel, was at the meeting. He'd been with the 2nd Armored for only three weeks and was supposed to give an update on the personnel status. "The division had been reporting the biggest lies, things like zero AWOLs," Maupin remembers. "So I was briefing the personnel status as honestly as I knew how, when Fair interrupted me."

"'You don't know what's going on—you don't know this division,' he said. 'Get out of here. I'll finish this—you're fired.'

"But Patton had spent a week in D.C. looking at the division before he came down," Maupin says. "The commander of military personnel was an old and close friend of his, and Patton had gotten with him and gone through all the personnel facts and statistics. He had it pretty well pegged before he hit the division. He got hold of me and said, 'Don't worry—I knew what was going on. Go back to work.'"

Within weeks, my father got special permission from his boss, III Corps commander Lieutenant General Bob Shoemaker, to make Maupin his chief of staff. It was a maverick act. "Normally, the chief of staff is the senior colonel in the division, and there were about eighty colonels to choose from," says Maupin. "I was just a punk lieutenant colonel. When I became chief of staff, three people on my own staff outranked me. But Patton had put the word out: He's going to be the chief—that's the end of it."

That was the lesson of my father's command: Honesty will get you everywhere. "But if you weren't honest with him," Maupin adds, "you were gone."

In a weird coincidence, all five of the brigade commanders in my father's division at Fort Hood changed over a four-month period. One of the incoming colonels was Dave Palmer; another was Palmer's old friend and classmate from West Point Jim Dozier. The two of them soon learned that their outgoing counterparts had clashed and never worked well together. "So Jim and I talked about it," says Palmer. "We decided that as each new colonel came in, we'd go to his office, lay out the situation, and bring him into the fold. We knew we'd only command at that level once in our careers. So we were determined to make it fun."

As part of their decision to have a good time together, the new team of colonels and their wives took off together every few weeks—to the beach, on a fishing trip, etc. I was about eleven at that point and knew Dave Palmer simply as another dad. His son Kersten and

I were good friends and played football together and trumpet in our school band. I'll never forget one night when all the other parents were busy, and Colonel Palmer took Kersten and me to our sixth-grade recital, where we performed "You're a Grand Old Flag" with another classmate. "While I enjoyed it, it was kind of painful as music," Palmer confesses. The kicker was that when we went back to the Palmers' house afterward, I felt so boosted by his compliments that I announced that I'd recorded the whole performance and offered to play it for him again. Gentleman that he is, he gamely sat through it a second time. I get to hear the story every time I see him.

Thirty-plus years later, the surviving members of Dad's former commanders and their wives still get together every year or two. Even in the military world, you wonder at the sheer tightness of the group. Palmer credits it to chemistry and the atmosphere of trust that my father created in the 2nd Armored. He was a master of delegating and then getting out of the way.

"George certainly didn't micromanage and he supported us to the hilt," Palmer says. "Not everyone's comfortable loosening the reins in that way, but within the rules and limitations of common sense, I could do anything I wanted."

Case in point: Part of the division commander's job was to hold counseling sessions with each of his senior officers. One morning around six, not long after Palmer arrived at Fort Hood, my father walked into his office. "He'd been up a good bit of that night, out in the field with the troops," Palmer recalls. "I expected him to ask me some tough questions. Instead, he said, 'Dave, everything's going very well in your brigade, but I do need a nap.' He closed the door, stretched out on the couch, and said, 'Wake me up in thirty minutes.'

"He was a very open person as a leader," Palmer adds. "You never needed to worry about what he was thinking because he told you. If he was happy with you, he let you know. And if he was unhappy with you, he let you know. Later, when I commanded a division, I aimed to delegate the exact same way."

INTERESTINGLY, my father and Dave Palmer had a chance to collaborate at West Point in the mideighties, and their different leadership styles came to the fore. Dad, now retired, sat on the board of trustees at West Point. Palmer had risen through the ranks to become the superintendent of the Academy—one of the most prestigious jobs in the Army. Among the things he wanted to take a hard look at was the unsanctioned tradition of hazing at West Point and its negative impact.

Yet the school's older alumni—my father included—had no intention of cooperating with the plan. They wanted West Point to stay just the way it was, and feared that Palmer was going soft on plebes. Some graduates even lobbied to have him fired. My father never went that far. Still, he grumbled at home about some of the changes.

Palmer, ever the consensus builder, quietly set about winning over my father and the rest of the old guard. "I knew, from the way he operated, that George would have bought into the new system completely," he explains. "He exemplified the idea that you don't browbeat your soldiers—he always looked to build self-esteem and professionalism in his men. This was a guy who would show up at a nighttime tank gunnery range around three o'clock in the morning, just to demonstrate that he was sharing the toughness of soldiering."

My father had to concede the point. He'd dealt with hazing in his own typically flamboyant way back when he was a first classman, or senior, at West Point.

As Dad told the story, it happened the day the new cadets arrived in the summer of '45: "I was on duty receiving these civilians who had decided to become cadets," my father told me. "In that group there were several World War II veterans from both the Pacific and Europe. And this guy walked in—his name was Hubbard—and he was in uniform in an Ike jacket and olive-drab trousers, dressed up. He walked up to [another cadet first-classman] and said, 'Corporal Hubbard reporting for duty.' Saluted. He was wearing a Silver Star, a Bronze Star, and a Purple Heart.

"The first-classman took his name and data down and gave him some instructions about where to go," my father went on. "Then he said to him, 'Well, you were the dumb guys in World War II. You're out fighting and we're around here chasing all these goddamn women. Look where we are and look where you are.'"

My father, overhearing this, walked up and stood between the two men. "Because I saw that soldier's patch," he said. "He had a 76th Infantry Division patch, so I knew he'd worked for my dad, you know, down at the bottom of the heap. I turned to Hubbard and said, 'Git. Post. Get out.'

"'Goddamn you, George,' his classmate said. 'I haven't finished talking to him yet.'

"And I said, 'You've finished talking to him.' I turned to Hubbard and said, 'I'm a cadet lieutenant and that's a cadet sergeant and I'm telling you to go.' And old Hubbard breathed a sigh of relief and grabbed his bag and took off.

"'You son of a bitch,' I said. 'That soldier was out there busting his ass for you, and you talked to him the way you did?'"

The two of them settled it later that day behind the barracks.

"Only time I ever laid hands on a cadet," said Dad, shaking his head.

In the end, my father got behind almost all of Palmer's plans for modernizing West Point and backed them in his outspoken way. The sweeping changes went through. "And, amazingly enough, they're still in place twenty years on," says Palmer. "They've stood the test of time."

My father liked people who pushed back, provided that their confidence was warranted. Despite their differences—and perhaps, because of them—he and Palmer taught each other a lot.

TEN

Glenn Finkbiner

On December 12, 1952, in his junior year at Texas A&M, Glenn Finkbiner eloped. This qualified as more of a renegade move than it might appear, since the twenty-year-old got himself kicked out of college in the process—school policy forbade students to wed until after graduation. He'd already changed his major three times. Now he lost a whole semester of work. "I had been spending all my time hitchhiking down to Houston, where my high school sweetheart was going to school," he says. "I was in love. That seemed more important."

He transferred to the ROTC program at the University of Houston. During its requisite three-week summer camp, the tall skinny Finkbiner—five eleven, 130 pounds, and with a shock of thick brown hair that was already turning silver—was singled out as an outstanding cadet. The experience turned him around. Soon after graduation, he joined the 29th Tank Battalion in Baumholder, Ger-

Major Glenn Finkbiner (second from right) and South Vietnamese soldiers carrying boxes of clothing for children in a village under Blackhorse's protection, Ben Co, Vietnam, Christmas 1968.   PHOTO COURTESY OF GLENN G. FINKBINER

many, as a first lieutenant. And he stopped thinking of the military as a limited venture.

"I'd never been in a tank before," he says. "I'd never even attended the basic course on tanks for officers." But he was already skilled in machinery: Growing up in Galveston, Texas, he'd spent his summers working at a shipyard, as a rigger on a crane. He also proved adept at learning on the fly.

"My tank team taught me everything I needed to know," Finkbiner says. "The first day, I didn't have a helmet or anything and off we went bouncing around: I didn't know how to keep my feet and ended up with a big gash on my head. But pretty soon I knew how to drive it, how to calibrate the sights, how to put a track back on, how to locate a target, how much fuel it burned." (How much? "It took four gallons to go one mile.")

This was precisely the chord that Finkbiner liked to strike, and his practice of getting the inside view would prove to be crucial to his success later on.

His first career reckoning came a few weeks later. Up to then, Finkbiner had demonstrated a striking capacity for disagreeing with his commander even when he didn't much care about the point he was disagreeing with. "Anything they said at the staff meeting, you could be sure I'd take a different tack," he says. "I thought I was pretty smart."

As Finkbiner was leaving headquarters after one such meeting, the XO came up to him. "We're going to take a walk," he said.

It was about 5 p.m., still lots of sunlight, warm enough to wear just field jackets. The XO was a straight-talking man with a compact build and a tough-looking face: Commanders tend to be the good guys; XOs, their enforcers, epitomize the bad cops on the block. The two of them walked out of the building and down by the motor pools.

"I appreciate your point of view, Finkbiner," the XO said. "But you're the most negative person I've ever met. Why don't you try it our way first? If you don't like it and have a better idea, then say no. But don't object to it right off the bat."

It was a basic value of the military: Unless you try hard to be part of the group, to be connected as a team, your work can't rise to the level of being truly honorable.

"From that day on, I was never able to say no," Finkbiner says. "Anything they wanted me to do, I'd try it. And that ability to just say, 'Okay, let's go,' helped me enormously in my career—it had a positive effect on all my assignments."

Cut to late 1967: Finkbiner was sitting in the instructors' office at Aberdeen Proving Ground in Maryland, where he'd spent the last few months teaching soldiers how to employ nuclear weapons, when the head of the combat arms department dropped a typed memo on his desk.

"I see you're going to the 11th ACR," he said.

"The 11th Armored Cavalry Regiment was the premier armored unit in all of Vietnam," Finkbiner remembers. "Any soldier would have been thrilled to be part of Blackhorse." His wife, Sylvia, a fair-skinned blonde with blue-green eyes and the woman who'd prompted him to drop out of Texas A&M, made plans to move back home to Galveston with their two young daughters. In the week before he shipped out, Finkbiner, now thirty-six and an avid golfer, bought an extravagant amount of new golf clothes and equipment. As Sylvia puts it, "I think he intended to let us know that he was coming back."

WHEN HE CLIMBED off the plane in "Ascom City"[1] in Vietnam in early July 1968, Finkbiner was assigned to a Quonset hut, a portable wooden building near the mess hall that held about twenty beds for him and the other soldiers who had just arrived. He threw his stuff on a bunk and walked over to the supply building, where he was given a bare mattress, a pillow, and a blanket—no sheets, no pillowcase. At about two o'clock in the morning, the personnel officer for the regiment shook him awake. "Major Finkbiner, you need to come with us," he said. "We're taking you to meet the CO."

"So I got in the jeep and they drove me to the 11th Cavalry headquarters deep in the jungle," Finkbiner says. "We were on a dirt road with no headlights on, and there was a machine-gun jeep in front of us and one behind us. I was scared to death."

At headquarters, he met the XO, Merritte W. Ireland. Ireland was popular and distinguished-looking; he had a barrel chest and held his chin up high like a blue blood. The two men spoke briefly. Then Finkbiner looked around and asked, "Where's the CO?"

"We got a new one coming," Ireland told him, enunciating every word with patrician accuracy.

"Yeah? What's his name?" Finkbiner asked.

"Colonel George Patton," said Ireland.

"For a second, I thought about the reputation of [Patton's] father," says Finkbiner. "Then I thought, 'Oh my God, I'm gonna get killed.'"

The next day, Finkbiner was milling around headquarters when the radio started squawking. My father, then forty-four, came on and announced that he was en route to the change of command and would stop by for a quick briefing on the way.

"How am I supposed to give him an update?" Finkbiner asked the regimental operations officer (prior to Dozier), Lee Duke, whom he describes as a brilliant, bald-headed guy with a warped sense of humor. "I just got here twenty-four hours ago."

"Well," said Duke. "*You* tell the old man that."

Finkbiner hesitated. Then he bolted out of the back of the command track to get a chart—"so I wouldn't sound like a blithering idiot"—only to run straight into Colonel Patton.

He had his helmet on and was wearing jungle fatigues, Finkbiner remembers. "He gave me a brief nod and said, 'You're Finkbiner!' I'd never met the man in my life, and he knew exactly who I was." And that was lesson number one, he says: "Patton did a lot of research before he took over a new regiment—what we'd done, where we'd been, and he even got photos, so he knew the names and faces on his team in advance."

A few days later, the sergeant major told Finkbiner that my father wanted him to fly with him in his helicopter. The rest of the crew came along, and after a quick spin, they descended rapidly and set down in a large clearing. It was heavily forested on all sides. The wash from the rotor blades ruffled the long grass, which shone a deep, emerald green. The men leapt out. "We were all kneeling in the grass with just our head and shoulders showing," Finkbiner says. "After a few minutes I asked the sergeant major, 'What in the world are we doing here?'

"'Well, we have a bunch of troops coming in by helicopter later,' the sergeant major replied. 'So the colonel took us all out here first to see if the landing zone is hot.'

"I remember tightening my grip on my weapon and sinking a little further down, thinking, 'Oh, good Lord, now he's *really* gonna get me killed,'" says Finkbiner. The rest of the team, seasoned veterans by this point, remained unmoved.

This was the second lesson: Prepare for the worst—and then act fearless. My father sought out new intelligence sources. He insisted on first-rate training for his soldiers and demanded a spit-and-polish perfection. He formed a team of officers (his "VIB," or Variety, Imagination, and Boldness Committee) to innovate new strategic tactics. He took what he personally felt were the necessary precautions. And then he went with his gut, whether it sent headquarters into a tailspin or not.

Soon, Finkbiner was flying with my dad four to five times a week, and not always at the safe, higher altitudes at which command and control helicopters generally traveled. "George had a thing where we would fly lower over the rice field—about five hundred feet off the ground—so he could toss out thermite grenades to burn the tall grass," he says. "It made a great hiding place for the Viet Cong soldiers. Our pilot, Charley Watkins, did a thing with the blades to create more of a downdraft and fuel the fire. We couldn't fly up high for that."

Although their helicopter would eventually be shot down while performing this very maneuver and its crew rescued after an extended firefight, "the colonel created a sense of invulnerability around us," Finkbiner says. "By the end of the first week, I felt completely safe around him—not any fear at all."

"If you do not have a disciplined unit and you get into battle, you're a potential murderer, period," Dad would say in a speech years later, after he'd retired. "That's the way you gotta look at that: They gotta be disciplined, because they're afraid. Anyone who's not afraid when that artillery starts coming in is either a liar or a fool." He insisted that a disciplined unit had a better chance at survival. "Troops in combat must react automatically—loading the rifle, loading the M16, picking up mines and all. They've got to be trained to have an automatic reaction which overcomes fear."

Another thing that impressed Finkbiner was my father's policy that if you earned two medals for bravery—a Silver or Bronze Star or a Purple Heart—you were pulled out of combat. "He believed that there was a gene that caused you to be brave and he wanted to preserve that," Finkbiner says. "He didn't want it to be killed off on the battlefield." Proven heroes were sent back to Blackhorse base camp to teach new recruits what to prepare for—how to protect themselves against mines and booby traps, search-and-destroy missions. And, adds Finkbiner, "George made them wear their medals to every class."

LIKE ANY SOLDIER, Finkbiner learned quickly that in warfare, rituals count. One precaution he took was to burrow his cot into a hole each night so that he could sleep almost level with the ground. "Being disciplined about that saved my life quite a few times," he says. Near the end of his ride in Vietnam, a year after my father had returned home, Finkbiner bedded down next to a command track at the regimental headquarters in Dau Tieng, later known as Rocket Alley. A large village crowned with the decaying remains of what had been a French country club, the base was filled with command-post vehicles and formed a major rearm and refuel point for helicopters. To keep off the rain, Finkbiner draped a tarpaulin from the top of the twelve-foot-high command track vehicle and tacked it to the ground to form a lean-to over his cot, which he'd dug into the ground. When the rockets came in a few hours later, the tarpaulin was shredded. Low-flying shrapnel missed him by an inch.

"The shelling stopped almost as quickly as it had started," says Finkbiner. "Then the regimental commander, Jimmie Leach, came out in his boots and his helmet and his underwear and yelled, 'Move the goddamn regiment!'"

But that was later. For the time being, Finkbiner was learning to keep his cool. And he was gaining his professional edge by borrowing one of my father's organizational habits.

"In Vietnam, George lived in a two-and-a-half-ton truck," says Finkbiner. "On the wall above his cot, he hung a chart on white poster board. Down the left side, in black ink, he listed the names of every unit that supported the regiment: logistical outfits, civilian units, the depot, the staffs, the hospital, the food people, you name it. Along the top of the chart ran a calendar, divided into weeks." Each week without fail, my father visited every one of these support organizations, dragging the appropriate staff officer along with him. Afterward, he'd check off the visit on the chart.

"George would go in with his pistols strapped on and all his regalia—I can see him right now, Lord have mercy," says Finkbiner. "Always loud and everyone knew he was in the building."

Dad didn't mess around. While he was at it, he regularly flew in the officers who worked back in Long Binh with General Creighton Abrams Jr., commander of U.S. military operations in Vietnam. "All these guys who were usually stuck behind desks loved getting a chance to come up to the front lines with the Blackhorse Regiment," Finkbiner says. "They'd get to spend the day with the unit and we'd always give them some kind of booty to take back—little things we captured like gas masks or a medical kit or a bayonet."

Plus, Dad and Finkbiner flew out to the different squadrons almost every day to see what supplies the soldiers needed.

The result? "It endeared him to all of them," says Finkbiner. "They all worshipped him. They'd do anything for him. And that was a trick I put in my bag. I always had my own chart after that, and made it a point to make friends with all the people in the supply chains."

All this strategizing wasn't for naught. For most regiments in Vietnam it took two weeks to get a replacement tank. But whatever the 11th Cav wanted, it got immediately.

Finkbiner's past experience in the military made an impact, too. "There was something about being a combat arms officer that gave me a leg up in the field of logistics," he says. Combat arms officers are the guys who use all the stuff that the supply people supply, and who put their lives on the line. "I had the advantage of looking at things from both ends of the supply chains," Finkbiner says.

"Because I had commanded tank platoons, I knew exactly what they needed and how much. I also understood the sense of urgency in a way that other soldiers might not."

This explains why my dad—a tough warrior not given to hyperbole—soon considered Finkbiner the guy who knew the supply business better than anyone else in the Army.

"People said that I could get anything, and that was almost true," says Finkbiner. "The one thing I couldn't get—which I still regret—was gas masks for dogs, which were in very short supply at the time." The weirdest order? A request for two dozen live ducks. "George secretly used them to patrol the Saigon River because the ducks would quack if anything came in the water," says Finkbiner. The annoying thing was that they had a tendency to go AWOL—scrambling up the banks or flying off.

IF THERE WAS a moment in which Finkbiner's training, talent, and character came together, it happened in early January 1969, near the Cambodian border.

It was one of Vietnam's perfect, balmy, blue-sky afternoons. Finkbiner was sitting inside the regimental command track listening to the radio traffic with Captain Jerry Rutherford, the officer in charge that day. Outside, his direct support maintenance company had been working on five Sheridan light tanks. A couple of them had already been repaired and were loaded with fuel and ammo. Their crew members were lying around, waiting for military escorts to take them back to their units.

Then, over the radio, came word that a convoy en route to their location had been ambushed and was under attack.

It was unheard of for supply guys to commit troops, and Finkbiner was not authorized to do so. "Still, I was still a combat arms officer and I figured we didn't have much time," he remembers. "We didn't have much intelligence either. All we did know is that our troops were getting fired at and that we were the closest guys at hand. And Colonel Leach and Major Jim Dozier, the regimental S3 in charge of operations, were fighting elsewhere."

Finkbiner turned to Rutherford, a short, bright officer who was feisty as hell. "I have some tanks back there and I'm going to see what I can do," he said. Rutherford, already on the horn, nodded.

"Go, get out of here."

Finkbiner ran to find the tank crews. Each Sheridan carried a crew of four—a driver, a gunner, a loader, and a commander. The soldiers were in the regiment but belonged to other squadrons. "Still, they were gung ho, absolutely," Finkbiner remembers. "There wasn't even a second thought."

Together, they quickly got the two tanks cranked up and headed off for the ambush. Finkbiner rode along with them in a jeep. He and his driver each carried an M16 rifle. Finkbiner also had a .45 pistol slung on his belt.

They got a few miles down the road—and that's as far as they got. News broke over the radio that the attack had ended and the convoy was moving again. Still, Finkbiner had been called upon, however briefly, and acted honorably—maybe not by the book, but in a way he could live with.

"When I saw Dozier later that day, he was annoyed with me for taking action," he remembers. "He said *he* was the only one in the regiment who committed troops." But George Patton? We never discussed it, but he would probably have been pleased as punch. That's exactly what he would have done."

UPON HIS RETURN from Vietnam later that year, Finkbiner joined the Pentagon as a lieutenant colonel. My father was passing through en route to Germany, where he'd been assigned to serve as assistant division commander for support. ("Being put in charge of logistics wasn't his thing at all," Finkbiner notes. "I think he figured he was being punished for some unknown deed he'd committed.") Dad stopped by Finkbiner's office. In case the younger man hadn't fully embraced my father's philosophy of doing business through plenty of face time, Dad now brought it home.

"Let me give you some advice, Finkbiner," he said.

"What's that, sir?" asked Finkbiner.

"Never pick up the phone."

"What's that mean?"

"You'll do a lot of coordination in the Pentagon," said my father. "You'll write papers, you'll process papers, and you'll always have to get approval on them. A lot of people get what they call a telephone chop: You call up your buddy and say, 'Hey, I've written this paper about whatever, and I need you to approve it.' And the guy says, 'Go ahead and put my initials on it.' Never do that. You can walk any-place in the Pentagon in eight minutes. And the more people you meet, the better off you'll be in the military. So look the person straight in the eye and do it that way."

"Of course, I got more done using that method," says Finkbiner, looking back on the experience. "There were twenty-seven thou-sand people working in the Pentagon when I was there. If I had put something on a buck slip and passed it around, it might languish in an in-box for a week or two. Hand-delivered, I got an answer right away. And I did meet a lot of people who helped me later on. Even now, if I have a problem or need to get something done, I get in my car and go see the person involved. That was really good advice."

What surprised Finkbiner most about my father, he says, was "the fact that he took such good care of us, not only when the fight was going on, but after the war was over. I trusted him on everything. And some of my assignments—including my last tour in Germany, where I served as a battalion commander under George—were so choice that I knew he was behind them all."

I got to know Finkbiner the year I turned ten. We'd just moved to Fort Hood and my brothers were both away at school, so my father and I were especially close then: I was his fishing and hunting partner. That meant that I got to spend a lot of time with Finkbiner, too. I remember him as disarmingly funny, with graying hair and an easy southern charm. The other kids and I loved him. On weekends, Dad and I would meet him and a few other bass-fishing soldiers at nearby Belton Lake before dawn. We'd launch our bass boat, *Plus Ultra,* and Finkbiner and others would climb into theirs. We always set a small wager, with the pool being split between the boats that brought home the first, the biggest, or the most bass. Finkbiner generally won. My father and I would come back with a pretty fair haul in our aerated bait well—or so we thought until we got a look in his. "Damn you, Finkbiner," my dad would say, and we'd all laugh. At some point Finkbiner made my father a beautiful, handcrafted bass rod to even the playing field, and painted *Fink Stick* on the side in white letters. Dad used it diligently, but Finkbiner kept winning.

In 1973, a package arrived for Finkbiner at his Pentagon office. Inside, he found a small white box and opened it. There, on a bed of white cotton padding, lay a set of my father's silver eagle insignia—the gold-trimmed metal ones that went on his dress mess uniform. With them came a note:

HEADQUARTERS 4TH
ARMORED DIVISION
OFFICE OF THE ASSIS-
TANT DIVISION COM-
MANDER OF SUPPORT

Memo to Lt. Colonel Glenn Finkbiner

Glenn, perhaps these will bring you luck some day. They did for me.

Patton

PART FOUR

SPIRITUAL INSPIRATIONS

MY GRANDFATHER FAMOUSLY believed in reincarnation. My mother is a devout Episcopalian. My aunt quoted mystics and read palms. My father fell somewhere in between. I sometimes got the feeling that he believed in anything that worked.

Sometimes on the way to church, he'd lean over and whisper that if we attended services that Sunday, we could build up enough credit with my mother and the Almighty to go fishing the next. That said, organized religion was an important element in his life—it's a primary source of community on a military base, providing grounding and inspiration for the troops, and hope in dire situations. My father saw the power in that and admired the people who were able to wield it in an inspiring and supportive way.

The people he chose as his spiritual advisers shared two common denominators: First, they were brilliant speakers and could get their point across quickly and with passion. (Any long-winded sermon got my father tapping his watch.) Second, according to Dad, they were tough and stood up for what they believed in—often at great personal risk.[1]

For me, finding out exactly what he meant by that has been one of the best parts of writing this book.

ELEVEN

Glenn Myers and Lamar Hunt

LT. COL. CHARLES R. CODMAN: *You know, General, sometimes the men don't know when you're acting.*
PATTON: *It's not important for them to know. It's only important for me to know.*

—FROM THE FEATURE FILM *PATTON*

IN THE WINTER of 1971, my father, then the assistant commandant of the Armor School at Fort Knox, agreed to lay a wreath on the tomb of Zachary Taylor, the former president and American military hero. Dad's chaplain, Glenn Myers, came along to offer a prayer.

"The mayor and some other dignitary from Louisville were supposed to be there, but it was snowing so bad, nobody came except us," Myers remembers. "God, it was cold. Finally, General Patton said, 'What the heck—put the wreath on that thing and say your prayer and let's get the hell out of here.'" Afterward, on their drive back to the base, they spotted a soldier hitchhiking in his summer uniform in the snow. Here's how Myers remembers what happened next:

"Stop the goddamn car," said General Patton. He beckoned the

Chaplain Glenn Myers
with orphans in Waegwan,
South Korea, 1964. The orphans are wearing clothes
and shoes purchased with
American soldiers' dona-
tions.

FROM THE PERSONAL COLLEC-
TION OF CHAPLAIN (COLONEL)
GLENN MYERS (U.S. ARMY-
RETIRED)

young soldier inside and yelled, "Don't you know how cold it is out there? What are you doing?"

"I'm on my way to hock my wedding ring so I can buy Thanksgiving dinner," the soldier said.

"Let me see that damn ring," said the general. It was just a cheap-looking thing. He turned to Myers. "What do you think, Myers? What do you think it's worth?"

"I don't know, sir," Myers said. "I'm not a pawnbroker."

Patton turned back to the soldier. "Why aren't you wearing your winter uniform?" he asked. The soldier replied that every time he visited the supply room, it was closed. Patton gazed at him for a minute. "Do you know who I am?" he asked.

"No, sir," said the soldier. "But you're some kind of general."

"You'll find out what kind of general I am," Patton said. "Take me to your headquarters. I want to talk to your commander."

When they arrived, the soldiers spotted Patton's uniform and shouted attention as he and the rest of his group walked up the stairs. The commander was a lieutenant colonel. He looked terrified.

"At ease," Patton said. He pointed to the soldier. "Do you see this poor shivering son of a bitch?"

"Yes, I see him," said the commander.

"He's never been issued winter clothing. By 4 p.m., I want him to have complete winter issue. You understand me, Colonel? And he better get it. If he doesn't, I'm after you."

"Yes, sir," said the commander. "I'll take care of it myself."

"You better, or you'll be doing something else tonight," Patton said. Then, as he was leaving the office, he wheeled around dramatically. "You," he said, addressing the young soldier. "Son, if you try to hock that ring, I'll court-martial you. That's a direct order."

"Yes, sir," says the soldier.

Back downstairs, Myers asked, "Can you really do that, General?"

Patton shook his head. "Myers, Myers," he said. "That's theater!"

"It was such a great moment," Myers says, looking back. "I remember thinking, 'This guy's an actor.'"

My father and grandfather relied on theatricality when dealing with soldiers, and prized the same asset in their chaplains. A soldier enjoys a specific rank and authority associated with that rank. Military clergy members, on the other hand, never turn up in positions of actual command—say, of a company, battalion, or corps. Their power comes from a different place: moral authority. And the Army chaplains my father most admired used it in a positive way, to get things done.

One of them was Myers. When, in 1964, at age thirty-two, he got orders to South Korea, he assumed that it would be a cushy preaching assignment in a large American community. Instead he was sent to Camp Carroll in a small rural area near Waegwan.

"Why am I going there?" Myers asked his supervisor.

"Because the unit has the highest rate of VD in Korea, and you're going to lower it," came the reply.

It was like trying to hold back floodwaters. At the time, Korea was racked by such poverty that many women were forced into prostitution to save their families from starvation. Camp Carroll had two doctors administering penicillin shots every day, one of them a Korean medic whom the soldiers dubbed "VD" Kim.

"It's impossible to send soldiers of a certain age over to a place where there's loneliness and dissolution and expect them all to behave like choirboys," Myers says. "The train would come in from Pusan or Seoul and drop off a few prostitutes, and within a day or two, they'd be hooked up with an Army guy and living in one of the villages. During the day, the woman would clean the hooch and wash the soldier's clothes, and at night, he would sleep with her . . . and this was all for so much a month."

Hoping to create more wholesome diversions, Myers began by launching a photography club. ("I know—it's almost laughable when I think about it now," he says.) Then, while driving in his jeep one night that winter, he came upon the Waegwan orphanage.

"There were over a hundred children there, and I couldn't believe how shabby they looked," he remembers. "They were barefoot—and it was cold outside. One kid had a belt made out of wire to hold his pants up. They didn't even have anywhere to take a bath—they just had helmets filled with water occasionally dumped over their heads. And, of course, most of them were GI babies who'd been fathered by soldiers and just left at the police station."

It was especially bad to be an orphan in Korea. "If you can't trace your family back five or six generations, you're nobody," Myers notes. So he decided to add some theater to his anti-VD campaign: to raise awareness about the orphans' plight in every crevice of the camp—and, true to his mission—use it as a reminder of sexual consequences.

Myers raised money among the soldiers to buy clothes and shoes for the orphans. He enlisted Army engineers to build them a proper bathhouse. At the end of every month, Myers sat at the head of the pay line with a "For the Orphans of Waegwan" donation can. Some of his in-your-face tactics hit too close. When Myers got permission from the mess sergeants to bring a group of children to the mess for Thanksgiving dinner, for instance, one of his commanders, a lieutenant colonel, lashed out.

"He pulled me aside and said, 'This is our Thanksgiving, not theirs. What the hell are they doing here? You have no business doing this and you'll pay for it'—the implication being that he'd get me," Myers remembers. "And this is a guy who'd just come from church!"

Did he have any impact on the VD rate? It was hard to tell. Still, Myers felt that he was making a difference. If anything, he boosted the image of U.S. soldiers in the eyes of the Korean locals, who began to wave and smile at Myers in the street. "They'd see me in a jeep with five or six children in the back, or taking a bus down to the orphanage, or teaching some of the teenagers English, and saw the good things we were doing for them," Myers remembers. "It helped to dispel the image of Americans just as whoremongers.

"On my last day in Korea, all of the orphans came to the train station and sang 'Arirang,' the Korean national song, and waved to me as my train was pulling out," he says. "I couldn't see a thing because of all the tears in my eyes."

IN THE SUMMER of 1971, when Myers was told that my father needed a new chaplain at the armor school, it was presented as one of the worst jobs in the Army. Hardly anyone showed up for services—on a good day, there might be thirty people in the pews. "In light of the poor attendance, the outgoing chaplain was at his wit's end," Myers says. "When I went down to see him, he sobbed, 'I'm so glad to get out of this place!' and threw his sermon notes on the floor. And I thought, 'Oh boy.'"

My father, then a brigadier general, had just arrived at the armor school himself. Among his other goals, he was determined to turn around the situation at the chapel. And he was very particular about his chaplains: He liked strong speakers, and had a strict twenty-minute time limit for sermons.

MYERS REPORTED TO duty at my father's office on a Monday. Here's how he remembers the scene:

"General Patton was writing and finally looked up and said, 'Myers, Myers, what are you, Myers?' "'Presbyterian, sir,' I said.

"'That's not what I asked you. Are you Regular Army or reserve?'

"'Reserve, sir,' I said.

"'Get out of my office, then. You're nothing but Christmas help.'

"I started to leave and he yelled, 'Get back here and stand at attention. And get those damn papers in by Friday.'

"'What papers?' I asked.

"'Whaddaya think I mean, the funny papers? I mean the Regular Army papers. In the meantime, I want good sermons out of you and they have to be short because I have a bad hip. If they're not short, I'll fire you.'

"'Yes, sir,' I said.

"'Oh, are you a yes-man? If you're a yes-man, I'll fire you now.'

"At that moment his wife, Joanne, called and the general said that she wanted to talk to me. I got on the phone with her and she said, 'Can you come for dinner this Friday?'

"And I said, 'If I survive this meeting with your husband I will.'"

Myers and my father ended up filling the chapel to capacity—170 people—within two months. "George spread the word in the staff meeting that we have a chaplain you ought to hear," says Myers. "And he could be pretty persuasive."

Here's an example of my father's use of theater, from a rare TV interview he gave in 1977. Most officers wear embroidered black insignia on their camouflage-patterned combat uniforms. My father wore white ones.

INTERVIEWER: Why do you wear white stars?

GSP: Two reasons, I'm glad you asked that. First, so that there's no problem with anyone recognizing who I am and then if I don't get the proper salute after I have given the proper salute, I can stop the jeep and take corrective action.

Second, to give the enemy a target to shoot at. In other words, if we have a war, to flaunt myself in front of them and give them a target.

INTERVIEWER: That shocks me.

GSP: I'm sure it would.

INTERVIEWER: Did you intend for it to shock me?

GSP: No, I just believe that a general should be seen. We have certain people around here that won't wear insignia in the field. Not in this division, although I did run into one the other day who now wears his insignia. But I believe in letting 'em know I am around.

INTERVIEWER: Is your life not more valuable than that?

GSP: Yes, I am enjoying it and we're a long time dead. But I happen to believe that I should set the example and be seen. I should not only be seen by the frontline soldier but if I show the enemy these stars, that shows them that I have a certain disdain for their accuracy of fire, and I in fact do retain that disdain. I don't think they're nine feet tall.

INTERVIEWER: You don't think you're going against Army regulations wearing those stars?

GSP: I'm sure I am. But there are other people who wear funny things on their uniform that go against Army regulations. Suffice it to say that no one has ever spoken to me about this. And I'll continue to wear them until I am ordered to take them off.

My father related to his other favorite army chaplain, Lamar Hunt, on a different level, because they'd both spent so much time in combat in Vietnam. Not that they ever really talked about it—it was just there, part of their background.

Hunt had been born dirt-poor in central Florida in 1932, in the midst of the Depression. Both of his parents were hard workers, but there were no jobs to be found in those years. They killed game for food. Unable to afford a toilet, the family used an outhouse. Hunt worked his way through high school and, in his senior year, beat out more than five hundred contestants to win a Voice of Democracy contest. The experience "helped me see the power of speech," says Hunt, and set his mind on the ministry. As it turned out, the president of his Bible school had served as an Army chaplain in World War II. The power of *his* stories prompted Hunt to follow suit.

Remarkably, he attended seminary while serving as full-time pastor of a church—and, in 1965, entered active duty. Following a tour in Korea and a couple of stints in Georgia, Hunt joined the 1st Cavalry Division in Vietnam, in the inhospitable stretch between Saigon and the Cambodian border. It turned out that he wasn't the kind of chaplain who felt comfortable staying at base camp. He spent most of his time out in the field: sleeping on the ground with the infantry soldiers and hitching a helicopter ride back to headquarters on weekends to take a shower and ward off jungle rot.

"When we knew where we were going to spend the night, we'd dig foxholes," Hunt says. "The first day I was there, the men told me, 'Don't worry, Chaplain. We'll take care of you.' We were attacked, so I crawled to the bunker and found that it was packed. The soldiers just pulled me on top of themselves. The next night, when we started digging in and they said, 'Don't worry, Chaplain, we'll take care of you,' I said, 'No. This time I want room for me in that foxhole and I'll help dig it!'"

He saw his share of unimaginable horrors. "One of the worst wounds that someone can get is a sucking chest wound, where his lungs fill up with blood," says Hunt. "You can't anesthetize a person in that situation—he'd drown in his own blood. Instead, you have to bore a hole in the right or left side of the chest while he's conscious to drain it. The doctors always wanted a chaplain there to hold the guy's hand." Hunt sometimes became so nauseated that he had to step outside of the medical tent to vomit.

In the face of death, denominations didn't seem important. Hunt remembers one time when a Catholic chaplain asked him to help him administer last rites.

"Protestants don't do last rites," Hunt notes. "Instead, we'll often say a prayer over the body. When the priest and I went to the mortuary, twenty body bags lay on the floor, and I started unzipping them to identify the men. Then I stopped and said, 'Jim, this isn't right. These are all God's children—all fellow soldiers whether Catholic or not.' In the end, we just unzipped all the bags and Jim gave them all last rites."

If Hunt ever doubted what he was doing, it was canceled out by the reception he got from the soldiers themselves. "They always acted glad to see me," he says. Though it was unconscious on his part, the fact that Hunt constantly put himself in harm's way—just to be there for the troops—constituted its own brand of theater.

On another occasion, he visited a company that hadn't received religious services in a couple of weeks. "The commander told me that they'd been in intermittent combat with the North Vietnamese," Hunt says. "He pointed to a tiny creek near our position and

Chaplain Lamar Hunt leading an Easter service for U.S. troops in the jungle, Vietnam, 1969.   PHOTO COURTESY OF CHAPLAIN (COLONEL) HENRY LAMAR HUNT (U.S. ARMY-RETIRED)

said, 'If they spot you, they'll shoot. The enemy's in bunkers there, so we can't make a sound or move without drawing fire.'

"I still felt that it was important to offer a service to the men, if they wanted one," Hunt says. "I believed it at the time and I still do. The soldiers welcomed me with warmth—they're not known for platitudes. So I felt that it brought them a lot of comfort. And it brought me comfort, too, to get to do it."

So the commander put the word out over the radio and the soldiers crawled to Hunt's position on their stomachs. "We drew ourselves into a tight circle, flat on the ground," Hunt remembers. "We whispered the whole service and I passed the wafers around and passed the wine in a ration cup. Before I'd left to go overseas, I found hymns that didn't have copyrights so I could hand them out. So I reached in my rucksack and pulled out 'Blessed Assurance.' We whispered the whole thing—it gave me chill bumps—and I murmured the benediction. Then I crawled back to the helicopter and all the guys lying on their bellies crawled back to the war. It was the most memorable service I've ever given, and I've preached in cathedrals."

FIVE YEARS LATER, in 1975, Hunt was put in charge of services at the 2nd Armored Division chapel at Fort Hood, Texas. My father was the division commander. After sitting in on a couple of sermons, he asked Hunt to become his personal chaplain. "He said he liked me because I had fire," Hunt says. And, together, they put their theatrical skills to work.

"The soldiers couldn't all live on base, and the nearby town of Killeen was a grubby little spot," remembers my father's chief of staff, Joe Maupin. "Soldiers were living in some pretty hellacious places and paying horrific prices." So my parents started visiting soldiers at their homes. They orchestrated these social calls almost like a play: Maupin would send someone down to the motor pool and ask a couple of soldiers if General Patton could stop by that evening. Then my parents, with Maupin and Hunt often in tow, would drive up to each soldier's apartment or trailer court.

"People would be looking at Patton from every window," Maupin says. "It was highly unusual for generals to go around visiting at home."

After a few pleasantries were exchanged, my father would ask the soldier a whole checklist of things: "How's it going? How much rent do you pay? Do all the appliances work?" In the meantime, my mother would be talking to the young wife: "Are you having trouble getting medical appointments for your children? Do you have a way to get to the commissary?" Et cetera.

"I was the most silent member of the team," Hunt says. "I was busy taking notes."

If something didn't work—say, the stove or the heat—or the rent seemed exorbitant, my father *himself* would call the landlords. "He'd tell them, 'If you don't fix it I'll be down there with Army trucks today and we'll move that soldier out lock, stock, and barrel,'" Maupin remembers. "All of a sudden the realtors knew that the command was watching them. The beauty of it was, once Patton started paying those visits, the brigade commanders started doing it and then the battalion commanders went around seeing how their men were living off post."

As Maupin saw it, it was simply an extension of what Hunt had found out on his own: the power of simply showing that you care.

"Many a Sunday night he'd call me and say, 'Chief, it's your division for a while,' and go out and spend two to three days in the field with the troops," Maupin says. "Another thing that impressed me: Every Christmas Eve he held a party for the staff, and around eleven-thirty he'd say, 'Chief, you're the host now.' And then he'd have his command fatigues on and go all through the division—thanking all his men out in an open jeep, telling those kids on guard duty, 'Thank you for your service—and I'm personally going to make sure you're off on New Year's Eve.' You think that doesn't go through a division? That was his way and the troops knew it."

What I remember about Chaplain Hunt from our days at Fort Hood was how colorful, animated, and to the point he was during his sermons. I have all sorts of images in my head of him playing guitar, singing, bellowing—and my dad and our family just ate it up. He was a fireball and made going to church bearable for ten-year-old me.

Funnily enough, the rivalry between the two divisions at Fort Hood—my father's 2nd Armored Division and General Julius Becton's 1st Cavalry Division—filtered down to the clergy. "The corps chaplain disliked Patton and told me straight out that I was hitching my wagon to the wrong star," Hunt remembers. "I felt just the opposite. The problem was that George's social skills didn't match his tactical skills: His macho side—which was designed to inspire the troops—could easily be mistaken for arrogance. Very few people got to see the tender George Patton, who would stand up and weep at a memorial ceremony. But when you got close to it, you saw that the drama came from the right place—it was genuine."

As Hunt saw it, "theater" was my father's way of cutting through bureaucracy to do the right thing.

During off-hours, the two of them often played guitar together. (My father could sing every verse of "Take a Cold Tater and Wait" and "I Heard the Wreck on the Highway but I Didn't Hear Nobody Pray.") "I was a refuge to Patton more than anything," Hunt says. "George didn't wear it on his sleeve, but he was regular in worship and he participated in church as a regular guy, not a honcho."

My father lobbied hard to be a lay reader at the church. Despite their friendship, Hunt kept putting him off. "I didn't trust him not

to swear," he says. "George didn't use the F-word or anything pro-
fane, but he said 'damn' every other sentence."

Finally, at the last service on the last Sunday before my father
left Fort Hood, Hunt let him read.

"He did a fine job," Hunt told me. "When we got to the last
hymn, I chose 'Onward, Christian Soldiers' because I knew it was
his favorite. And then, just at the start of the final verse, he put his
hand on my shoulder and leaned into the microphone and shouted,
'Let's give 'em hell!'"

TWELVE

Tom Bowers

"GET THE ____ out of here." That was an awful thing for an Episcopalian minister to tell anyone, much less a longtime parishioner. He couldn't believe it had come out of his mouth. He'd been in the war; maybe he still had a lot of that in him. He'd been getting harassing phone calls and even death threats for weeks.

It was at the start of the crowded 11 a.m. service on a Sunday. After he stopped shaking so much and the heat of the moment faded, he worried what the bishop would say. And then he thought, *I'm going to lose my parish because of this thing.*

"I never had to go looking for trouble," he said later. "It came to me."

FOURTEEN YEARS EARLIER, in the summer of 1950, Tom Bowers had left for Korea as a member of the 39th Field Artillery Battalion of the 3rd Infantry Division. A twenty-two-year-old lieutenant

Lieutenant Tom Bowers en route to Korea, summer 1950.

PHOTO COURTESY OF TOM BOWERS

freshly minted from the Virginia Military Institute, he'd been born into a charmed life. He was the son of a wealthy businessman. In photos from the time, Bowers looks like a movie star, with brown eyes and dark wavy hair.

As part of an invasion that was hastily planned by General Douglas MacArthur, Bowers's battalion landed on November 10 at Wonsan, a port town on the east coast of North Korea. Like so much of the country, it was rugged, barren, and hilly; the air was bitterly cold. To Bowers's eyes, it looked like the end of the world.

"At that point the United Nations had no direct front line that cut across the whole Korean peninsula," he recalls. "We were going up the east coast. Meanwhile, the Chinese were secretly coming south along a mountain range that ran down the center of the peninsula." The approach of UN troops toward the Yalu River, on the border between China and North Korea, prompted a massive onslaught by the Chinese. "Suddenly all of us were cut off up in the northern part of Korea," Bowers remembers. "It was just a massacre. The Chinese overran us with thousands and thousands of men—they just kept coming."

Both the 1st Marine Division and the 7th Infantry Division had been up at the Yalu and needed to evacuate immediately. Bowers's task force was assigned to guard the perimeter of the port town, holding the dirt roads and the high hills on each side in order to help UN soldiers escape. "It was the largest evacuation of troops in history," Bowers remembers. He watched an endless line of vehicles roll through to the harbor in Hŭngnam, where they'd be loaded onto Navy ships. The Marines, following their tradition, brought back as many of their fallen comrades as possible. "Their vehicles were loaded with frozen bodies," Bowers remembers. "Bodies were even tied all over the trucks."

Bowers's division was evacuated, too, and taken in a naval vessel to Pusan, the major port in South Korea. From there, the troops disembarked and began moving up the west coast toward the capital city of Seoul.

Bowers's role was to make sure that his division's communications were constantly in service. Sometimes he filled in for a forward observer who had been lost or wounded. This put him with the infantry, anywhere from a hundred to five thousand yards in front of the division artillery, and even farther out from the bigger guns. The days ran by in a blur. He worked all the time. He slept standing up or in a hole he had dug. When he was exhausted, he simply lay down in the snow. He saw many soldiers killed. He participated in the killing. There were moments when it all felt utterly futile.

"I had to tell the troops why we were there all the time, but I didn't believe any of it," Bowers admits. Occasionally, he and a couple of lieutenant friends shared a quick whiskey behind the lines and talked about what a damned mess they were in. Bowers told them the theory he'd hatched: "If we could get all the world leaders together—Truman, Kim Il-sung, Mao, Stalin, all of 'em—and put 'em all on top of one of these damn hills we're always fighting over, fire this white phosphorus at them, starve them to death, and let them freeze up there like the rest of us, they'd bring this to a conclusion pretty quickly."

On what might have been the bleakest night of his life, on the night he was sure he would be killed, there came a small miracle. "We had just taken Seoul again and were going up to the Imjin River there," he remembers. "An ROK [Republic of Korea] division was placed on our division's left flank. They were expecting a big Chinese push that evening."

Bowers's superior, Leon Lawrence, a friendly, thoughtful colonel with a black bushy mustache, needed a forward observer to place with the South Korean infantry. He and his driver drove Bowers to their front line. "Tom, I hate to do this," Lawrence said, "but I have to leave you with them tonight."

None of the ROK soldiers or officers spoke English. Since Bowers didn't speak Korean, there was no way to communicate verbally. He went to see the Korean captain, who was crouched down in his headquarters—a foxhole equipped with a telephone and backup radios in case the phone lines were blown out by shells. The captain looked busy and serious. He waved Bowers to a foxhole with a group of other soldiers. Bowers's head, behind field glasses, stuck out of the top.

I have to communicate somehow, he thought. The sun had begun to sink behind the ridge. Bowers thought of another forward observer he knew, a young American lieutenant who had recently lost it after a battle, sobbing into his hands. The other soldiers had promptly ostracized him. Everyone there feared the sound of panic above everything else; more and more, they had the uneasy apprehension that they, too, might crack.

Bowers clambered out of the foxhole and borrowed the Korean captain's phone to call back to headquarters. A Korean soldier answered. Bowers repeated the word *American* over and over and there followed a long silence. Then, all of a sudden, he heard a familiar voice: "Lieutenant Branch here."

Bowers froze, stunned. "Wait—is this Beanie Branch?"

"Yes," came the reply.

Improbable as it seemed, the voice belonged to Cary Branch, a classmate and close friend of Bowers from their days at VMI and Fort Sill, Oklahoma. Branch was a handsome devil from a humble background, an industrious guy who kept everyone laughing. He'd headed over to Korea before Bowers, and had been taught Korean and trained to work with the ROK troops. He'd also been part of the advance on the Yalu River when the Chinese had hit at least six months before.

Branch's entire ROK division was blown apart in the attack. Alone, he wandered behind the lines in North Korea for more than eight weeks, carefully avoiding capture before finally making contact with UN forces.

"All I'd heard was that Beanie was ill, starving, and near death when they found him, and that he'd been sent to a hospital in

Japan," says Bowers. "I had no idea if he was still alive, much less that he'd reunited with ROK troops—with the very division I was with on that hill." Now here came Branch's voice hurtling out of the blue.

"Beanie!" Bowers exclaimed. "My God, I can't tell you how good it is to hear your voice again!" The two friends spoke for a minute. Then Bowers remembered where he was. "Listen, Beanie," he said, "it's getting dark. I want you to fire some rounds out here so if the Chinese come I will know where to direct the fire."

"Sorry, Tom, I can't do it," said Branch.

"What do you mean you can't do it?"

"We've been ordered to orient all of our howitzers and guns on other targets," Branch said.

"All of your guns? Go talk to your colonel and tell him we need some support right here, now!"

After a minute, Branch came back on the line. "Sorry, Tom— they're not gonna do that."

"My Lord, what am I doing up here? I'm utterly impotent!" Bowers had a pistol but knew perfectly well that it couldn't save his life. The Chinese attacked in such great numbers that they often overwhelmed the first infantry units in their path. They'd run right over them.

"Listen, Beanie," Bowers said. "If we get under attack, for goodness' sake, get on the phone and talk to me . . . 'cause I figure I'm gonna go tonight."

Time seemed to slow down over the next eight hours. Until first light, amid the constant wondering and worrying, Bowers thanked Providence—not only for sending the Chinese in a different direction that night, but also for sending him Beanie.

The next morning, as Bowers walked around wondering what to

do next, Colonel Lawrence drove up. "You're useless up here," Lawrence admitted. "I can't afford to lose you for no good reason. Get in the jeep—we're taking you back to the unit."

As THE MONTHS dragged on, Bowers saw dead and wounded men all the time; he felt almost immune to it. But one particular enemy corpse shook him to the core.

"It was a bright morning just after a battle and we were walking up a hill, looking for high ground to do some reconnaissance," he remembers. "Everything was frozen—there was a lot of naked rock and some battered-looking trees amid the snow. We had our pistols out. There weren't a lot of bodies right at that spot, but there was a dead Chinese soldier laid out on his back in the snow, and what I noticed about him first of all was that his arms had been burned off, leaving just ash and bone. We were using a lot of white phosphorus, and when it hits you it burns right through your skin: Nothing can stop it; nothing can put it out."

Somebody had been by and pulled out the dead man's pockets. Little pieces of paper propaganda, which said things like "I died for a new China," lay in the snow.

Bowers went closer. Like all Chinese soldiers, this one wore a quilted khaki uniform and carried seven small packets of rice, one for each day of the week, in a bandolier across his body. "He had a little hat on with earflaps which framed his face," Bowers says. "And as he lay there and I looked at him, I thought, 'That's one of the most beautiful faces I've ever seen.' He looked almost like a pretty girl. And then I thought, 'This man isn't my enemy. Why are we doing this?'" The image of that Chinese soldier's face still haunts him. "It led to other thoughts I had about my own life, and my own part in killing people," he says. "It impacted me considerably."

When he came home to Norfolk in late December 1951, Bowers thought he might want to become a writer and decided to go back to school. Princeton couldn't take him until the fall, but Bowers, realizing that he couldn't go back to his country-club life after what he'd been through, felt restless. He wanted to start school right away. With his minister's help, he ended up at Sewanee, the University of the South. There, he signed up for seven different courses—including subjects he'd never studied before like philosophy and religion.

"I was searching," he admits. As it turned out, the religion class he'd signed up for was underenrolled and had to be canceled. The professor was a balding priest, a cultured man, thoughtful and direct. Seeing Bowers's disappointment, he suggested they meet for three hours every Wednesday afternoon in his office.

What started out as an impromptu seminar course morphed into an extended therapy session. "I told him about Korea—how it had affected my life and had raised a lot of questions for me," Bowers says. 'Why do we kill everybody? Why are we at war all the time?' I had always been a religious person, but now it didn't make any sense." After each meeting, the priest assigned him three books to read and had him write a short paper on each one—just the main points and how he felt about them. It was all very Socratic: The priest asked a lot of questions, and then undercut Bowers's answers with an incisive observation or two. It got him thinking in a whole new way.

"One afternoon, I was walking home from one of our meetings," Bowers says. "It was a gorgeous day in early spring, the sky was blue and the dogwood and redbud were starting to bud up there in the mountains, and it hit me: 'This man has changed my life. He's changed my life!'" It moves him just to say it, even now. "I thought if I could just do one thing like this for some other person, I'd feel like my life wouldn't be in vain. I'd been part of a killing machine; now, as a way to atone, I wanted to do something different."

He promised his bishop back home that he'd go to the seminary for a trial semester. "I knew all my friends would think I was crazy, because I had quite a reputation for raising hell," he said. "And then I actually tried to back out of it. But I hadn't been at the seminary very long before I said, 'This is what I've been looking for.'"

My mother, Joanne Patton, joined the parish of St. Patrick's Episcopal Church in northwest Washington, D.C.—where Bowers had become rector at the age of thirty-three—while my father was in Vietnam. The two men met after services one Sunday in 1963 when Dad came home on leave. As Bowers recalls, "I preached a sermon and brought in the problem of Vietnam, and as I came out the front door George was there in his uniform."

"Father, that was the best goddamn sermon I've heard in my life!" he said.

"George," Joanne exclaimed. "You're at church!'"

My parents invited Bowers and his wife to dinner and struck up a friendship. My father liked that Tom had been in a war. And Bowers still was at war, in a sense, because this was Washington in the 1960s.

Bowers oversaw St. Patrick's from 1961, on the verge of the Vietnam War, until 1971. The decade in between was rocked by war protests as well as the civil rights movement. John F. Kennedy, Medgar Evers, and Malcolm X were assassinated. The women's liberation movement was gathering momentum. The immense social uproar of the era burned so hard—particularly in Washington—that the District threatened to combust at any moment. When Martin Luther King Jr. was assassinated in 1968, five days of riots ensued in D.C. Twelve people were killed and twelve hundred buildings burned to the ground. Marines set up machine guns on the steps of the Capitol while troops from the Army's 3rd Infantry guarded the White House. (Shortly after King's death, St. Patrick's held a service at which my mother first heard—and joined in singing—"We Shall Overcome." "It was a very moving moment," she says. "We were all gathered in.")

"All of these terrible things happened during that time, and everyone in my parish was dealing with them, politically and emotionally," Bowers says. "That was the world in which I was enmeshed. It was a tough time to run a church."

St. Patrick's served an upscale, heavily military neighborhood; at one point it had five generals on its vestry. Bowers was a southerner who hated racism, an admirer of the military who believed that war should be an absolute last resort. It meant walking a fine line. "As a military wife with a husband coming and going from the war zone, I always felt supported by Tom and St. Patrick's," says my mother. "There was never any heavy-duty 'antiwar' rhetoric, even when the sentiment was toward peace. I think Tom's southern grace prevailed, even when he was taking bold actions."

Like so many others, Bowers felt the racial struggle deeply. In the early 1960s, he worked with St. Patrick's to establish a mission in D.C.'s inner city—a largely black community of galling poverty. He wanted it to be a place where people could not only worship but also come with their problems and get help with jobs and housing. In 1964, he organized a committee to select a clergyman to run it.

"We interviewed all kinds of people and narrowed down to three," he says. One of them was black.

"I knew, I felt that it was going to be the black priest," he says. "And when we brought our decision to the vestry, they said, 'Absolutely,' and voted for it. The new minister, Jesse Anderson, came from Philadelphia and was in his late twenties. Slender, quick-witted and confident, with a Vandyke goatee and a forcefulness that would emerge later on, Anderson signed on to work at the mission during the week and serve at St. Patrick's on Sunday. "It wasn't meant to be a big dramatic thing," says Bowers. "But it was. Remember that Washington was still a very southern city; no other white churches in the area did that kind of thing."

He tried to make the official announcement as soon as possible. But the news leaked out before he could do so and set off a backlash. The worst part was the death threats; his wife, Margaret, started to dread answering their home phone. "I was damn sure frightened," Bowers says. "But I wanted a black priest on my staff to say to everyone, when they came in each Sunday, that we're open to all people—that nobody is denied, that Christ came for all of us. It's one thing to say it, it's another thing to do it."

On the Sunday that autumn when the new priest arrived, Bowers felt exhausted and nervous as a cat. "There was a lot of anxiety," he says. "I could feel it in the congregation." The church was packed. Faceted, stained-glass windows lined the whole north side of the church and wound around the baptistery. Bowers remembers how the sunlight splintered through them and sparkled in the air.

The two men walked up the long aisle together. When they reached the altar, they turned to the congregation. "I'd like to introduce the Reverend Jesse Anderson," announced Bowers. One by one, fifty families stood up and walked out.

As emotionally wrecked as Bowers was at that moment, he knew that it was nothing to what Father Anderson must have felt. Both priests did their best to rise to the occasion. It wasn't long before Bowers realized that in his distress, he'd forgotten to bring along a passage that he wanted to quote in his sermon.[1] While the choir was still singing, he slipped out and scurried down the secret passage through the vesting and altar rooms to his office. On his way back, in the room just outside the pulpit where the altar guild fixed flowers, a place where regular churchgoers weren't supposed to be, a man stepped forward. He had on a suit and glasses, and although a little bent over, he spoke with vehemence.

"It's one thing to put a nigger in the congregation," the man said. "But if you put a nigger up front, I'm getting out of here."

Bowers recognized him as a parishioner, a man in his eighties who'd moved to Washington from Alabama. Already on edge, Bowers exploded. "Well then," he shot back, "get the _____ out of here!"

Back at the altar after this ugly exchange, the actuality of what had just happened began to sink in. "I had to preach with all that going on inside me," he says. "I thought, 'Oh my Lord, I'm going to lose my parish because of this thing.'" Still, he felt that even if he hadn't *said* the right thing, he'd done it.

"I just knew that that was what was demanded of me as a leader in that situation, in that time and place," he says. "That's the code of the demand of the Gospel—that you be true to it in some way. I'm not just talking about not saying bad words, or never touching a drink, or never going to the movies, or not dancing. That's ridiculous stuff. That's really not what the Gospel's about. The Gospel is about what you represent and who you represent."

At the end of the service, Bowers walked outside, feeling numb. Then, in the tense seconds that followed, another man approached.

"Father Bowers, I'm really proud of what you've done," he said. "I'll help you if you'll let me."

"I HARDLY KNEW the man at all," says Bowers, "just that he was new to the parish and worked for IBM." But Tom Bloomer, an easygoing guy with a wide smile and the build of a hockey player, proved an answer to his prayers. With Bowers's permission, Bloomer studied all of the parish books and the giving process. Then he called the vestry and associate vestry to a meeting. About twenty-five people showed up one night after work and sat at a couple of long folding tables in the parish hall.

"Gentlemen," said Bloomer, "this is our situation: You've lost a significant group of pledgers—a small percentage, but an important one. Without their support, a lot of our programs will suffer. So I ask you right now to write on a card what you're willing to do to make up for the money we've lost."

"He was dealing with the financial thing, not the emotional problem of losing people," Bowers remembers.

Bloomer set a pad of paper in front of everyone in the room and asked each one of them to write down what he or she could give every year for the next three years, in addition to what they were already pledging. Then he collected the pages and added all the numbers up. "The final number was more than double my budget," says Bowers. "It was unreal."

The vestry then decided to do the same thing for the whole parish. "Instead of having the terrible financial problems we had feared, the parish became alive in a whole new way," Bowers says. "All sorts of new people joined the church—a lot of Foreign Service types and people in the State Department and others who were concerned about racial and social justice. They said that they'd been waiting for something like this to happen."

My father backed him up completely. "Some of the older generals actually left our church, but George applauded what I'd done," Bowers says. "He said, 'That's what you've got to do—in battle we have blacks and whites together.' They were trying to integrate people in the armed forces, too.

"George's support meant a lot to me at the time," Bowers continues, "because he seemed like a kindred spirit: the kind of man who takes risks, who's willing to try something he believes in even if other people say, 'You're out of your mind.' He didn't like wishy-washy: Even if he disagreed with you, he respected people who took a stand. What he couldn't stand was someone who never wanted to take a position on anything. I just loved that about him. And I think he saw the same quality in me."

Indeed, Bowers has always been there as a support whenever members of my family have turned to him. For starters, he baptized most of my siblings and me. In the years since we were stationed in Washington, our whole family has stayed in touch with him. For me, he's always been a source of great calm and wisdom sprinkled with southern wit. And boy, could he preach. I was always amazed at how he could keep an audience rapt with his inimitable ability to, say, quote Scripture or recite a William Blake poem from memory, then tell an off-color story and, using both his superb intellect and old-fashioned charm, drive home a profound and timely point.

For Bowers, that Sunday in the church with Father Anderson—like the night on the hill in Korea when Beanie Branch's voice had bobbed up the phone lines like a life raft—had made one thing clearer, more resonant. The Lord giveth and the Lord taketh away.

"Sometimes," says Bowers, "when you launch out into the deep and think there's no bottom on which to stand, God's hands reach underneath and hold you up."

TOM BOWERS'S ACCOUNT of the young Chinese soldier whose dead face shook him so profoundly reminds me of a similar experience my father had in Korea. Approximately twenty-four hours after an official cease-fire had been declared on July 27, 1953, he got orders to move his two-hundred-man unit west, from Kumhwa—a town in the southeast corner of the Korean peninsula—to the Pusan River Valley. There, they were to hook up with the 64th Tank Battalion and form part of the division reserve in the event that truce talks fell through.

My father remembered it vividly. "We left our position in the Punch Bowl about maybe eight or nine o'clock at night. And the war was over. The war was over—we weren't blacked out or anything. We moved with headlights and all that . . .

"It was a long, long drive, up and down over the mountains . . . We got in there about three o'clock in the morning and I told my mess sergeant, 'I want to feed these troops soup, coffee, and sandwiches now—after they refuel and check their weapons—before they hit the sack . . .' And to make it a little [nicer], I had a truck pull up and shine its headlights on the chow line so these guys could see what they were eating. Normally you don't do that in combat, you know. You eat in the dark.

"So I went up there with Sergeant Vaillancourt, my first sergeant . . . we were standing on a slope about a hundred feet away from the chow line watching these troops go through. And it was very, very wet; raining like hell and a little bit of wind blowing . . . lousy, lousy weather. And all of a sudden I heard this voice booming out over the chow line, 'What you doing here, motherfucker?'

"And down comes a cleaver on this guy, this poor guy—and the cleaver was wielded by [this NCO] who was a giant. [It] entered the left collarbone of a Chinese soldier who had sneaked into my chow line and stopped about eighteen inches above the right hip.

"I went running down there with Vaillancourt and said, 'What in the hell are you doing? The war's over!' "'Sir,' he said, 'my war ain't over.'

"I'll never forget it as long as I live . . . Well then, I had the body, and I mean, there was blood all over the goddamned place and these soldiers were so tired and so beat up that it didn't bother 'em. They just stepped over the body and got their coffee and stuff.

"I called the 140th Tank Battalion . . . on the radio and I told them what had happened . . . and they said, 'Who was it that killed him?' And I told them a lie: I said, 'I'm not sure.'

"Francis Xavier O'Leary was my battalion commander at the time. He said, 'Well, I'll tell you what you do. You just dig a hole with your shovel and you bury him on the banks of the Bukhan River, and you put a little stick up there with any kind of identification he's got and somebody'll pick him up someday.'

"So I said, 'Yes, sir. I've done what I'm required to do, [which] is report that to you.'

". . . He said, 'I'm not even going to tell the 40th Division. We'll just leave it.' And that was the right thing to do. You know, it was a shaky situation politically. We didn't know whether they were going to start up again or not. But I'd say this body, I looked at him pretty close under the light at his face and all, and I'd say he wasn't a day over fifteen and he didn't have hardly any food in him. He had a couple of cornucopias of rice and some bread and a couple of pieces of fish and that's it. He didn't have any ammunition on him to speak of—maybe three or four rounds. But it just goes to show you that the Chinese were pretty well finished. I mean I don't think they could have gone any further."

My father feared that reporting the incident would end his career. "I thought I was going to be relieved, oh yes," he said. "But I knew I had to report it. I knew I had to report that and I did. Things were really confused. There were Chinese behind us that had been cut off, they didn't know the war was over."[2]

I'm sure my father couldn't help looking at the dead teenager, killed one day after the truce, without thinking of his South Korean tent boy and friend, Geasung Choi, who was about the same age.

PART FIVE

SCENES FROM A MARRIAGE

Somebody once said that the greatest gift a father can give his children is to love their mother. And my father gave that gift to my mother every day.

—FROM MY BROTHER BOB'S EULOGY FOR OUR DAD,
MASSACHUSETTS, JULY 7, 2004

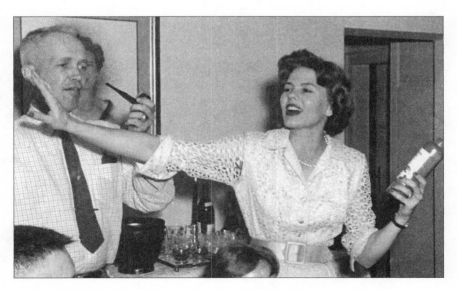

Celebrating George's Christmas Eve birthday, Stuttgart, Germany, 1959.

PHOTO COURTESY OF THE PATTON FAMILY

THIRTEEN

Joanne Patton

IN 1968, my mother, Joanne Holbrook Patton, was awarded the Outstanding Civilian Service Medal, the highest honor the Army can bestow on a civilian. It's the same award the Army gave Steven Spielberg for directing *Saving Private Ryan*. Later, in 1981, she was awarded the Decoration for Distinguished Civilian Service, recognizing her many achievements during nearly thirty years as an Army wife.

These tributes celebrated the fact that my mother had shaped a private experience into a public movement that helped countless military families across the globe. What had started out as a quiet act of volunteering had turned into something much bigger—my mother could never have foreseen her accidental career, much less the splash it would create. And it reveals something about my father's character that he chose to marry someone who was so strong in her own right: More than an equal partner, my mother bloomed into the consummate problem solver, capable of turning a bad situation into a greater good and calmly bagging new tricks along the way.

Joanne Patton with Bob and Margaret after receiving her Army Service Medal, 1968.

Like my father, my mother enjoys a military pedigree that stretches back to the Revolutionary War. Both of her grandfathers, Willard A. Holbrook and John K. Herr, served as chief of cavalry of the U.S. Army, a generation before the advent of tank warfare. West Point graduates in her family began with the Class of 1812, and included her father and brother, Willard Holbrook Jr. and III. Her mother, Helen, was also an Army brat—a beautiful, independent, headstrong girl who cannoned from career to career (jockey, missionary, songwriter, journalist) before finally agreeing to marry my grandfather, who had fallen in love with her on sight at an Army social six years before.

By the time my mother was born in September 1931, her parents were stationed at Fort Myer, Virginia. The troops had gone out on maneuvers, and my maternal grandfather, who'd been chosen to stay back and handle needs at the post, ended up driving two other Army wives to the hospital to deliver their babies. A few days later, when it was my grandmother's turn, the hospital registrar looked at him from behind the counter and shook her head. "Young man, one of these days they're going to catch up with you," she said. My grandparents found this hilarious.

Little Joanne—a pretty, musical child with blue eyes and a head of bouncy brown hair—came by her wanderlust naturally: When World War II called for Willard to join a newly forming armored division that was training in Louisiana, his wife gathered her three children and took off, promising to follow him until he went overseas. At various times, my mother attended a one-room schoolhouse in rural Louisiana; rode across the California-Nevada desert on borrowed gas coupons, with bottles of water hanging out of the windows; lived in a casino-motel in Las Vegas; and in a final quick-change flip, camped out at a dude ranch (where she attended school with the children of Mexican railroad workers whose families lived in boxcars). By September of 1944, her father's unit—the 11th Armored Division—was combat ready. He and his troops left the hot desert and plunged almost straight into the freezing Battle of the Bulge. Meanwhile, thirteen-year-old Joanne and the rest of her family returned to Washington, D.C., to wait out the war.

Not long before then, in 1943, my paternal grandfather, George S. Patton Jr., had written to my father at West Point with this advice about women: "Should I again become front line news you will probably have a lot of females running after you, so look out. The girls that have to run after a man are usually not worth having."

Fortunately, this wasn't an issue when my parents met in June 1951; my mother was all but running in the opposite direction. She'd just finished her junior year at Sweet Briar College. My father was fresh from a tour in Germany and about to head off to Fort Knox. While he was in Washington, his sister Ruth Ellen took him to an anniversary party in honor of Joanne's parents.

One of the Holbrook relatives, Bob Stillman, had once dated Ruth Ellen. As my mother remembers, "When Bob and his wife came in, my mother, who was kind of a tease, said 'I thought you'd like to know that one of your old girlfriends is coming today with her brother, George Patton.' And Bob said, 'Oh, that awful guy—he used to hold me up for fifty cents to be alone with sister.' That didn't sound like anybody I wanted to spend time with, so when George came in the door, I said, 'Nice to meet you, the bar is over there,' and walked away. I guess that the fact that I was so standoffish intrigued him, but that wasn't the intention at the time."

The next morning, "that awful guy" called and asked her to play tennis. "I was surprised but I went," she says. "After we'd batted about a bit, he stomped over and said, 'You are the laziest tennis player I've ever had the misfortune to play against—pick up your racquet and hit the ball!' So I picked up my racquet and tried to kill him with the ball, and possibly ended up playing my best tennis in years. In any event, I went home and told my parents he was the rudest man I'd ever met and that he swore, which I thought was terrible. And they looked at each other and chuckled and said, 'Wonder where he got that?'—the implication being that it was from his father, the World War II general."

The turning point in my parents' relationship came a few weeks later. My mother's father—who had taken the Nazi surrender of Linz, Austria—was now retired from the Army and working at the Federal Services Finance Corporation in Washington, D.C. (He later became its president and chief executive.) My mother was working in the city that summer; her family had taken a place in Gibson Island, Maryland, where she often joined them on the weekend. One day a telegram arrived from Fort Knox: *Look forward to seeing you in Gibson Island on Saturday. I arrive on the 3 p.m. plane. —George Patton.*

My mother was in shock. "I went out to my parents and said, 'Good grief. This is outrageous—this fellow has invited *himself.*' And my mother said, 'Oh well, there's room.' I thought, 'Well, if he thinks he's going to see anything of me, he has another thing coming.'" When my father arrived, she scheduled a golf lesson for herself, sent him sailing with her twelve-year-old sister, and cooked up other ways to torment him, hoping he'd leave soon.

At the end of the weekend, he found her sitting alone on the porch. "I don't know what kind of game you're playing," he said. "But I'm not accustomed to having someone invite me for the weekend and then treat me like this."

"But you invited yourself!" said my mother. My father pulled a telegram out of his pocket. It read, *Please come for the weekend at Gibson Island—Joanne.*

"I said, 'Oh, my Lord,'" my mother recalls. "My mother never admitted that she'd done it, but I knew that she had. And of course, once I realized that he'd been misled, I felt horrible for having treated this man so badly. It seemed only kind to sit down and get to know him. And then I realized he was something more interesting—and better—than I'd given him credit for."

By August my father had declared his feelings. "I can remember studying my face in the mirror and trying to decide who was there and if I had the courage," my mother says. "I knew it was going to be a different life and I wondered if I was up to it. But the more I thought about it, the more I thought I'd hate to miss the adventure."

That November, six months after they met, my father ordered up the best table in the Palladium Room of the Shoreham Hotel in Washington, D.C. "The best table turned out to be the one right under the orchestra, which is okay if you're there for the music, but not if you're there for conversation," says my mother, depicting the scene. "We made little noises at each other throughout the evening. Finally, George gave up, reached in his pocket, and threw something across the table. It was a little brochure with an advertisement for a ring company, and he had circled one of the rings.

"'Do you like it?' he asked.

"'What?' I said.

"'Do you like it?'

"'Does this mean you have honorable intentions?' I screamed back.

"'I guess I forgot!' he yelled. 'Will you marry me?' It just so happened that the orchestra stopped playing at that very moment, and the whole dining room, which was packed with people, sat up to find out what I was going to say." And: "I was too embarrassed to say no, so I said yes."

"ONE THING WE did have from the beginning was teamwork," she says. Even my father's friends will admit that he got away with a lot of his salty, shoot-from-the-hip behavior because my mother was diplomatic enough, and gentle enough, to balance the ratio of grace to grit. "In the first years of our marriage, the most frequent phrase out of my mouth was, 'Oh, George,'" she says. "But in later years I learned to parry. He challenged me to be feisty."

Peering back, my mother would appear to be the archetypal 1950s housewife, raising children and baking brownies while her husband was often away. On top of which, she had to constantly pull up stakes and move to his latest post. (Over the course of their marriage, they lived in twenty-seven different houses.) To a feminist, it would sound like a nightmare, yet that's not the way my mother saw her life at all.

For one thing, she had been hardwired for Army living—she was in her element. It's worth noting that, although she adored my father, she stayed cool whenever he was off at war. "We who were raised in the military tradition understood there were risks," she says with a shrug. "I did my praying, but I didn't really feel the anguish of worrying every day that my husband wouldn't come home." Talk about a steady hand on the tiller: After he was wounded in battle, she simply noted, "Well, he takes his chances."

Second, my mother found a surprising amount of freedom as a wife in the Army. In an era when most of the fairer sex was making do with more traditional roles, the military's volunteer world offered an infrastructure that trained women to become leaders. It also promised a chance for some genuine trailblazing, which is what ultimately roused my mother to action. "Never underestimate the power of ego," she says. "There's nothing more satisfying than having people trust you to do something innovative."

Naturally, it was expected that officers' wives would participate in life on the post. My mother came into formal volunteering as a "Gray Lady," an American Red Cross aide at Fort Leavenworth, Kansas. She and my father were subsequently stationed at three different posts in Germany. The last was a very small base in the Bavarian countryside, so rural that sheep had to be routinely shooed off the runway. My mother went to see the field director there and offered to present her modest qualifications to his chairman of volunteers. "You're my first volunteer," he told her. "So you're the chairman. Let's get to work."

This marked my mother's entrée into management. Conferences with more experienced leaders and social workers across Europe followed. By now, she was a twenty-nine-year-old mother of three—Margaret, George S. Patton V, and Robert. By now, it had also become apparent that my brother George had definite developmental disabilities. So my mother quickly went from being a comfortable housewife who arranged community services to being someone who needed them desperately.

GEORGE, BORN IN 1955, has been tested by every kind of expert under the sun, but there's no definitive diagnosis for his condition: not Down syndrome, not autism, not Fragile X. My mother has her own (not scientifically proven) theories: At the time George was conceived, four people on my parents' block were struck down by polio; it was the summer before Salk's vaccine was released. Meanwhile, the Army quarters were routinely sprayed with DDT. That winter, my mother and a close neighbor, Mary Pharr Love, both delivered children with special needs. George looks pretty normal, handsome even—in fact, he looks a lot like my father: six two and strapping, with blue eyes. He's a sweet guy with better manners than most able-bodied people you'll ever meet. But by the time he was two or three and the doctors finally recognized that he was intellectually challenged, George's vocal muscles had atrophied, so he didn't speak, really, and his coordination was off.

Resources for military family members with handicaps were almost nonexistent in those days. And disabled children were often considered an embarrassment and institutionalized, even in 1960. So my mother, loath to part with her child, tried home therapy and sought advice from Children's Hospital in Washington. She also cajoled local kindergarten teachers into accepting George in their classes, even if he couldn't keep up. Later, when our family returned to Washington from Germany in 1961, my mother applied for six-year-old George to attend a special-needs class there.

It's hard to believe, but there were only two such classes in the

George at Devereux
School, circa 1972.

PHOTO COURTESY OF THE
PATTON FAMILY

entire D.C. public school system at the time, and the children in them represented every disability you can think of: ADD, hearing impairments, autism, you name it. A school-appointed doctor and social worker evaluated my brother and then sat my mother down. "We understand that your military lifestyle requires you to move from post to post," they told her. "But if you want this boy to have the best opportunity for success, he needs the stability of a permanent residence. You have no constant in your life, and although you're trying to help him, your efforts aren't enough."

By now, my father already had orders for his first tour in Vietnam. When he left, in April 1962, things really fell apart. My mother, who had just given birth to my sister Helen, developed a collapsed lung and had to undergo major surgery. Meanwhile, her own mother suffered a major stroke that left her partially paralyzed. My parents had brought our unflappable German housekeeper back to the States with them, and she proved invaluable. Still, in the months that followed, my mother put all her volunteer activities on hold and, when she emerged from the wreckage, threw herself into finding a solution for my brother George.

It was expected that the other children in our family would attend boarding school at some point, as did many military kids at the time. "But I wasn't a bit sure that I could find any place I'd feel comfortable leaving my disabled child as a boarding school student," she says. "I visited some pretty gothic-horror institutions—and they definitely were 'institutions' in that era." Showing her respect for George, she included him in the process, and a few months into their fact-finding mission, my mother discovered the Devereux Foundation. Started in California by a woman who gathered special-needs children into her home, the now professionally run foundation had expanded into Pennsylvania, where backers acquired Main Line estates so that the children could be housed and taught with others of similar age and disabilities.

The place that my brother would be eligible for, as it turned out, was run like a family. "It really was a system that was functioning," my mother notes. "The staff had a way of zeroing in on each child's strengths to bring out his or her potential." (George was quickly identified as an outdoorsman, athlete, and someone who was good with animals.) Best of all, George, who was with my mother when she visited, was happy to see that the foundation had a farm and kids his own age; he was ready to move right in.

After that, no matter where we were stationed, my mom arranged for George to come home to visit at least twice a year and made sure that he was fully integrated into our activities and circle of friends. To this day, he remembers each location, when we talk about past years, because he was there with us. "George was never hidden away, and he could always visualize wherever we were posted, which I thought was important," my mother says. That arrangement lasted until he was in his midtwenties and moved home with my parents for good.

By the time she had George settled at Devereux, my mother, a quick learner, had stored up a lot of information. Armed with the training she'd acquired in community service at various Army bases, she found her true calling. "I was very conscious of my child's situation and that we had the means to support it, whereas many families might not," she says. "So I contacted Dorothy Johnson, the wife of the chief of staff of the Army, and said, 'I really want to do something for other families who have a member with a disability, particularly children. At the least, I think we need to have a center where people can go for information.'

"'You know, something like that is already starting,' said Mrs. Johnson. 'It's called Army Community Services. If you want to get involved, here's where to go.'"

WHEN MY MOTHER found her way into the very first Army Community Service (ACS) office, tucked in a tiny building in Fort Myer, Virginia, the staff was just moving in. Seeing as the organization had only two volunteers—and the other woman's husband was the social worker at the Pentagon charged with writing the regulation to create ACS—my mother was made volunteer supervisor right off the bat.

"It was a time when the military was beginning to realize that the welfare of military families affected the morale and efficiency of the troops," she says. "We set ourselves up to be a one-stop shop for people's problems—and if they couldn't find the aid they needed, we dreamed it up."

One early innovation was the *Waiting Wives* newsletter, which they began sending out in 1968 across the D.C. area to women whose husbands were stationed in Vietnam. They started with twenty-five recipients; by the end of the following year, twelve hundred women had subscribed. Eventually, the program went nationwide. It was uncommon for the different military branches to share resources at the time. My mother and her colleagues respected tradition, yet weren't afraid to cut through the red tape. For instance, my mother got a call from the wife of the Air Force chief of staff, Mrs. Ryan, the head of the Air Force family service program. "She wanted to know if the Army would be willing to let our volunteers and hers serve in each other's offices when it was more convenient," my mother recalls. "I told her that I was only the volunteer supervisor for our ACS program, so I probably couldn't make that decision. But Mrs. Ryan said that *she* could, and since the Army had no equivalent to her role . . . if I agreed, that was that." So it was—no Pentagon approval required, or sought.

As it happened, the Army Community Service program was growing at a time when soldiers were leaving for Vietnam in greater numbers. The wives of those men became the ACS volunteer corps. When the first ACS training manual was published by a team of social workers at the University of Maryland and the Department of the Army, based on what my mother and her friends had done, the introduction read, "Army Community Services is a program that incorporates innovation." For my mother, that was doubly significant, she says. "It contradicted the Army's reputation for being stodgy and resistant to change."

At every new post, my mother recruited her friends, and together they sowed the seedlings for more family aid. At Fort Knox, Kentucky, in 1971, they found that a lot of wives were at the base reluctantly: Their husbands had been drafted and their families uprooted; many of the younger wives had been forced to put their own careers on hold. My mother worked to dispel the gloom by helping to whip up a flurry of special-interest programs—sports, the environment, the arts, charitable ventures—that let the wives make use of their talents and learn new skills. The programs morphed into something bigger. And no problem was too small to address. When a young Army wife wrote to the local newspaper complaining that she couldn't find anything to eat in the commissary, my mother chased her down. "I'm really worried," she told the woman. "What don't you find?" It turned out the girl had grown up with frozen meals and didn't know how to cook from scratch. Voilà: a gourmet cooking class was born.

I think it's only now that I have come to appreciate how amazing my mother was as an army wife, mom, and innovator. My dad was the main attraction when I was a kid, I suppose, but Mom made everything about our complex lives run smoothly. Every year she threw each of us a birthday theme party—there was an Olympics party, a rock-and-roll party, the obligatory military party, even a political party where everyone had to make campaign posters and give stump speeches. And every party featured an obstacle course— the goal being to wear out a bunch of supercharged kids, no doubt. She always dressed up in a costume for Halloween. Through everything she dealt with, including my dad being MIA for a few days on one occasion and being wounded on another, she never lost her cool or got too excited. Admittedly, that unruffled, move-the-ball-forward way about her drove all of us crazy at times, although I now see it as one of her most valuable survival skills.

There were different needs among Army families in each place we lived, and over time my mother's efforts snowballed into a top-level career in community service. Back in Washington, she became the senior volunteer consultant for both the American Red Cross Services to the Armed Forces and the Army Community Service program. Soon after my father retired in 1980, she formed her own successful consulting firm, a national resource agency for nonprofits based at our home in Massachusetts. She went on to cofound and administer a recreation program for mentally challenged adults from twenty Massachusetts communities, cofounded a public-access television program targeting the families of physically and developmentally challenged individuals, became active in military family organizations such as Operation Troop Support and the National Military Families Association, and became a revered voice of the community.

During the time that my mother was starting her company, my father—eager for another adventure—was in the process of whipping some of the parkland surrounding our house (which his parents had bought in 1928) into an actual farm. Ambitiously for the era, he pictured it as a commercial operation that could serve the local community. My father wasn't a farmer; he was also ahead of the curve in the sustainable-food movement. Luckily, my mother, who knew less about farming than my father did, had learned plenty about networking and vetting people. Proving what a good match they were, she was the one who ultimately found the right team to bring my father's vision to life—making the farm certified organic and profitable.

"My best role has been putting the pebble in the pond," she concludes, shrugging. "After that, the ripples make the waves."

. . .

WHEN MY EIGHTY-YEAR-OLD father was dying of a form of Parkinson's disease in 2004, my sister Margaret, a cloistered nun, made a few rare trips to the farm to see him. My father was virtually living in a chair at this point, and he wanted my mother near him. Margaret remembers him, on one of her visits, telling her, "Your mother is like God to me."

"He repeated it," says Margaret, "and that was really profound to me—that he saw God in another person and was that sensitive to her worth."

The winter after my father died, while my mother was still cataloging the more than one thousand condolence letters that had flooded in, she bumped into a box of his papers in the basement. Inside she found a small red journal from 1951, the year she and my father met: She'd never seen it before, and saved it for Christmas Eve, my father's birthday, to share it with the rest of us.

THURSDAY, JUNE 7, 1951
I met Joanne.

FRIDAY, JUNE 8, 1951
Well when I got up there I made up my old mind I was interested in this gal . . . it didn't take me very long to discover that I'd fallen in love with her.

FRIDAY, JULY 13, 1951
This is when I first kissed Joannie. Told her I was planning on waiting until Xmas [but he did it anyway]. WOW!!

THURSDAY, SEPTEMBER 6, 1951
Letter from J—Special delivery A/M. Christ wotta woman.

MARCH 1, 1952
Called my honey . . . I always get the damndest warming feeling when I talk with her. I've got it terrible bad and that's a fact. Terrible, terrible bad: I am a whole helluva lot in love.

SATURDAY, JUNE 14, 1952 [MY PARENTS' WEDDING DAY]
"D"-Day
This is the day that I have waited for . . . This is the day all my dreams come true. It's going to be a great life.

Joanne and George Patton on their wedding day.   PHOTO COURTESY OF THE PATTON FAMILY

FOURTEEN

Wartime Correspondence Between George and Joanne Patton (1968–1969)

IT'S INTERESTING TO look at my parents' separate lives during my father's third and last tour in Vietnam—my father immersed in a doomed fight with men he loved; my mother in D.C., raising children in the thick of the civil rights and women's liberation movements while seeing her own career in social work take off.

Fortunately, we have a record of all this in the audiotapes that they sent back and forth.

On my mother's end, you hear the familiar sounds of family life: laughter, tantrums, sniffles, and heavy breathing (three-year-old me leaning into the microphone) or the hum of traffic, since my mother often took the tape recorder while she tore around town for work, errands, and car pools. Occasionally, my siblings—Margaret was fourteen when Dad left in January 1968; George, nearly thirteen;

Robert, ten; and Helen, five—would chime in with greetings and updates about sports and school trips. On my father's end, you get the other extreme: The growl of his voice is punctuated by the ominous rhythm of mortar shells, the clatter of helicopter blades, or the buzz of B-52s skimming thunderously through the air.

Occasionally, my parents finished tapes for each other. On some of the cassettes, their voices overlap and you can almost picture the split screen: Mom at home in our leafy, northwest Washington suburb; Dad camped in his small trailer in Vietnam, eight thousand miles away.

It's shocking to discover how many of the tapes were made at midnight or even 2 a.m. We're talking about a mother with five young children and a busy volunteer life, and a soldier who worked twelve-hour days at a minimum. That's how much they longed to talk to each other, even if the conversations were one-sided.

My father left for Vietnam just after New Year's 1968. His initial assignment was a staff position in the Force Development Office in Long Binh, a sprawling, Fort Hood–style base about fifteen miles northeast of Saigon.

JANUARY 17, 1968

From George:

We left Long Binh this morning . . . and went out to all the brigades . . . My impression was that overuse of helicopters, not using the roads, too much talk on kill ratios . . . I don't see an end to it. I really don't see any end to this thing, it's just a constant breaking the bushes. George Ware's brigade had a big fight a week ago right on the beach just south of Quàng Ngãi city . . . I mean the Marines had been in there for almost three years. And of course they're no longer there, the Army's there. But that's not what I'd call a real high degree of progress.

On April 4, 1968, Martin Luther King Jr. was assassinated in Memphis, Tennessee, triggering four days of riots in D.C.

APRIL 6, 1968

From Joanne:

When we sat down to dinner, we had the news on and they began to report the outbreak of fires, about a half a dozen . . . and the roaming and breaking in began to increase . . . I'm going to send you some pictures, and so on, but it really does look just like a war . . .

This is certainly quite an education in our modern-day world for the children. Helen was quite concerned last night, and needed to have an in-depth explanation after she asked the question "Mommy, why do the colored people hate the white people so much?"

JUNE 6, 1968

From Joanne:

I had a great time in San Francisco. I just am so glad that I swallowed my pride and got over my "mad at the Army" for being unable to finance me and went on out there, because it really was worth it to me . . . And I got up that morning and I got over my nerves and I just knew that the talk was gonna be a success. And the main reason I knew it was that after going to conferences and listening to other people's lectures all week long, I knew that I had as much to say as they did. And I knew that my paper was in line with the current thinking that I had heard expressed in various ways on other platforms. And that really the ACS [Army Community Services] had something to brag about because they had already put into action a program that was being proposed by a lot of other people . . .

The dean of [the] social work school at the University of Maryland . . . got up and announced that he was very much impressed with this paper . . . that it had attacked this in a different way and . . . there were new theories that he was surprised I'd picked up . . . And then the director of volunteers for the Red Cross raised her hand and stood up and said, "I consider her one of the Red Cross's failures . . . we let her get away because we didn't offer her a challenging enough job"— which was really true, though I didn't say so . . .

Then anyway, they started to ask me questions: One man who'd given a very academic paper . . . began to pump me: "Did I think the way we were running ACS could work for the ghetto neighborhoods?" And it was really very exciting to be suddenly the target of all these questions as they were asking me as an authority, whereas up to this time I'd been the little girl tagging along. Everyone afterward came up pumped my hand and all these people wanted a copy of my paper. I've been told that if the conference doesn't publish it, the Army will publish it for ACSs around the world . . .

Oh gosh, it was exciting. A lot of good things happening, I feel.

About six months after arriving in Vietnam, my father was promoted to commander of Blackhorse, the 11th Armored Cavalry Regiment, which was composed of four thousand men.

JULY 26, 1968

From George:

I've been in command of this sterling outfit for about eleven days and nine hours. Today was very easy. I went up to see the 1st Squadron . . . I raised hell with their maintenance and came on back . . . [They'd been having trouble pacifying the East-West Village.] From the second of July [it] has cost us two tanks, three or four armored personnel carriers, one M88 tank retriever, four killed in action . . . and thirty-eight wounded . . . by mines and claymores, two of those with both legs blown off. The village is completely VC and you cannot fire on it—because under these rules of engagement, how do you return fire when you are moving a tank up the road and a mine goes off under [it], detonated by some clown hiding in a field a hundred yards away? . . . This village is about fifteen to twenty air miles form Lai Khe, where the 1st infantry Division main CP and one brigade have been . . . for three years. It just kind of shows the progress we are making in this war, which in my opinion is very little.

The last two days are the only two days that we have not had a fairly major contact since I've been here . . . The whole thing is trying to get people to fire on ya . . . just trying to get them to do something. It's a real bad thing, you can't get your hands on 'em. They're just like ants—they're all over the place, the place is just crawling with VC, but they're not in any big unit configuration where you can tie into 'em.

Our major problem here is mines—mines and booby traps and RPGs fired by an unknown hand from a populated area from which we cannot return the fire. I had an interesting experience [with] ARVN [the Army of the Republic of Vietnam] the other day in this village, which we had wiped out. [They cleared the town] so as to not show too much U.S. presence . . . Of course some of the houses were put together with mortar shingles on top, and . . . slate shingle [is] very dear to the Vietnamese. So trying to have some compassion for these people—they were weeping and wailing, of course, this was the home of their ancestors—I tried to get the district commander and the district chief to load up some of these shingles and tiles . . . in their trucks and take it up to the refugee camp and redistribute it among the people there. And they refused to do it . . . They did not have the time the energy or in effect the interest to load this material on the trucks . . . Actually, they just didn't give a damn, you see . . . We're getting nowhere in this war; we're losing people unnecessarily and we're getting nowhere . . . It's an extremely frustrating and saddening experience . . .

AUGUST 3, 1968

From George:

About three days ago this fellow [combat photographer] Al Chang was here from the AP. [We were conducting] a mine-clearing operation in really quite deep jungle and . . . a soldier stepped on one right next to me and he was blown seventy-five feet, both arms and both legs off . . . I thought I was hit pretty bad because I had blood all over me from him. And Al Chang wanted to take a lot of pictures and I wouldn't let him and then we went forward and the soldier was dying and died before we got him to the chopper . . .

He'd walked off of the trail . . . we'd cleared about five mines out in five hundred feet, most of which were antitank. They're put in very, very skillfully: They have a little stick sticking out of the middle of the road—and of course, on a lot of these trails there are sticks sticking out. And when the front-slope plane of the vehicle hits the stick, it bends the stick over and the mine is detonated.

SEPTEMBER 18, 1968

From Joanne:

I got your letter yesterday saying that you had received the feeler . . . and had submitted your application to extend, with which I entirely concur, as I have told you in the past. I feel that if you can keep your beloved command, you certainly should do it—I would do it in your place . . . I'm sure this is setting a precedent about the first commander of that regiment who will have been allowed the privilege of extending. I'm extremely proud of you, I really am . . .

From Joanne:

[At eight o'clock this morning] the doorbell rang...and Helen came rushing up and said, "Mom, Mom, there's a man downstairs with a colonel's hat on," and in my stupor I thought it was a special-delivery postman or something...

First of all, [it was] pouring rain...and ink black outside for the hour—and here, standing in the darkness in the corner of the front hall, was this man who was immediately identified as a chaplain by the flashing crosses. And somehow, not for one second did I think that he was bringing me the ultimate bad news...Poor fella...He got out the telegram that was going to be sent to me later in the day...The secretary of the Army felt that there might be some press coverage of this and wanted to...make sure [I] got the message first: "...Your husband...was lightly wounded in Vietnam while engaged in combat against hostile forces..." I really thought it was so good of him to come out in the rain and everything...

Well, darlin', I think this is another time the Lord has been good to us...it's a thing to be extremely thankful for. I love you with all my heart and I am very proud of what you are—and hope that you can let this be the only Purple Heart that you bring home next April 6.

From George:

Well, here we are, and I find myself in the 93rd Evac Hospital with a little hole in me that doesn't amount to much...The way all this happened was, about a quarter to seven this morning, we got word that B Company, 2nd/16th Infantry . . . had seen Charlie moving east, near just this little town Binh Mai, that we've had a lot of trouble with . . . I went up there and we were huddled on the banks of this little stream and I said, "Well, why don't you go get Charlie?" And they said they wanted more artillery and gunships, and I said, "Bullshit. Let's go."

So we went into the woods, which wasn't too thick . . . and we crossed a little stream and . . . saw three bunkers and we decided to recon by fire. And I don't know how I was hit, but I was hit . . . in the right side with a piece of shrapnel. It could have been Charlie, it could have been anything, but it was probably friendly. So I told McHenry to go on with the goddamn fight and clear the woods and I went back to my chopper . . .

And now here I am . . . so I got a Purple Heart the easy way . . . The boy in the next bed to me has both legs off . . .

So best of love to everybody. Nobody worry, everything's okay.

NOVEMBER 10, 1968

From George:

We lost, as you probably have heard by now—Captain Hays, B Troop, was killed day before yesterday . . . uh, one of the things that has shaken me up [clears his throat] more than anything else [his voice catches] since I have been here. We also believe that we have found the wreckage of Major Cunningham's aircraft, which is way, way up to the northeast. They found it on the ground, one Air Force and one Army in it. The thing went straight in and has been impaled on a tree lengthways, which means the tree went through the two people in the cockpit. So it seems to me there is no longer any doubt on Major Cunningham's fate. He was a very exceptional fellow, as was Captain Hays. It always makes you feel tough to lose the good ones, and those two were two of the best.

Hays, I believe, is in for a posthumous DSC [Distinguished Service Cross]. The story on him was his company didn't do particularly well up here in the Lang Son in September. He had told the squadron commander that he had had enough company commander time and he was beginning to get a little shaky and he wanted out. I talked him into staying so that he could bring his company up and then I would take him out. In the meantime, he got killed. And of course this is one of the things that you have to go through as a commander that's kind of hard to go through. But anyway, he's gone and I'm gonna write his wife . . . a special letter . . .

We're fighting a defensive war here—we're fighting a war of attrition. I wonder how these gold-star mothers feel, and gold-star wives like Mrs. Hays and Mrs. Cunningham, I wonder how they really feel when they stop to consider, if they're sensitive enough to the problem, how they feel about this bombing halt . . . We're going out here and losing guys to mines and RPGs and all, and we have stopped the one thing the North Vietnamese asked us to do with no compensation, no compensation whatsoever. It's a pretty important thing to think about . . . It's like getting into a fight in a ring with a fellow and he says, "Look, let's fight but you can't use your right, you can only use your left . . . [but] I'm going to use both my right and my left 'cause I'm weaker than you. And then we'll go for fifteen rounds and then we'll do another five and then we'll do another twenty-five."

I don't know how long this thing will last . . . We can still lose this war. That's a real clear statement. I wouldn't be a goddamned bit surprised but that we will lose it. And then you can just write those casualties off and those ever-increasing names on those ever-increasing monuments . . . You can just keep putting them on the monuments and giving out all this crap, all this posthumous DSCs and Purple Hearts . . . but there's no end to this thing.

DECEMBER 17, 1968

From George:

I think I sent you the citation that I got and I'm sure I didn't earn it but I'm glad I got it . . . It really wasn't as scary as the citation reads. . . . Andy [O'Meara, the regimental intelligence officer] and I went down there and got that VC out of that hole . . . and he was scared to death that we were gonna kill him. And I did shoot him in the foot, because I saw his ol' foot hanging out there on the creek bed there outside the hole. And Andy shot him in the other foot and that kind of lamed him a little. We hauled him up on the side of a ravine and we put him in a chopper. And as he lay there in the stretcher, I came to attention and saluted him, because he put up a pretty good fight. And he returned the salute. And I'll just never forget that, it was really quite a thing . . .

I always admire a good soldier—I don't give a goddamn what uniform he's wearing. I just admire him. And this was a pretty good soldier . . . He was up against it—I mean, he had gunships and tanks and ACAVs [armored cavalry assault vehicles] and ARPs [aero rifle platoons] and me all around him . . . and he put up a good fight. So he got a salute from me and I'd do it again.

This isn't a very good Christmas message, is it? . . . I don't know what to say except that I miss you . . . Wishing everybody very seriously a very Merry Christmas and a Happy New Year. So Merry Christmas, everybody. Good night.

On February 28, 1969, Thomas A. McAdams, a beloved Blackhorse captain (F Troop, 2/11) was killed while pulling soldiers out of a bombed and burning APC (armored personnel carrier). He was posthumously awarded the Silver Star. My mother attended the funeral in D.C. and, at the request of McAdams's widow, took their five-year-old daughter to the Army Community Services office during the graveside portion of the ceremony at Arlington Cemetery.

MARCH 9, 1969

From Joanne:

The ceremony was really very fine. Little Anita [the widow] came down the aisle and [her] darling little girl . . . was wearing a tam-o'-shanter and coat knit by her grandmother in this beautiful raspberry red. It was such a note of bravery coming down that aisle with everyone else in somber black . . .

As soon as the family came out, I slipped behind and I didn't know if the little girl would be willing to go with me, but she . . . took my hand right away and we went out together . . . I'd brought a little doll with me inside my pocketbook and I made up a story about how she had appeared looking for Sheri McAdams [Captain McAdams's daughter] and so the little girl was touched by that . . .

[After the burial] I went back to the [ACS] center and found [her. She'd drawn a picture with] a little girl in the middle with a big smile on her face and up above her were big thunderclouds threatening and underneath her was a big red devil . . . And I thought, maybe that was just a sign of this little girl working out how she was gonna be happy and smiling in spite of the troubles coming along.

But anyway, so much for symbolism. I took her back to the chapel, and by this time the crowd had thinned out, and it was just the family there. I . . . introduced myself to his parents, Colonel and Mrs. McAdams. First of all, the father said, "Tom was . . . kind of hard to handle as a boy, a real fighter, but he wrote home and said, 'Colonel Patton is my kind of commander, this is really a fella I'd like to go all the way for.'" And then the little widow came up and said, "Yes, you know what we're proudest of? We were able to arrange for Tom to be buried on Patton Drive, the same name as his commander." And then Colonel McAdams said, "Yes, he's the first person to be buried on Patton Drive."

And I thought, "Well you know, that's one of the loveliest compliments I've ever heard . . ." that they sought out this privilege for this young boy and that they're proud to have him buried on the street that bears your family name because you were his commander . . .

They were all so brave and looking at everything in such a positive way—of course, they were brokenhearted, don't let me say they were anything but—but I just felt this was a family that was really showing us how. This was the only son of this father, you know . . . and that brave little girl—I was just proud to know 'em. Anyway, I think I said all the right things . . .

And I was driving away in my car and the first thing I heard on the radio was that lovely song from [the Broadway musical] *I Do, I Do:* "My Cup Runneth Over with Love." And for the first time I really felt tearful . . . it was very moving . . .

I guess that's about it except to say I love you very much. And oh, we're getting so excited—we can say, "Next month, next month, he's coming home next month!" It's just almost more than we can stand, but I guess we'll just have to bear with it. God bless, the last days are the hardest. I love you.

APRIL 23, 1969

From George:

Christ, I'm busy and there's a lot of people who wanna give parties and I've got to go by and say good-bye to the troops. And Jesus, we've got some great troops here, just great. I'm so kinda sad leaving them, just kinda sad. I was sittin' in the chopper today and I just bawled my goddamn head off, I just did. Funny . . . It isn't that I don't want to come home; I want to come home and I'm sick of this war a little bit. But leaving this unit is tough, that's all there is to it.

PART SIX

MOVING FORWARD

In each generation, as long as we are to remain a great nation, a group of us are somehow chosen, perhaps by the Almighty, to serve our country and our Army and to serve our nation. Perhaps it is a small group, woefully inadequate, but it is there, and regardless of how we see it, regardless of the dwindling budget, the ancient out-dated tanks of the 1920s and equipment, the congressional pressures to cut, cut, cut, that group will stay, and as the poet said: "Some for honor, and some for pay."[1]

—MY FATHER, MAJOR GENERAL GEORGE S. PATTON, FROM HIS FAREWELL STATE OF THE DIVISION SPEECH TO THE 2ND ARMORED DIVISION, OCTOBER 16, 1977

FIFTEEN

Charley Watkins and My Brother George S. Patton Jr.

THESE LAST TWO heroes, Charley Watkins and my brother George S. Patton Jr., are linked by the fact that they're both horsemen, they now live less than an hour's drive from each other, and they were both dear to my father in different ways.

IT WAS OCTOBER 2003, in the Sunni Triangle in Iraq: The impact from the roadside IED flipped Specialist Justin Widhalm's Humvee, flinging the first sergeant who was riding with him into the road. On cue, a group of Al Qaeda snipers bobbed up on a nearby rooftop and opened fire. Widhalm, twenty-five, managed to crawl out of the overturned vehicle with a basic M16 rifle—no scope—and killed all five shooters. Sensing an expert marksman, his commanders promptly sent him to sniper school.

Charley Watkins at Blackhorse Base Camp Vietnam, May 1968.

Fast-forward to July 23, 2006: another tour in the same area of Iraq. The winds in the desert were blowing too hard for the Army helicopter to take off. Around dusk, after waiting for hours, Widhalm and his six-man crew finally received clearance to fly. Their mission was to kill a notorious Al Qaeda warlord in a nearby village; the team's job was to protect Widhalm, now a certified sharpshooter and platoon sergeant, so he could take the shot.

It was already getting dark as they closed in on the drop zone. Widhalm stood by the open hatch, ready to rappel down, when a powerful updraft rocked the helicopter. Knocked off balance, Widhalm tumbled thirty feet into a concrete drainage canal. The impact fractured both of his feet, dislocated his knees, and broke his back in three places. Then his head hit the ground.

He was medically evacuated back to the States, to Evans U.S. Army Hospital at Fort Carson, Colorado. It was a wonder that he was alive, but it was also immediately clear to his doctors that they were dealing with more than broken bones. Nuclear imaging tests showed damage in five of the seven regions of Widhalm's brain—some of it due to his fall in July, some undoubtedly due to other concussions he'd sustained in IED attacks in Iraq.

He was barely verbal, with almost no short-term memory: He'd go through a bottle of shampoo in less than a week because even while he was in the shower, he couldn't remember whether or not he'd just washed his hair. Before the accident, Widhalm had been an elite athlete and trained for the 2000 U.S. Olympic wrestling team. Now he felt so helpless that he dreamed of suicide. At his lowest point, he overdosed on painkillers and woke up in the hospital.

Soon after, Widhalm met Charley Watkins, a Vietnam veteran and retired helicopter pilot who, along with his wife, Donna, volunteers a couple of days a week at the Soldier and Family Assistance Center at Fort Carson, Colorado. If there's not a particular job for him to do at the center that day, Watkins usually positions himself by the coffee machine in the lobby and talks to people who feel like talking. He and Widhalm struck up a conversation and started meeting regularly.

"I'd had a lot of sessions with psychologists, but the biggest thing I needed was to get out of my pity party—and Charley gave me that," says Widhalm. "First off, as a former pilot, he pointed out how horrible my pilot must have felt about what happened. Secondly, he made me see all the other things that could easily have gone wrong: I could have been crushed under the helicopter, or the wind could have inverted the aircraft, rolled it, and everyone could have been killed. It gave me a reality check that I was lucky to come out of that alive. And, excuse my French, but it really made me pull my head out of my ass and wipe the shit out of my eyes and get on with it."

Today, Widhalm is a champion in the Wounded Warriors cycling program. He's still a little foggy at times and gets terrible headaches, and he can't run—he can't handle the force on his joints. But he can work: He's now a program coordinator for the USO. And he can walk and play with his three-year-old son, and he can bike. His goal now is to be a Paralympic cyclist as well as a biathlon champion in cross-country skiing and shooting.

"Justin's a young guy," says Charley Watkins. "We had to keep reminding him, 'You just have a new norm, but you can still have some dreams.'"

BORN IN 1944, Watkins started out as a cowboy. Compact and sinewy, he grew up on a cattle ranch twenty-five miles south of Las Animas, Colorado, which he helped work on horseback. He was the first member of his family to attend college. But when he took off a semester to earn more tuition money, a draft notice hit his mailbox. Basic training, a tour in Europe, and flight school followed. And then, in 1968, he landed in Vietnam.

Assigned to an Air Cavalry Troop, Watkins first helped insert reconnaissance soldiers into enemy territory, hauled mail to the squadron, and delivered food to remote units. Next, he became a copilot for my father, who'd just been named commander of Blackhorse, the 11th Armored Cavalry Regiment. After about three weeks, the job for lead pilot opened up.

Nobody wanted it, with good reason. My father lived in the air.

He was in charge of four thousand men, and if any of them were seeing action, he wanted to be there. And if there wasn't any action going on, he wanted to scare some up from the sky.

"By no means were we a command and control helicopter," says Watkins. "We were more like a single assault helicopter out looking for trouble."

Watkins loved to fly just for the sake of it, and wasn't the type to sit around anyway, so he volunteered for the job. He remembers my father being very polite to him and the crew that first week. But he also noticed that the regimental safety officer had started to come down every morning and watch his preflight check. When Watkins asked why, the officer admitted, "The colonel doesn't like the way you preflight the aircraft. He thinks you're too rough on the equipment."

"I used to pull pretty hard on the pitch change links to make sure there wasn't any play in the bearings," Watkins says. "If things are loose, they wear quickly. Those helicopters can shake apart."

Watkins chewed on the situation for a couple of days. Then, one night, he decided to go down to my father's hooch—an M109 truck van—and speak to him himself. "Sir, I understand you're not happy with the way I preflight the aircraft," Watkins told him. My father looked a little taken aback—he wasn't accustomed to being confronted.

"Well, yes," he said.

"You know, if I can break the equipment, it's not safe to fly anyway," Watkins said. "I have a lot of responsibility and I want to make the aircraft safe—that's why I do my kind of preflight. But I know what the aircraft will do. I know what I can do with this aircraft. And I plan to go home in twelve months. If you want to do the same, you can stick with me or you can find another pilot."

My father slid his chair back. "Chief, I like a guy who's not a 'yes, sir' or 'no, sir' all the time, who has a mind of his own," he told Watkins. "From now on, whenever we get in that aircraft you're the boss and whatever you say goes. But when we land, I'm the boss."

"We agreed, and from that day forward we never had a problem and he never questioned my judgment on what we did or how I flew."

Army helicopters have to be maintained constantly: an intermediate inspection after twenty-five hours and a periodic inspection after one hundred hours, in addition to preflights before every flight and a postflight check after every flight. My father didn't like to wait around for maintenance, and he liked to be able to carry a lot of men and ammunition. So he managed to secure two H-model Hueys, the kind of powerful, workhorse helicopters that are generally used to recover downed aircraft from the jungle. While maintenance was being pulled on one he had another to fly. He had them fitted with double machine-gun mounts on the command side and named them both *Little Sorrel,* after Stonewall Jackson's famed war horse.

As soon as my father and Charley and the crew landed for an inspection, they'd immediately shift their gear to the other chopper, hop inside, and take off again. Their gear included guns, map cases, a radio rack, four thousand rounds (bullets), a case of "frags" (fragmentary grenades), a case of M79 grenades (which were shot out of a small launcher), CS tear gas, and a case of incendiary grenades and flares. The aircraft would be rearmed two or three times a day, depending on the volume of contact. In this case, calling the craft "command and control helicopters" seems an inadequate description. Each *Little Sorrel* was more like a flying death machine.

Most pilots have mortality hovering in the back of their minds already. Why take on additional risk when you already have so much hanging out? But there's a particular kind of soldier mind-set: an absolutely macho, invincible, let's-defy-death-every-day approach. It's usually reserved for jet-fighter pilots. But both my father and Watkins fit the mold.

Most pilots flew 300 to 400 hours over a twelve-month tour. Watkins officially logged a staggering 2,300 hours in the same time period. He and my father often spent more than ten hours a day in the sky. They'd go to meetings, check on units, drop in on firefights, visit wounded soldiers in the hospital, or zoom down Highway 1, where the Viet Cong routinely placed mines to blow up U.S. convoys.

"George liked to fly along the highway at night with all of the helicopter's lights blazing, and intentionally try to get someone to fire at us," says Watkins. "Then we'd kill the lights, climb up, shoot out an M79 flare, and take them under fire. Then we would contact units to move into the area and attack them from the ground. Sometimes, Patton couldn't sleep and we'd go out and fly at one o'clock in the morning."

My father was supposed to be flying between 1,500 and 2,500 feet—the official height for command and control aircraft. Instead, Watkins flew what later became known as the map of the earth, averaging about 50 feet or less above the trees, eyeballing it, and varying the airspeed to fit the situation. He flew in a different pattern every day so that the enemy wouldn't be able to guess which way they were going to take off or which way they were going to fly en route to the daily command briefings at 1st Infantry Division headquarters.

"I can't remember a single day in Vietnam when I wasn't shot at," Watkins says. "Some of the other guys couldn't handle it. For a while I changed copilots as often as I changed flight suits."

The situation made high command crazy, since the regimental commander was supposed to stay out of danger. Yet my father and Watkins were hit by enemy fire so often that their helicopter regularly limped back to base, and they were shot down five times. It's amazing that both of them lived. Andy O'Meara, the Blackhorse intelligence officer, was along for one of these rides in September 1968. A senior Viet Cong officer had just defected and given O'Meara the details of VC battalion positions. My father, directing from his helicopter, moved in with a cavalry squadron, a mechanized infantry battalion, and a Vietnamese Ranger Battalion.

O'Meara wrote about the battle years later in an article titled "The Bravest of the Brave."[1] Here's an excerpt:

> The area occupied by the enemy was cut by deep ravines, formed by erosion during the rainy seasons. Patton told Watkins to fly over the forested area of the enemy position to observe the Blackhorse units as they surrounded it.
>
> A Chinese Communist .51 caliber MG opened fire as our chopper approached. The green tracers of the machine gun rounds passed on either side of us. They were followed by the sounds of rounds thudding as they struck their target. Suddenly, we were without power.
>
> Watkins maintained control of the chopper, auto-rotating the blades to slow the descent. He succeeded in directing the crippled bird into a clearing with a crash that damaged the chopper and shook up the occupants, but no one was seriously injured.
>
> I asked Watkins to report our situation to the Operations Center; then, pulling off my flight helmet and replacing it with my steel helmet, I took my M16 and looked for Colonel Patton. He was gone. We were

taking small arms fire from a wood line directly ahead of the chopper. Patton was running directly toward it and hit the ground.

He began firing at the muzzle flashes in the tree line with his revolver. I ran after him and hit the ground beside him.

"Colonel, you're the point man in the attack of the Regiment," I told him. "You are the lead man in the attack." [It was a reminder that he needed to stay out of harm's way.]

He replied, "F—you, O'Meara." Grabbing my M16, he resumed firing.

Looking around, I observed an American mechanized infantry platoon closing in, and ran in their direction. By the time the platoon leader reported to Patton, his chopper crew had set up the M60 MGs [Little Sorrel's door guns] in the bottom of the ravine. Patton turned to the infantry platoon leader and the platoon sergeant and said, "The enemy is holed up in the ravine on the right side of the chopper. I've set up an ambush at the base of it. Take your platoon to the head of the ravine and drive the enemy into our ambush."

The lieutenant's eyes opened wide as he turned to his platoon sergeant, whose eyes were just as large. It was a difficult challenge. It was beginning to get dark and driving the NVA soldiers from their prepared defensive positions was no small challenge.

Patton sensed the problem. He drew his .357 Magnum and said, "Follow me."

Remaining on high ground to spot enemy movement ahead of them, I observed the platoon as they made their way down. A few times, I called out, "Hold what you've got. There's movement ahead of you. Throw grenades." In each case, two grenades sailed down and exploded with devastating force.

When they reached the base of the ravine, they found a wounded enemy soldier. I climbed down to join Patton and the platoon. A medi-

cal evacuation helicopter had arrived on the scene. Two medics helped us load the enemy soldier on a stretcher. Charley Watkins and I took up positions at the rear of the stretcher to make our way up the steep slope of the ravine.

Before we could lift the stretcher, Patton drew himself to a position of attention and saluted the soldier who had fought against us. And the enemy soldier, lying on his back on the stretcher, returned the salute.

Back in the helicopter, Patton turned to me with a broad grin, slapped me on the thigh and said, "That was better than sex!" He was in his element. He was a fearless warrior. Patton intuitively recognized that as long as we pressed the enemy, it became a protective shield. Prisoners we captured told us that they were told never to fire on a Blackhorse vehicle "because the Blackhorse never breaks contact."

It was the ultimate compliment to the man who taught the regiment to find the bastards, then pile on.[2]

Medical-evacuation (medevac) helicopters didn't have weapons, so, as a rule, they didn't rescue wounded soldiers if the landing zone was hot, but waited until a battle was over. If a soldier was hurt and medevac wouldn't go in, Watkins would park my father and the sergeant major at a defensive position nearby and go get the wounded man himself. In the evenings, he often had to use a hose to rinse the blood from the helicopter.

In April 1969, before my father shipped back to the States, Watkins and his crew rescued a young soldier with a terrible chest wound. He was bleeding profusely.

"Any of that gruff side of George Patton completely went away in those situations," Watkins says. "He and Sergeant Major Bill Squires had this guy in their arms and Patton was talking to him and asked, 'Son, what can we do for you?' And the soldier, as he was dying, said, 'Please sir, just take care of our kids—and don't let people forget who we are.'"

That was the start of the Blackhorse Association, a scholarship fund that my father, Charley, and about ten other Blackhorse troopers started for the children of slain Blackhorse soldiers during the Vietnam War. The Blackhorse is now fighting in Afghanistan and the organization is still providing scholarships and family support for those soldiers killed in the global war on terrorism.

"Being a good soldier wasn't my goal in life when I was growing up," says Watkins. "That was Patton's thing. But when you see someone set the example over and over again, it gives you a different perspective. Once I started working with him, it became my goal, too."

In December 2010, I visited the Soldier and Family Assistance Center (SFAC) at Fort Carson with Charley and Donna Watkins. I'd known Charley by reputation—the intrepid Vietnam Huey pilot—for most of my life. He played a part in many of my father's favorite Blackhorse stories and saved Dad's life more than a few times. But it's only in the last few years, in the wake of my father's death, that Watkins and I have become good friends. And my visit with Charley and Donna at Fort Carson to meet several wounded warriors was a critical step in coming to know and understand my father.

The SFAC is a big modern building, all glass and steel, set in rolling plains near the mountains. It serves over four hundred wounded warriors, most of whom suffer from serious wounds, traumatic brain injuries, post-traumatic stress disorder, or some other kind of physical or psychological injury. SFACs such as this one operate in close coordination with the Army's thirty-five Warrior Transition

Units (WTUs) located around the world, which provide crucial rehabilitative medical care and counseling to wounded soldiers.[3]

That day, Watkins, sixty-six, a sturdy, compact man, was dressed in black from head to toe. "You're all Johnny Cash on us today," said Tiffany J. Smith, SFAC director, as she walked up. "Charley and Donna are known as the grandparents of the SFAC," she told me. "They bring that little touch that makes this place home. Charley has a gift for knowing how to be genuine and the soldiers flock to that."

Watkins introduced me to Justin Widhalm, the sniper who was wounded in Iraq. Widhalm, blond and blue-eyed, could pass for a college student. "He's come a long way," Watkins says. "Last year, Justin was still a basket case—now he's just doing great."

We met another young sergeant whose vehicle had hit an IED in Iraq. He had dragged one of his men to safety before succumbing to his brain injuries. He's so light sensitive from the blast that he has to wear sunglasses indoors, and so violent and confrontational at home that he's lost visitation rights with his children. He can't remember things from one minute to the next: His second wife has become his memory bank. He has an iPhone programmed to remind him when to eat. He's Donna and Charley's new project.

"The other day the soldier whose life he saved came in, and this guy just sat there and cried like a baby," Watkins told me. "It just brought back all those memories. These men go from running a whole platoon to not being able to run their own lives. You take them to the mall and they're constantly watching alleys and rooftops—it's very difficult for a soldier to desensitize to a point that he's careless. Now his whole family's broken apart."

Charley and Donna worry that the sergeant's wife might leave him. "He's a big suicide risk for us," Donna admits. "And without her, he's lost. His brain is still making connections, though—that was how Justin was when we first met him. We're going to get him back. The thing I keep telling them, what I tell all these kids, is that it will never be the same, but it will be okay."

Charley and Donna would know, because they've been through it. Charley self-medicated with alcohol for years after his Vietnam experience. "I think we all did," he says. After living on adrenaline for months, he was paranoid, jealous, on edge, always ready to fight a battle, whatever that might be.

"Our son asked me once, 'Mom, why do you stay with him?'" Donna says. "My answer was that he'd do it for me. And it's hard to find someone who would take a bullet for you. Loyalty is something you don't walk away from."

When Watkins returned from Vietnam, he came home alone. Donna picked him up at the airport. "For months afterward, people called me a baby killer, or came up and acted like they were going to spit on me," he says. Now every time a soldier finishes his or her tour and comes back through Fort Carson—whether as part of a group or individually—Charley and Donna find out in advance and are there, even if it's three o'clock in the morning, and they welcome them home and thank them for their service.

"It's a happy-sad occasion," Watkins says. "There's always someone whose wife doesn't show up, or a wife who comes out of the bleachers with divorce papers. I make sure I'm there to offer the soldiers a ride home, buy them dinner, or get them some groceries to last a couple of days.

"I don't want them treated like we were treated," he continues. "Regardless of whether we support the war or not, we've got to support the troops. So many soldiers become suicidal because they think they've done something wrong. When really, they just did what our country asked them to do. They volunteer to serve, of course, but they commit their lives to serve our country and their fellow soldiers. They're true patriots."

LIKE CHARLEY WATKINS, my fifty-seven-year-old brother, George—my father's oldest son and namesake—is a cowboy. He has a developmental disability, possibly caused by the DDT that was routinely sprayed in Army quarters while my mother was pregnant with him. George is a man of few words. But ever since he started riding at age five, he's been a natural, and he's poetry in the saddle: George has won multiple awards for barrel racing, trail classes, and even English riding (begrudgingly—English riding's not his thing).

As sad as George's impairment made him, my father dealt with it. "He was really very understanding and tolerant and never ranted or raged about it," my mother says. "We all grew into it because George's differences weren't apparent from the beginning. Your father was accepting of him; there was never any shame about it all. It was also perfectly apparent to everyone that he was an involved dad—although he was a very busy guy and couldn't do all the things he wanted to do, like coaching. But George was wholeheartedly accepted as a member of our family."

IN AUGUST 1987, my parents flew to South Bend, Indiana, for the International Special Olympics. That year, George competed in a number of English riding events. "We were sitting in the stands and had just watched him ride when a voice came over the loudspeaker and announced that George was a gold medal winner in the equestrian category," my mother remembers. "One of the Shrivers slipped

My parents with my brother George at the International Special Olympics, South Bend, Indiana, 1987. PHOTO COURTESY OF THE PATTON FAMILY

the medal around his neck. Then your dad elbowed me: 'You know,' he said, tears running down his cheeks, 'I used to worry that George wouldn't be able to do all the things that the rest of our kids could do. And look here, now he's the only one to make the Olympics.'"

When I was growing up, George and I had an unusual relationship. He's ten years older than I am, and as a child, I looked up to him because he was big and strong and athletic. Yet things shifted as I gradually realized that I was so much further along mentally. In the summertime, when George came home from Devereux, the special-needs school in Pennsylvania where he boarded for many years, the two of us used to play war games with toy models. Since the instructions came in pictures, George could look at them and build a tank even though he couldn't read or write.

His models were invariably covered in glue and splotches of paint, but he worked hard to build up his forces. I usually won the battles by outwitting him, though, amazingly, he somehow always managed to help his troops limp back up the stairs to his base on the third floor.

The problem was that his own models weren't enough; George helped himself to mine. Often I'd go looking for whatever kit I'd just received, only to find it in his room, already built. The turning point in our relationship came in 1979. We both lived in the attic in our house in D.C., and I'd just gotten an aircraft carrier kit for Christmas. When I went to build it the next day, it was gone.

I headed across the hall. George's bedroom was filled with military models, a Bearcat police radio so he could hear where the latest fires were, and lots of weather equipment. (George has always followed the weather religiously.) On the dresser sat my finished aircraft carrier, the glue still wet.

I lit into him. Caught red-handed, George apologized and started crying. I refused to forgive him and stormed out of the room. He chased me down the stairs, around the first floor, and back up to my room. He banged on the door violently, demanding that I accept his apology. He was twenty-three. I was thirteen and intimidated by his anger, but suddenly no longer afraid of him. Finally, I came out and said, "George, I'll forgive you on one condition: that you never steal from me again." And he never did.

As the rest of us grew older, we got cars, apartments, significant others, and independent lives of our own. George still lived at home. While he can't express things very well, he feels them deeply. He hated his lack of independence. One day, in frustration, he punched my seventy-year-old father in the chest, knocking him down. Not long after that, George got his own wheels, an all-terrain John Deere mini–dump truck that he could drive around the farm. My parents also built him a separate house on their property, designed with a private suite so that a caretaker could live with him.

As my father's strength decreased and his dementia grew, George seemed to come into his own. My sister Margaret remembers a moment near the end of Dad's life when he got mad at George for not showing him some photographs that George, in fact, *had* just shown him. "They had a big blowout and George stormed out," Margaret remembers. "I went out to him and said, 'George, you know, sometimes you know more than Dad knows. This time he doesn't remember that you showed him the photographs, and I know you did, but he doesn't know that.'" George didn't even wait for her to finish, he just went back in and said, "Sorry." My father shook his hand.

After Dad died, George began walking over to our parents' house each day at breakfast time to kiss my mother good morning, since our father wasn't there to do it anymore. "I have two jobs now: barrel-racing champion and head of the family," he told me. But having just turned eighty, Mom wants to prepare George to have his own life. So she just bought him a home in Colorado—in the plains not far from Fort Carson, a good place for riding—and he and his longtime caretakers moved there last summer. George has worked with handicapped children and adults in the past, helping them ride and interact with horses. My hope now is that he may come to play a role at the Air Force Academy Equestrian

Center, where wounded warriors and their families can come and ride for free.

Charley Watkins has promised to look into it.

"It would be a nice symbol, a nice way to carry on the family tradition," Watkins told me as we said good-bye. "I think your father would have liked it."

Epilogue

WHEN I WAS seventeen and made the (in our family) pivotal decision not to enter the military, my aunt Ruth Ellen—whom we knew as Gagi, my father's only surviving sibling, sent me a typed, three-page letter.

She, for one, supported my decision. "I am very proud of what you have done," she wrote. "The decisions you make at 17-going-on-18 are not the ones that you will make in 4 years of so, but the important thing is that *you* have made a decision—that you have taken the first great step from being a child to being an adult who will have to make decisions the rest of his life, on his own actions and future, and those of his as-yet-to-be family." Ruth Ellen went on to remind me that in her generation of the family, my grandfather gave all the children quotations to live by. "He said the knights of old had mottos that were signposts of what they had to live up to," she wrote. Ruth Ellen wasn't sure if the mottos were a blessing or a curse, but she cited them all in the letter.

My grandfather, paraphrasing Tennyson, gave the first quotation to his eldest daughter, Bee: "Be loyal to the royal within yourself." Undoubtedly, he envisioned her as the young princess of the family—Bee was renowned for her beauty, very bright, and a wonderful rider. As it happened, she went on to marry someone my grandfather saw as a prince—the handsome John Knight Waters, captain of two sports at West Point who went on to become a four-star general.

The next quotation went to Ruth Ellen: "To whom much hath been given, much shall be required" (from Luke 12:48). My grandfather had fully expected his second child to be a son; just before the birth, he even rushed my grandmother back to San Marino, California, so his namesake could be born in the ancestral home. Instead, he settled for raising Ruth Ellen as a tomboy, tossing her into the ocean to teach her to swim, and so on. That alone required a certain degree of patience from Ruth Ellen; more than that, she eventually married into the military—to James W. Totten, who rose to the rank of major general—and over the course of his career was required to move forty-six times. Since Bee died young, Ruth Ellen and my father also became the gatekeepers of the family memory, to whom everyone turned to for the inside dope on my grandfather. After the movie *Patton* lifted him to a kind of folk-hero status, the focus could be relentless.

For my father, the youngest, my grandfather settled on his version of an Alexander Pope quotation: "Act well thy part, therein the honor lies." To me, it's about staying true to who you are and who you're meant to become.

Ruth Ellen closed her letter by offering me a quotation to live by—Polonius's advice to his son Laertes in *Hamlet:*

This above all: to thine own self be true,
And it must follow, as the night the day,
Thou canst not then be false to any man.

Of course, part of being true to yourself is being true to your history. At least in our family, the initial, necessary impulse was to push it away—our grandfather's fame and our father's personality loomed too large. But once we'd staked out our own turf psychologically, as my brother Bob puts it, it was easier to look back and see where our family had been and maybe figure out where it needed to go. Maybe that's true of every family. Either way, sidling back to those memories has felt like a useful exercise.

Now that I think of it, my brothers and sisters and I each picked up a prize from the paternal Cracker Jacks box; we're all paying something forward. Bob, an acclaimed writer and historian, carries forth our father's and grandfather's skills as raconteurs and their great love of history. My older sister, Margaret, shares their powerful sense of vocation and purpose. (She's also an accomplished poet, picking up on my dad and grandpa's love of verse.) George, despite his handicap, upholds their sense of humor, courage, egotism, and sense of adventure. In his stubbornness alone, he may have more of the Patton DNA than any of us. Helen inherited a romantic streak and love of theater and music. Through her nonprofit, the Patton Stiftung Sustainable Trust in Germany, she uses the arts to bring people from different cultures together and is very involved with veterans abroad—she honors that history from a visceral place.

Ironically, just when we thought this book was finished, an Army hospital agreed to test a filmmaking workshop that my friend and business partner Scott Kinnamon and I developed to help soldiers and military families struggling with post-traumatic stress disorder (PTSD). The project evolved naturally from our film workshops with teenagers, but on reflection, it seems like progress on a different level, too. My grandfather notoriously slapped two shell-shocked soldiers. A decade later, my father, in turn, savagely beat a young lieutenant who'd deserted his foxhole during a battle. But both men were products of their time, when PTSD wasn't even in the vocabulary.

Through my work with wounded warriors, things may have finally circled back. The workshop we designed, with input from clinicians at Massachusetts General Hospital, allows soldiers with PTSD to make short films about their experiences, as a way to sort out all the painful images crowding their minds and make sense of what happened to them in combat. The soldiers are the directors, shaping their stories in a way that only they are qualified to do. We instructors simply serve as the banks of a river, helping to facilitate the flow of their narrative. During our first three-day workshop in the spring of 2011, a dozen men and women produced eight powerful short films. The feedback from the base commander, our medical advisers, and the soldiers themselves has been overwhelmingly positive.

It's a pilot program for now, but my dream is to take it global, and make it a standard part of soldiers' post-traumatic therapy.

I'd like to think my father and grandfather would approve.

Dad and me observing a firing demonstration at Fort Hood, Texas, circa 1977.

INTERVIEWS CONDUCTED

Brigadier General (Ret.) Creighton W. Abrams III; General (Ret.) John N. Abrams; Shirley Fischer Arends, PhD; Brigadier General (Ret.) John C. Bahnsen; Colonel (Ret.) David Beckner; Lieutenant General (Ret.) Julius W. Becton Jr.; J. Wesley Becton III; Martin Blumenson; Reverend Mother Irene Boothroyd, OSB; Reverend Thomas Bowers, PhD; Geasung "Sammy" Choi; Reverend Mother Placid Dempsey, OSB; Major General (Ret.) James L. Dozier; Lady Abbess Benedict Duss, OSB; Colonel (Ret.) Glenn Finkbiner; Reverend Mother Dolores Hart, OSB; Colonel (Ret.) Lieutenant General (USAF-Ret.) J. D. Hughes; Colonel (Ret.) James Hildebrand; Lamar Hunt; Sergeant Sammy Kay; Colonel (Ret.) Joseph Maupin; Colonel (Ret.) Glenn Myers; Lieutenant General (Ret.) Dave Palmer; Colonel (Ret.) Andrew P. O'Meara Jr.; Major General (Ret.) George S. Patton (IV); George S. Patton Jr. (V); Joanne Holbrook Patton; Robert H. Patton; Helen Patton Plusczyk; Reverend Mother Margaret Georgina Patton, OSB; Honorable Manfred Rommel; Lilo Rommel; Tiffany J. Smith; Colonel (Ret.) Charles Watkins; Donna Watkins; Baron Rüdiger von Wechmar; Justin Widhalm.

ACKNOWLEDGMENTS

I'm thankful to have been born into my family for many reasons—not only for our colorful history, but also because my ancestors had the foresight to collect stories and write things down for future generations. Better yet, they saved *everything*: letters, diaries, scraps of clothing, even the fatal shell fragment that had embedded itself in my great-great-grandfather George S. Patton's hip during the Civil War.[1]

Although most of the subjects who found their way into this book aren't related to me by blood, they've played such key roles in my life that I think of them as family. Each one has a story that's compelling as a narrative, and instructive as well. I'd like to thank them all for their time, candor, good humor, and patience throughout the process of creating this book. Their lifelong efforts in the service of others have made the world a better place. I'd also like to thank their wonderful spouses and families, most of whom I know well.

For anyone who might look at the book jacket and see the word *with* between my name and Jennifer Scruby's, I confess that this is only *my* book insofar as it is largely about my family and written in my voice, as it were. But I happily confess that the book would not, could not, exist were it not for

Jennifer, a former Georgetown University classmate, and now—lucky for me—my collaborator. We've known each other's family for a long time, and it helped that Jennifer loved and admired her own father, the late Frank Scruby, as much as I admired mine.

Jennifer is a dear friend, a great listener, and as gifted a writer as there is. Supreme thanks to her husband, Alex Ryshawy, and their two kids, Miranda and Nicholas, who gave up so much of their mom's time to enable her to make this book a reality.

Special thanks also go to Natalee Rosenstein, our editor at Caliber; Robin Barletta; Melissa Broder; and our agent, the inimitable Harvey Klinger, for making this book possible. And for publishing the article that gave birth to this book, Carey Winfrey, Tom Frail, and all the wonderful folks at *Smithsonian* magazine.

I'd also like to thank my mother, Joanne Patton, for her generous help and encouragement. For their advice and help on getting the facts straight, my brothers and sisters: Mother Margaret Georgina, George, Bob, and ever-creative and unstoppable Helen. Bob's terrific 1994 biography, *The Pattons: A Personal History of an American Family,* proved both an invaluable resource and something to live up to.

For unearthing the most obscure gems in our giant family archive, Carol Mori. For assistance at the Library of Congress, Bob Patrick of the Veterans History Project; Dr. Daun R. van Ee, Chuck Henning, and the other incredibly knowledgeable members of the library staff. For helping me conduct the on-camera interviews for this book, producer Gia Amella and her crew, and cinematographer Kevin Malone. For sharing his historical knowledge, meticulously copyediting our manuscript, and letting us reference (and re-reference) his celebrated book on Creighton Abrams, *Thunderbolt,* author Lewis "Bob" Sorley. For allowing us to rely heavily on her wonderful, definitive biography of Lady Abbess, *Mother Benedict, Foundress of Regina Laudis Abbey,* Antoinette Bosco. For supporting, inspiring, and challenging me over the past two decades, Mother Abbess and everyone at the Abbey of Regina Laudis (particularly my sister, Mother Placid, Mother Dolores, and Mother Irene) and Father Robert Tucker of St. Anthony's Church in Litchfield, Connecticut. For his thoughtful and necessary book, *The Fighting Pattons,* his genuine regard for my dad and the importance of *his* story, and his willingness to provide assistance to me whenever I have sought it, Brian Sobel. For his friendship, ongoing advice, and generosity in digitizing many hours of old family film footage, Duart's Charles Darby, and his incredibly capable and caring color-correction specialist, Tim Bond. For the care and support they've offered my brother George over the years, Gregg and Shirley Halliday, John Michaud and Peter Nichols.

For contributing the book's foreword and believing in our work, Bob Woodruff, and his wife, Lee. For her friendship and wisdom, Kayce Freed Jennings. For advice and expertise on everything else: Jackie Arends and Dr. Shirley Arends, Wes Becton, Frank Bender, my amazing assistant Katie Carman, Timm Chartier, Pam Dedeo, Cristina Del Sesto, Lance Dildine, Steve Friedman, Chris Galazzi, Jean Godfrey-June, Jonathan Groome, Jamie Hedlund, Tim Hodgin, Shannon and Jeff Henderson, Lois Hunkins, Georgina Keefe-Feldman, Brian Kennedy, Kevin Kennedy, Scott Kinnamon and Liz Westerfield and their family, Susan Korey, Art Labriola, Ellen Lees, Caleb Loring III and everyone at the 1911 Trust Company, Kris Mack, Bob Marty, Lynne McPhail, Muffie Meyer, Christina Morano, Martha Morano, John Musto, Ali Nichols, Alison Pace, Steve Reade, Ken Ringle, Jamie Robinson, Andrew and Diana Rodgers, Catherine Rommel, Gillian Rose, Tony Vaccaro, Drew Schiff, Lorraine Scruby, Mayy Selim and her incredible family, Michelle Taylor, Jeffrey Sachs and Jonathan Walsh.

For helping me understand her family's experience of wartime loss, Leslie Hays Campbell—thank you.

I regret that we were unable to include stories from many of my father's other friends and colleagues—particularly those I had the good fortune of knowing as a boy. These include my much-beloved maternal grandfather, Brigadier General Willard A. "Gaga" Holbrook Jr.; my aunts and uncles Colonel and Mrs. Robby Roberson, Colonel and Mrs. Willard Holbrook III, and Ruth Ellen Patton Totten. Also Brigadier General John C. "Doc" Bahnsen, Lieutenant General Charlie Brown, Duke Doubleday, Colonel Lee Duke, Rear Admiral Gene Farrell, Major General Hal Hallgren, Margaret

Vinson Hallgren, Colonel Sidney "Hap" Haszard, Colonel Jim Hildebrand, Lieutenant General Don Hughes, Colonel Joe Love, Colonel Joe Maupin, General Montgomery Meigs, Colonel Andy O'Meara, Colonel John Reitzell, Lieutenant General Tom Rhame, Colonel Jamie Totten, Colonel Mike Totten, Brigadier General Gary Turner, Major General Wilbur Vinson, and Lieutenant Colonel Tom Vogt.

Finally, I want to thank all the men and women who have served in harm's way on behalf of this great country, along with the families that support them. Many have died, many have been wounded—some physically, while others carry wounds of a different sort, including post-traumatic stress disorder. We can never do enough for the soldiers and families who rise to the call when it comes—and it has come all too often in recent years, and at far too great a cost.

It is to them, so many of whom may never receive the recognition they deserve from those of us who, as my dad used to say, "have never missed a meal or heard a shot fired in anger," that this book is dedicated. On behalf of myself, and all members of the extended Patton family, past and present, THANK YOU FOR YOUR SERVICE.

NOTES

INTRODUCTION

1 Brian M. Sobel, *The Fighting Pattons* (Westport, CT: Praeger Publishers, 1997), p. 352.
2 Ibid., p. 353.
3 Technically, my brother is George Smith Patton V. But my father dropped the IV from his own name soon after my grandfather died—he thought it pretentious ("It sounds like the king of England," he said). The simpler George Smith Patton didn't carry as much baggage with it.

PART ONE

CHAPTER ONE

1 The complete version of *Gentlemen-Rankers*, by Rudyard Kipling.

To the legion of the lost ones, to the cohort of the damned,
To my brethren in their sorrow overseas,
Sings a gentleman of England cleanly bred, machinely crammed,
And a trooper of the Empress, if you please.
Yea, a trooper of the forces who has run his own six horses,

And faith he went the pace and went it blind,
And the world was more than kin while he held the ready tin,
But to-day the Sergeant's something less than kind.
We're poor little lambs who've lost our way,
Baa! Baa! Baa!
We're little black sheep who've gone astray,
Baa—aa—aa!
Gentlemen-rankers out on the spree,
Damned from here to Eternity,
God ha' mercy on such as we,
Baa! Yah! Bah!

Oh, it's sweet to sweat through stables, sweet to empty kitchen slops,
And it's sweet to hear the tales the troopers tell,
To dance with blowzy housemaids at the regimental hops
And thrash the cad who says you waltz too well.
Yes, it makes you cock-a-hoop to be "Rider" to your troop,
And branded with a blasted worsted spur,
When you envy, O how keenly, one poor Tommy being cleanly
Who blacks your boots and sometimes calls you "Sir".

If the home we never write to, and the oaths we never keep,
And all we know most distant and most dear,
Across the snoring barrack-room return to break our sleep,
Can you blame us if we soak ourselves in beer?
When the drunken comrade mutters and the great guard-lantern gutters
And the horror of our fall is written plain,
Every secret, self-revealing on the aching white-washed ceiling,
Do you wonder that we drug ourselves from pain?

We have done with Hope and Honour, we are lost to Love and Truth,
We are dropping down the ladder rung by rung,
And the measure of our torment is the measure of our youth.
God help us, for we knew the worst too young!
Our shame is clean repentance for the crime that brought the sentence,
Our pride it is to know no spur of pride,
And the Curse of Reuben holds us till an alien turf enfolds us
And we die, and none can tell Them where we died.
We're poor little lambs who've lost our way,
Baa! Baa! Baa!
We're little black sheep who've gone astray,
Baa—aa—aa!

Gentlemen-rankers out on the spree,
Damned from here to Eternity,
God ha' mercy on such as we,
Baa! Yah! Bah!

Source: http://www.daypoems.net/poems/1803.html

2 From a letter to Frederick Ayer. Martin Blumenson, *The Patton Papers, 1885–1940* (New York: Da Capo Press, 1997), pp. 161–162.
3 Sobel, *Fighting Pattons,* p. 33.
4 Blumenson, *Patton Papers,* p. 23.
5 From GSP Interviews, 1987–1992; the Patton Family Archives.
6 Sobel, *Fighting Pattons,* p. 52.
7 Ibid., p. 81.
8 Letter from GSP Jr. to GSP IV from Palermo, Sicily, January 14, 1944; Patton Family Collection.
9 Sobel, *Fighting Pattons,* p. 204.
10 Blumenson, *Patton Papers,* p. 55.
11 From Ben's interview with Blumenson, 2001.
12 From video of GSP IV speech, Abrams Lecture Series, Patton Museum, Fort Knox, Kentucky, March 20, 1991.
13 Ibid.
14 Sobel, *Fighting Pattons,* p. 119.
15 Ibid., p. 214.
16 From GSP IV Speech, October 16, 1977.
17 Robert H. Patton, *The Pattons: A Personal History of an American Family* (New York: Crown Publishers, 1994), p. 262.
18 As my father himself admitted, this rule might have been enforced in World War II, but not in the Korean War.
19 From GSP IV Interviews, 1987–1992, p. 47.
20 From GSP IV speech at the Patton Museum of Cavalry and Armor, Fort Knox, Kentucky, March 20, 1991.
21 Ruth Ellen Patton Totten, *The Button Box: A Daughter's Loving Memoir of Mrs. George S. Patton* (Columbia, MI: University of Missouri Press, 2005), p. 155.
22 Blumenson, *Patton Papers,* p. 6.
23 Sobel, *Fighting Pattons,* p. 327.
24 From Ben's GSP IV Interviews, 1987–1992.

CHAPTER TWO
1 Blumenson, *Patton Papers,* p. 71.
2 The word "make" is cadet slang for an appointment or a promotion or attaining some recognition, as in making corporal or making an academic honor

roll. The word "skinned" is slang for being reported or receiving a demerit for some offense. Thanks to Dave Palmer, a former West Point Superintendent, for providing this clarification.

3   The letter here, from General "Hap" Gay, is interesting on more than one front. He probably was taking a special interest in young George because it is General Gay's daughter, Alzina, whom the cadet had written about as the one he was smitten with. (She later married another soldier—and, sadly, committed suicide in later life.)

4   Lewis Sorley, *Thunderbolt: General Creighton Abrams and the Army of His Times* (New York: Simon and Schuster, 1992), p. 93.

PART TWO

CHAPTER THREE

1   Sobel, *Fighting Pattons,* p. 290.
2   Blumenson, *Patton Papers,* p. 608.
3   Sorley, *Thunderbolt,* p. 57.
4   Ibid., p. 77.
5   Ibid., p. 80.
6   Ibid., pp. 95–96.
7   U.S. Army Center for Military History, *Department of the Army Historical Summary: FY 1972* (http://www.history.army.mil/books/DAHSUM/1972/cho2. htm#b1): "Against a background of diminishing war in Vietnam, sustained withdrawal of American forces from the combat zone, substantially reduced draft calls, fiscal constraints, and returning peacetime conditions, Army demobilization continued through fiscal year 1972. Actual military strength declined from 1,124,000 to 811,000 during the year, while major units leveled off at 13 divisions, including 5 unmanned brigades, below the Army's postwar goal of 13 fully manned divisions.
8   Sorley, *Thunderbolt,* p. 348.
9   Ibid., p. 316.
10 Ibid., p. 54.
11 Ibid., p. 15.
12 Ibid., pp. 16–17.
13 Ibid., pp. 28–29.
14 Ibid., p. 53.
15 Ibid., pp 50–51.
16 Sobel, *Fighting Pattons,* p. 276.
17 Sorley, *Thunderbolt,* p. 109.
18 Sobel, *Fighting Pattons,* pp. 275–276.

19 Sorley, *Thunderbolt,* pp. 142–143.

20 Ibid., pp. 114–115.

21 Ibid., p. 174.

22 From GSP Interviews.

23 Sorley, *Thunderbolt,* p. 119.

24 Ibid., p. 169.

25 MACV stands for Military Assistance Command, Vietnam.

26 Sorley, *Thunderbolt,* p. 237.

27 Sobel, *Fighting Pattons;* original in Patton family collection.

28 Sorley, *Thunderbolt,* pp. 353–354.

CHAPTER FOUR

1 The producers of *Patton* chose to alter the book's title to *Tank Attacks.*

2 Samuel W. Mitchum Jr., *The Desert Fox in Normandy* (Westport, CT: Praeger Publishers, 1997), p. 191.

3 Benjamin Patton interview of Manfred Rommel, 2000.

4 Richard Huffman, "The Baader-Meinhof Gang at the Dawn of Terror—Timeline," 2009, < http://www.baader-meinhof.com/timeline/timeline.html > (accessed November 19, 2010).

CHAPTER FIVE

1 It is doubtful that Captain Patton was actually carrying a whip. It was more likely a riding crop.

2 Sobel, *Fighting Pattons,* p. 74.

3 The rank of E4 is also known as "Specialist."

CHAPTER SIX

1 Becton was awarded both the Distinguished Flying Cross and the Silver Star for his actions during that battle.

2 Benjamin Patton interview of Colin Powell, March 16, 2006.

3 Lieutenant General Julius W. Becton Jr., *Becton: Autobiography of a Soldier and Public Servant* (Annapolis, MD: Naval Institute Press, 2008), p. 296.

4 I often heard my father express the same sentiment: "Don't ever get mad except on purpose."

5 Becton, *Autobiography of a Soldier and Public Servant,* p. 296.

6 Ibid., pp. 40–41.

7 Ibid., p. 55.

8 Ibid., p. 102.

9 Ibid., p. 103.

10 GSP IV speech, Abrams Lecture Series, Patton Museum, Fort Knox, Kentucky, March 20, 1991.

CHAPTER SEVEN

1   For the story of Lady Abbess, the authors are hugely indebted to Antoinette Bosco, author of *Mother Benedict: Foundress of the Abbey of Regina Laudis, A Memoir* (San Francisco: Ignatius Press, 2007), the superb and epic history of Duss's life.

2   Bosco, *Mother Benedict,* p. 115.

3   Ibid., p. 105.

4   Ibid., pp. 122–126.

5   Ibid., p. 132.

6   Ibid., pp. 137–139.

7   Ibid., pp. 140–141.

8   Ibid., p. 100: From the perspective of Abbot Langdon, "it would have to be the Abbey of Jouarre, and not an individual nun, that would start a foundation. Mother Benedict was trying to establish a precedent that had never before happened in the history of the Benedictine order. The usual procedure was that a Bishop would invite the Order to come and establish a monastery, not that one member of the Order would begin with a decision to start a Foundation in a certain place and then try to find a Bishop to welcome them."

9   Ibid., p. 166.

10   When the constitutions of Regina Laudis were at last approved by Rome, the monastery had sufficient stability to be elevated to the dignity of abbey. An election was held and Mother Benedict was elected abbess, and was known from that time forward as "Lady Abbess." The ceremony marking the foundation's transformation from Regina Laudis Monastery to the Abbey of Regina Laudis took place on February 10, 1976.

11   Two relevant entries from *The Rule of Saint Benedict:* Chapter 31, "What Kind of Man the Cellarer of the Monastery Should Be": "Let him look upon all the utensils of the monastery and its whole property as upon the sacred vessels of the altar. Let him not think that anything may be neglected . . . nor be wasteful and a squanderer of the monastery's substance . . . "; and Chapter 32, "The Tools and Property of the Monastery": "If anyone treat the property of the monastery in a slovenly or careless manner, let him be corrected."

12   She was later clothed as a novice and eventually became Mother Frances of Rome.

13   This was a mandate given to Lady Abbess by Pope Paul VI as communicated to me by Mother Placid Dempsey, OSB.

PART THREE

1   From a famous speech that my grandfather gave the troops in the run-up to D-Day. Blumenson, *Patton Papers,* p. 457.

CHAPTER EIGHT

1 Richard Oliver Collin and Gordon L. Freedman, *Winter of Fire: The Abduction of General Dozier and the Fall of the Red Brigades* (New York: Dutton, 1990), p. 40.

2 Ibid., pp. 68–71.

3 Ibid., p. 120.

4 Audiotape from GSP IV to Joanne Patton, recorded July 26, 1968.

5 The complete version of "The Children's Hour" by Henry Wadsworth Longfellow:

Between the dark and the daylight,
When the night is beginning to lower,
Comes a pause in the day's occupations,
That is known as the Children's Hour.

I hear in the chamber above me
The patter of little feet,
The sound of a door that is opened,
And voices soft and sweet.

From my study I see in the lamplight,
Descending the broad hall stair,
Grave Alice, and laughing Allegra,
And Edith with golden hair.

A whisper, and then a silence:
Yet I know by their merry eyes
They are plotting and planning together
To take me by surprise.

A sudden rush from the stairway,
A sudden raid from the hall!
By three doors left unguarded
They enter my castle wall!

They climb up into my turret
O'er the arms and back of my chair;
If I try to escape, they surround me;
They seem to be everywhere.

They almost devour me with kisses,
Their arms about me entwine,

Till I think of the Bishop of Bingen
In his Mouse-Tower on the Rhine!

Do you think, O blue-eyed banditti,
Because you have scaled the wall,
Such an old mustache as I am
Is not a match for you all!

I have you fast in my fortress,
And will not let you depart,
But put you down into the dungeon
In the round-tower of my heart.

And there will I keep you forever,
Yes, forever and a day,
Till the walls shall crumble to ruin,
And moulder in dust away!

Source: http://www.bartleby.com/42/788.html

6   Sobel, *Fighting Pattons*, p. 315.
7   Collin and Freedman, *Winter of Fire*, p. 174.
8   Ibid., p. 177.
9   It should be noted that Sherry Brown's husband, the late lieutenant general Charlie Brown, had served with Dozier under my dad at the 2nd Armored Division. He had commanded the Division Support Command (DISCOM) and was another of my father's favorites.
10   This is excerpted from a letter written by Sherry Brown.

CHAPTER NINE

1   GSP speech, Abrams Lecture Series, Patton Museum, Fort Knox, Kentucky, 1991.
2   Sobel, *Fighting Pattons*, p. 127.

CHAPTER TEN

1   This was a nickname for "ASCOM," the Army Services Command in Vietnam.

PART FOUR

1   There are at least three other chaplains who, although I did not know them when they worked with my father, deserve to be mentioned:

First Chaplain Walthour, who was the chaplain at West Point when Dad was a cadet and the one he insisted on having at his wedding or he wouldn't feel properly married, since the man had been such a fine influence on him. When my parents sought him out (not knowing where he could be, since Dad had not kept in touch), they finally discovered that he was the Episcopal bishop of Atlanta. Even so, he agreed to come to Washington and marry them in the Washington National Cathedral. A few months later he died of a heart attack.

Next was Chaplain Bob Hawn, the 11th Cavalry chaplain when my dad was CO. He was on hand when the battalion psychologist passed out a fake prayer making mockery of Dad, when Dad was departing the regiment. Hawn was furious. Later he retired to civilian life and became one of the first "breakaway" priests who rejected the formal traditions, and was, I think, an Anglican bishop.

Finally, there is Father Berberich, the Roman Catholic priest who married my sister Helen and her husband, Thorsten, and who recalls Dad taking such good care of him when he arrived to serve in Blackhorse.

CHAPTER TWELVE

1   The passage Tom used in his sermon: "Jesus would say, 'Go out to meet reality courageously and completely . . . Do not look for the easiest way; look for the way that leads to the richest fulfillments. Do not shun pain and hardship as though the main purpose of existence were to build shelters of ease and isolation. Let your mind face great new thoughts even if they break up your comfortable ideas and force you to hard intellectual readjustment. Let your heart share other people's distresses, in order that sympathy may make you gentle . . . A knowledge of the depths in other may make your own emotions deep. Do not fear to be disturbed: fear to be undeveloped. There is only one death which can matter and that is the dying-by-inches of a mean existence in the universe where God's spirit is at work. Dare to live!'" Dr. Walter Russell Bowie, *Remembering Christ* (New York: Abingdon Press, 1940).

2   From GSP Interviews.

PART FIVE

1   The complete version of "The Islanders" by Rudyard Kipling, (1902):

NO DOUBT but ye are the People-your throne is above the King's.
Whoso speaks in your presence must say acceptable things:
Bowing the head in worship, bending the knee in fear—
Bringing the word well smoothen-such as a King should hear.

Fenced by your careful fathers, ringed by your leaden seas,
Long did ye wake in quiet and long lie down at ease;
Till Ye said of Strife, "What is it?" of the Sword, "It is far from our ken";
Till ye made a sport of your shrunken hosts and a toy of your armed men.
Ye stopped your ears to the warning—ye would neither look nor heed—
Ye set your leisure before their toil and your lusts above their need.
Because of your witless learning and your beasts of warren and chase,
Ye grudged your sons to their service and your fields for their camping-place.
Ye forced them glean in the highways the straw for the bricks they brought;
Ye forced them follow in byways the craft that ye never taught.
Ye hampered and hindered and crippled; ye thrust out of sight and away
Those that would serve you for honour and those that served you for pay.
Then were the judgments loosened; then was your shame revealed,
At the hands of a little people, few but apt in the field.
Yet ye were saved by a remnant (and your land's long-suffering star),
When your strong men cheered in their millions while your striplings went to the war.
Sons of the sheltered city-unmade, unhandled, unmeet—
Ye pushed them raw to the battle as ye picked them raw from the street.
And what did ye look they should compass? Warcraft learned in a breath,
Knowledge unto occasion at the first far view of Death?
So? And ye train your horses and the dogs ye feed and prize?
How are the beasts more worthy than the souls, your sacrifice?
But ye said, "Their valour shall show them"; but ye said, "The end is close."
And ye sent them comfits and pictures to help them harry your foes:
And ye vaunted your fathomless power, and ye flaunted your iron pride,
Ere ye fawned on the Younger Nations for the men who could shoot and ride!
Then ye returned to your trinkets; then ye contented your souls
With the flannelled fools at the wicket or the muddied oafs at the goals.
Given to strong delusion, wholly believing a lie,
Ye saw that the land lay fenceless,
and ye let the months go by
Waiting some easy wonder, hoping some saving sign—
Idle—openly idle—in the lee of the forespent Line.
Idle—except for your boasting—and what is your boasting worth
If ye grudge a year of service to the lordliest life on earth?
Ancient, effortless, ordered, cycle on cycle set,
Life so long untroubled, that ye who inherit forget
It was not made with the mountains, it is not one with the deep.
Men, not gods, devised it. Men, not gods, must keep.
Men, not children, servants, or kinsfolk called from afar,
But each man born in the Island broke to the matter of war.

Soberly and by custom taken and trained for the same,
Each man born in the Island entered at youth to the game—
As it were almost cricket, not to be mastered in haste,
But after trial and labour, by temperance, living chaste.
As it were almost cricket—as it were even your play,
Weighed and pondered and worshipped, and practised day and day.
So ye shall bide sure—guarded when the restless lightnings wake
In the womb of the blotting war-cloud, and the pallid nations quake.
So, at the haggard trumpets, instant your soul shall leap
Forthright, accoutred, accepting—alert from the wells of sleep.
So, at the threat ye shall summon—so at the need ye shall send
Men, not children or servants, tempered and taught to the end;
Cleansed of servile panic, slow to dread or despise,
Humble because of knowledge, mighty by sacrifice. . . .
But ye say, "It will mar our comfort." Ye say, "It will minish our trade."
Do ye wait for the spattered shrapnel ere ye learn how a gun is laid?
For the low, red glare to southward when the raided coast-towns burn?
(Light ye shall have on that lesson, but little time to learn.)
Will ye pitch some white pavilion, and lustily even the odds,
With nets and hoops and mallets, with rackets and bats and rods
Will the rabbit war with your foemen—the red deer horn them for hire?
Your kept cock-pheasant keep you?—he is master of many a shire,
Arid, aloof, incurious, unthinking, unthanking, gelt,
Will ye loose your schools to flout them till their brow-beat columns melt?
Will ye pray them or preach them, or print them, or ballot them back from your shore?
Will your workmen issue a mandate to bid them strike no more?
Will ye rise and dethrone your rulers? (Because ye were idle both?
Pride by Insolence chastened? Indolence purged by Sloth?)
No doubt but ye are the People; who shall make you afraid?
Also your gods are many; no doubt but your gods shall aid.
Idols of greasy altars built for the body's ease;
Proud little brazen Baals and talking fetishes;
Teraphs of sept and party and wise wood-pavement gods—
These shall come down to the battle and snatch you from under the rods?
From the gusty, flickering gun-roll with viewless salvoes rent,
And the pitted hail of the bullets that tell not whence they were sent.
When ye are ringed as with iron, when ye are scourged as with whips,
When the meat is yet in your belly, and the boast is yet on your lips;
When ye go forth at morning and the noon beholds you broke,
Ere ye lie down at even, your remnant, under the yoke?

No doubt but ye are the People—absolute, strong, and wise;
Whatever your heart has desired ye have not withheld from your eyes.
On your own heads, in your own hands,the sin and the caving lies!

Source: http://www.poetryloverspage.com/poets/kipling/islanders.html

PART SIX

CHAPTER FIFTEEN

1 Andy O'Meara, "The Bravest of the Brave," http://www.goldcoastchronicle.com/recognitions/the-bravest-of-the-brave/ (accessed August 30, 2010).

2 My father credited Andy O'Meara for saving his life more than once on the battlefield. Like my grandfather, my father hated to take casualties. So on February 13, 1969, when he learned that O'Meara had been shot multiple times in the leg, my father rushed to the hospital. By that point, O'Meara had lost consciousness.

"The leg has to come off," the doctor told him. "We can't save it."

In response, my father pulled out his revolver, pointed it at the doctor, and said, "You cut him and I'll kill you." Then my dad quickly dispatched his chopper to bring in another, older Army surgeon from Saigon for a second opinion. The leg was saved.

"I didn't learn about that until later, but I really appreciated it," says O'Meara. "I still have that leg and it works pretty good."

3 From the Warrior Transition Command Web site, http://wtc.army.mil/about_us/wtu.html

ACKNOWLEDGMENTS

1 Patton, *The Pattons,* pp. 58, 61.

INDEX

Page numbers in *italics* indicate photographs; those followed by "n" indicate notes.